International Series on Public Policy

Series Editors

B. Guy Peters, Department of Political Science, University of Pittsburgh, Pittsburgh, USA

Philippe Zittoun, Research Professor of Political Science, LET-ENTPE, University of Lyon, Lyon, France

The International Series on Public Policy - the official series of International Public Policy Association, which organizes the International Conference on Public Policy - identifies major contributions to the field of public policy, dealing with analytical and substantive policy and governance issues across a variety of academic disciplines.

A comparative and interdisciplinary venture, it examines questions of policy process and analysis, policymaking and implementation, policy instruments, policy change & reforms, politics and policy, encompassing a range of approaches, theoretical, methodological, and/or empirical.

Relevant across the various fields of political science, sociology, anthropology, geography, history, and economics, this cutting edge series welcomes contributions from academics from across disciplines and career stages, and constitutes a unique resource for public policy scholars and those teaching public policy worldwide.

All books in the series are subject to Palgrave's rigorous peer review process: https://www.palgrave.com/gb/demystifying-peer-review/792492.

B. Guy Peters · Philippe Zittoun
Editors

Contemporary Approaches to Public Policy

Theories, Controversies and Perspectives

Second Edition

Editors
B. Guy Peters
Department of Political Science
University of Pittsburgh
Pittsburgh, PA, USA

Philippe Zittoun
LAET-ENTPE
University of Lyon
Lyon, France

ISSN 2524-7301 ISSN 2524-731X (electronic)
International Series on Public Policy
ISBN 978-3-032-06025-9 ISBN 978-3-032-06026-6 (eBook)
https://doi.org/10.1007/978-3-032-06026-6

This Palgrave Macmillan imprint is published by the registered company Springer Nature Switzerland AG
The registered company address is: Gewerbestrasse 11, 6330 Cham, Switzerland

If disposing of this product, please recycle the paper.

CONTENTS

NOTES ON CONTRIBUTORS

Christopher Ansell is Professor of Political Science at the University of California, Berkeley. His research focuses on understanding how public institutions handle risk, uncertainty, and turbulence. He is an author or editor of more than ten books, including *Pragmatism and Political Crisis Management* (2019) and *Pragmatist Democracy: Evolutionary Learning as Public Philosophy* (2011). He is currently the Director of Berkeley's Center for Catastrophic Risk Management

Peter deLeon was CU Distinguished Professor and School of Public Affairs Emeritus Professor at the University of Colorado, Denver.

Jennifer Dodge is Associate Professor of Public Administration and Policy at Rockefeller College, University at Albany. Using interpretive and critical theories/methodologies, her research focuses on environmental policy-making, especially policy conflict and grassroots policy advocacy. She is currently researching "intersectional coalitions" as a political strategy for addressing climate change, and developing theory on sustainability transitions in the interregnum. She is former Editor of *Critical Policy Studies* and serves on the board of several policy journals.

Anna Durnova is Professor of Political Sociology at the Department of Sociology, University of Vienna. She is also a Faculty Fellow at the Yale University Center for Cultural Sociology. She serves as a member of the Editorial Board of the journal *Policy & Politics* and *Critical Policy*

Studies. She is the Recipient of the 2024 Mattei Dogan Foundation Prize for European Political Sociology.

Rebecca Eissler is an associate professor at San Francisco State University. Her research interests include public-policy processes, agenda setting, and political institutions, specifically the U.S. presidency.

Frank Fischer is a research scholar at Humboldt University in Berlin and Faculty Fellow at the University of Kassel.

Patrick Hassenteufel is Professor of political science and Director of the Graduate School for Sociology and Political Science at Paris-Saclay University. His main research field is the comparative analysis of health policies in relation with the theoretical discussion on approaches of the policy process. He published in several political science and public-policy journals including the *Journal of European Public Policy, Social Policy and Administration, Public Policy and Administration, Comparative Politics, Comparative European Politics, European Policy Analysis*, and the *International Review on Public Policy*.

Christopher Hood was Gladstone Professor of Government at All Souls College, University of Oxford

Helen Ingram is a Professor at the Southwest Center, University of Arizona.

Hank c. Jenkins-Smith is currently a George Lynn Cross Research Professor of public policy at the University of Oklahoma and directs OU's Institute for Public Policy Research and Analysis. Hank has published books, articles, and reports on public-policy processes, risk perception, national security, weather, and energy and environmental policy. In his spare time, Hank engages in personal experiments in risk perception and management via skiing, scuba diving, and motorcycling.

Michael D. Jones is the Thurmond Professor of Political Science at Clemson University. He earned his PhD from the University of Oklahoma and holds both an MA and BS from Idaho State University. From 2010 to 2013, he was a postdoctoral fellow at Harvard's Safra Center for Ethics. His contributions to the study of narrative and public policy have been recognized with Idaho State's Distinguished Alumni Award and the Policy Studies Organization's Enduring Contribution Award.

Bryan D. Jones is Professor of Government at the University of Texas, Austin, and co-founder of the Public Agendas Project.

Peter John is Professor of Public Policy at King's College, University of London.

Helen Z. Margetts is Professor of Society and the Internet, and Professorial Fellow of Mansfield College, University of Oxford.

Rachel McGovern is a PhD candidate in Public Policy in Clemson University's Department of Political Science. She holds an MPA and a BS in Political Science from Idaho State University. Her research focuses on policy theory, particularly the role of narratives in shaping policy processes. Her recent publications have appeared in *Review of Policy Research* and *Ecosystems and People.Corresponding*

B. Guy Peters is Maurice Falk Professor Emeritus at the University of Pittsburgh.

Anne Schneider is Professor, School of Politics and Global Studies, Arizona State University.

Christopher M. Weible is a Distinguished Professor at the School of Public Affairs, University of Colorado Denver. He is the Co-Founder and Co-Director of the Center for Policy and Democracy (CPD). He is the former editor for *Policy Studies Journal, International Review of Public Policy*, and *Policy & Politics*. He holds an Honorary Doctor of Philosophy and is a Guest Professor at the Luleå University of Technology, Luleå, Sweden.

Nikolaos Zahariadis is the Mertie Buckman Chair and Professor of International Studies at Rhodes College in Memphis, TN, USA. He researches comparative policy-making at the intersection of domestic and international affairs with substantive emphasis on European political economy.

Philippe Zittoun is Research Professor of Political Science at LAET-ENTPE, University of Lyon, and General Secretary of IPPA.

List of Figures

Introduction

B. Guy Peters and Philippe Zittoun

In the first roundtable focusing on contemporary approaches to public policy at the 2013 International Public Policy Conference, one of the participants described the field of policy sciences as populated by "warring tribes." While the degree of conflict among different approaches to policy can easily be exaggerated, a number of important, and at times contradictory, approaches are commonly used when studying public policy. These approaches offer alternative explanations for policy choices and provide a range of means for understanding the consequences of those policy choices. The approaches have different intellectual backgrounds and epistemological assumptions associated with different ideas about the dynamics of policy, so that the same set of data about policy-making may be perceived in quite different ways. The number of approaches continues to increase, making the field if anything more open to conflict and incoherence.

B. G. Peters
University of Pittsburgh, Pittsburgh, USA
e-mail: bgpeters@pitt.edu

P. Zittoun (✉)
LAET-ENTPE, University of Lyon, Lyon, France

1

The above said, these various approaches often tend to ignore each other as much as they conflict with each other. To a degree this is a function of the perspectives of the different academic disciplines involved in policy studies. Economics, political science, decision sciences, and a host of other disciplines are all involved in studying policy, and have their distinctive perspectives. More surprisingly, some of this mutual indifference is the consequence of different epistemological approaches within the same discipline. The case of Political Science, one of the most important disciplines for public policy—which considers public policy to be an entire sub-discipline—constitutes a relevant example of this indifference. Within the field of public policy, we can identify more than ten different approaches which are relatively indifferent to each other, and make little or no effort to offer contending explanations for the same phenomena.

From a scientific perspective, this indifference is problematic because discussion, even if it is apparently divisive and contentious, can help to guide hypotheses, concepts, empirical observation, understanding, and conclusions and can ultimately help to produce more rigorous knowledge. To borrow a term from Karl Popper, the testing and argumentative exchange around a theory can help to consolidate its "scientificity." This book proposes to contribute to this debate between approaches by focusing on political science approaches to public policy. Therefore, it tends to largely ignore the importance of economic analysis, ethics, and substantive fields such as public health (as it concerns public policy). If this selectivity is in some ways limiting—given that other disciplines do have a great deal to say about policy—we consider it a first step which, by restricting the universe of discourse, offers a real opportunity to initiate the debate.

To better understand the policy field in political science, let us first present a quick mapping of the different approaches that have been developed. The tendency of these approaches to policy to ignore one another may be understood firstly in relation to fundamentally different purposes in studying policy. We identify two different dimensions which produce an initial conception of the difference in Policy Studies. The first dimension distinguishes the key object of the studies: policy versus policy process. This first dimension, which we call "Policy Analysis," attempts to study policy itself as an object and to produce understanding and normative knowledge for the policy process. A Policy Analysis study generally tries to identify the different elements which compose public policy—for example, instruments, problems, causes, consequences, laws, decisions, public concerns, and so on—to understand the link between them or/ and to propose some new connections. Policy Analysis is often prospective and may attempt to provide advice about the feasibility and desirability of policies.

Within Policy Analysis, we can group different subcategories like "Policy Design," which contribute to produce "clear connections between the assumed causes of the problem being addressed, the instruments used to attempt to remedy this situation, and an understanding of what desirable outcome would be" (Peters 2015, p. 2). We can also include "Policy Evaluation," which proposes to produce normative knowledge between the outcomes and the outputs and the goals of policy. In addition, many studies based in economic analysis would fit into the Policy Analysis category. Policy Analysis, which has been widely developed in the USA, since the 1950s, is exclusively produced not only by researchers but also by practitioners and experts.

The second dimension, the one that we call "Policy Process Studies," aims at producing knowledge on the policy process itself to enable us to better understand the dynamics of policy-making and the different factors which play a key role in the development of policies. These kinds of studies are very interested in the different elements composing the whole process—like problem agenda setting, decision-making, policy formulation, implementation, and so on, and they focus on the normative and causal link between them. In these kinds of studies, where temporality is a key dimension, there is specific attention to the role of context, of the different kinds of practitioners (bureaucrats, politicians, companies, citizen, etc.), of the different institutions, and of the different kinds of ideas and discourses, among other things. In Policy Process Studies, we can regroup different subcategories like "policy-change studies," "policy-making studies," and "policy-implementation studies."

Another reason it can be difficult to define Public Policy Studies is the distinction between some approaches concerns the roles of theory and practice. Some approaches consider that the theoretical dimension of understanding policy or policy process and the applied dimension of recommendations to produce advice are complementary. Other approaches consider that these two dimensions are incompatible and contribute to biased understandings. If, in the first approach, the purpose is to affect the political process, in the second approach, the purpose of studying public policy is most often to simply understand the political process (Zittoun 2014), as manifested in the way in which policy proposals are processed through the "issue machine" (Braybrooke 1974). This is an old debate, present in all social sciences. It can be found, for example, in David Easton's critiques of Lasswell's work when the latter began to develop policy sciences. Easton spoke about two Lasswell studies—the first one, before the Second World War, aimed at creating knowledge to assist the government in understanding the elite process and the propaganda machines—and later Lasswell works intended to help the government implement the "good" decision (Lasswell 1956; Easton 1950). But this difference is not only epistemological, but also influenced by the research policy of the countries involved and their relationship to political science. This is probably why we find more researchers in the second category from Germany and France and in the first one more researchers from the USA and UK.

All of these approaches are valid and can contribute to policy studies, but because they focus on different objects and different questions, they do not necessarily connect with one another. As we suggest in the sub-title of this volume (Theories, Controversies, and Perspectives), the aim of this book is to present some different approaches to Policy Studies and thus promote the debates, exchanges, and mutual understanding to be gleaned from new perspectives. For this reason, we selected eleven contemporary approaches (which we judged to be most commonly used in the research community) and asked the leading experts in each approach to consider not only the nature of contemporary policy studies but also paths for future research. This book therefore provides significant insight into contemporary public policy studies and the continuing questions that arise in this field of study. In addition to those eleven, there is an historical chapter that outlines the development of the field of Public Policy Studies.

The remainder of this introductory chapter examines some basic questions found in the public-policy literature. We discuss these questions in general and then point to the ways in which specific chapters in this volume address these issues.

WHAT IS PUBLIC POLICY?

The most basic question that must be asked is: how do we conceptualize public policy and the role of the state in policy? There are probably as many different definitions as there are different authors, and the twelve chapters in this book do not break this tradition that Thomas Dye (1972) already observed in 1970s. Beyond this multiplicity, the most fundamental epistemological question concerning defining policy is the extent to which it is an empirically defined phenomenon versus one that is more constructed by political and social processes. The bulk of the work done in public-policy analysis takes an essentialist position: scholars argue that the understanding of policy is constructed by political processes and its meaning is more a matter of interpretation than of essence (Zittoun 2014; Fischer and Gottweiss 2012). For the policy studies strand of research, the opposite is true, and most scholars treat policies are empirical realities.

The second definitional question is to what extent public policy is confined to the activities of the state—or does it also include the actions of groups and individuals that act in the name of the state or who have influence as if they were public-sector actors. At one end of this spectrum are scholars who focus almost exclusively on the public sector—although these tend to be an increasingly small segment of the population (see Bell and Hindmoor 2009)—while at the other are scholars who argue that governance (and hence policy-making) without government is both possible and desirable (Rhodes 1996; Koppenjan and Klijn 2004). If we eschew that extreme position, it remains undeniable that contemporary public policy involves significant levels of interactions between public- and private-sector actors, whether those private-sector actors are market or non-market (Torfing et al. 2012).

There can be, and are, other definitional debates about public policy, but the study of this field has tended to be a "big tent" that has been capable of containing a range of approaches. Indeed, the diversity of perspectives and methodologies for addressing public policy within political science has contributed to the vibrancy of the field. Not only do the policies actually adopted and implemented continue to change, but so too do the intellectual approaches used to understand them. And if we include work in other scholarly domains such as economics, sociology, and planning, the research becomes even more diverse and more challenging.

chapter "History of Public Policy Studies" in this volume discusses the nature of policy and alternative ways of thinking about these actions of governments and their partners. Anna Durnova, Frank Fischer, and Philippe Zittoun in chapter "The Advocacy Coalition Framework for Comparative Analyses of Contentious Policy Issues" examine how the definition of, and the arguments for, policy constitute a major discursive activity between practitioners in the policy process that researchers need to grasp not in order to judge the process or to propose a new one, but to understand the policy process and its political dimension.

chapter "History of Public Policy Studies" is complemented by chapter ""The Narrative Policy Framework: A Storied Understanding of Public Policy", in Contemporary Approaches to Public Policy: Theories, Controversies and Perspectives" by Christopher Ansell, Patrick Hassenteufel, and Philippe Zittoun that develops a transactional approach to public policy. It stresses that policy processes are always a form of valuation where values are discovered and invented and through which interests are staked out and identifies are forged. To understand the Policy Process, the article proposes to grasp it as an assemblage of interviewing policy situations where policy valuation, problematization, and policy formulation take place, where the collective action and the problem/solution are built and be testing.

Policy Stages

The political science approaches discussed in this book can be divided into several camps, and those different camps can help to identify the modes of thinking in this discipline about policy. Perhaps the dominant strand in political science approaches to policy is to consider the policy process.[1] This concern has been central in this discipline, since before the study of public policy became institutionalized within the discipline. Legislative scholars, for example, would discuss "how a bill becomes a law," and this is what we might now call a study of formulation and legitimation of policy. The stages model of the policy process (Jones 1984) contains five stages, beginning with agenda setting and proceeding through evaluation that became institutionalized as a standard means of understanding how the policy process functioned.

This stages model has been elaborated with specialized studies of individual process stages. One of the most notable of these perhaps was the Pressman and Wildavsky (1974) study of implementation that preceded the development of the stages model per se, but which clearly developed the ideas relevant to one of the stages. The study of implementation remains a mainstay in public policy and public administration, although some would argue (but see Sager and Mavrot 2024) that there has been relatively little intellectual development in the field after publication of the original book and perhaps the ensuing discussion of backward mapping as an approach to implementation (Elmore 1985; Linder and Peters 1989).[1]

Evaluation research represented a second major elaboration of one of the stages of the policy process. This literature has both a more applied dimension and a more political dimension. The applied work is perhaps best represented by works such as Rossi et al. (2014) and Weiss (1972) that provided insights into the techniques of evaluation, as well as some of the difficulties encountered in this research. The more political evaluation studies (see Vedung 2013) emphasized the particular political obstacles to evaluation and the manner in which evaluation could be used within the political process. Both lines of research, however, pointed out how important understanding the consequences of policy interventions was for government, and for the society being served by government.

Policy formulation is a third stage of the policy process that has been elaborated significantly. The literature on formulation spans the theoretical and practical dimensions of public policy. For example, policy design has been discussed primarily in theoretical terms (Peters 2018) but it also has significant implications for the development of policies by governments. Other research that is directed at understanding how best to formulate policies (Jordan and Turnpenny 2015) also has substantial relevance for the development of public policy as an academic enterprise.

Finally, the basic policy process model has been elaborated significantly in the study of agendas and agenda setting. This area of research began with first identifying the importance of agendas for the outcomes of the policy process, and later began to elaborate dimensions of agendas and mechanisms for setting agendas (Cobb and Elder 1972). In addition, this literature identified the need to define policy problems and the importance that particular definitions of those policy problems may have for the outcomes of the process (Dery 2000; Payan 2006). The agendas literature has further developed in the punctuated-equilibrium model, which will be discussed in some detail in chapter "The Transformation of Ideas: The Origin and Evolution of Punctuated Equilibrium Theory".

Beyond the research on the separate stages, one principal consideration of researchers is to understand the link between the different

---

[1] Although Hood's book has been very influential in political science and public adminis-tration, economists actually began to think about this issue somewhat earlier. E. S. Kirschen (1964), for example, identified 64 instruments that were available in economic policy.

stages. Although being identified here as political science, a good deal of the evaluation literature actually might be located more appropriately in sociology, using methodologies better developed in that literature and focusing on social problems that are to a great extent the province of sociology step than chronologically linked steps, the debate begins with Wildavsky, who proposed a Policy Cycle model in 1979 (May and Wildavsky 1978). This question takes a new dynamic path with the work of Kingdom (1984), who suggests considering three independent streams (problem agenda, political process, policy formulation) and transforming the condition of their coupling into a research question.

One chapter in this book (chapter "The Transformation of Ideas: The Origin and Evolution of Punctuated Equilibrium Theory") addresses a stage in the policy process. Rebecca Eissler, Annelise Russell, and Bryan Jones in chapter "The Transformation of Ideas: The Origin and Evolution of Punctuated Equilibrium Theory" first examine agenda setting and particularly the punctuated-equilibrium theory that has become central to the study of agendas. This approach has become a major comparative project on the ways in which governments develop agendas for action. That said, this chapter might well fit with the following section on approaches to policy-making more generally, given that the idea of punctuated equilibrium has become more pervasive throughout the study of public policy, as is in fact the authors of this chapter argue.

EXPLANATIONS OF POLICY CHANGE

A second line of thinking about public policy is to attempt to explain policy choices made by governments and their allies in the private sector. Some of these explanations involve the application of general theoretical approaches in political science to the study of policy, while others have been more purpose-built to deal with policy-making. These approaches also attempt to deal both with problems of initial policy-making as well as the dynamics of change. Further, these approaches to explaining public policy can be seen in part as explanations for political action taken more generally, given that the ultimate purpose of politics and government is to make policy.

One of the major questions which arises in the study of policy choices is the extent to which rationality can explain those choices. Although rational-choice theories in political science have been applied relatively rarely in the study of public policy, economists have applied some aspects of their usual armamentarium to the field. These applications have been mostly in the evaluation of policies—the usual cost-benefit analysis—but also in the explanation of the formation of coalitions around particular policy choices in legislatures or coalition governments (Martin and Vanberg 2011). Many scholars have argued that the demands of strict rationality do not fit well with the complexity—substantive and political—of public policy and have argued that less comprehensive approaches to policy are more suitable.

Herbert Simon, the father of the bounded rationality approach to policy, argued that policy-making involved too many uncertainties and too many possible choices for full rationality to be possible (Simon 1947). Attempting to behave in a fully rational manner would require too much time and resources to be a practical possibility. Simon therefore recommended "satisficing"—making decisions that were good enough—rather than optimizing, with that decision-making being bounded by organizational commitments, the availability of information, and a host of other factors. Those decisions that are good enough could then be reviewed and there could be continuous improvement of policies. This logic of bounded rationality is similar to the logic of incrementalism (Lindblom 1965; Hayes 2006) that has been central in American thinking about public policy—both in academia and in practice.

The need to revise policy continuously brings up another challenge in understanding public policy—policy change. To some extent the explanations for the adoption of policy and explanations for policy change have a number of things in common. But explanations for change involve the political issues of coping with entrenched interests and entrenched policy ideas. For example, while the incrementalist literature may make the continuing change of policies appear easy, in reality that change typically will encounter significant opposition. That said, however, most existing policies do represent the overlays of a number of episodes of change (Carter 2012).

chapters "Introduction, The Advocacy Coalition Framework for Comparative Analyses of Contentious Policy Issues, Institutionalism and Public Policy, Tools Approaches, and Bounded Rationality and Garbage Can/Multiple Streams Models of Policy-Making" in this volume address alternative explanations for policy change. In chapter" Introduction", Christopher Weible and Hank Jenkins-Smith examine the Advocacy-Coalition Framework (ACF) that has become a central approach to

understanding policy change. This approach has been especially important for dealing with policy issues which are characterized by high levels
of political contention. This framework explains how actors, especially
working with different policy ideas and different perspectives on policy,
interact and how those interactions can produce change.

Guy Peters in chapter "Institutionalism and Public Policy" provides
a discussion of alternative conceptions of institutions and the manner in
which institutions can shape policy choices and policy change. While institutions are not usually associated with change, they are not as unmoving
and inflexible as the stereotype assumes. Even more fundamentally, institutions can be the carriers of policy ideas and therefore can shape the
policy choices made by governments.

chapter "Meaning in Public Policy Approaches: Discursive Practices,
Emotions, and Political Power" (by Eduardo Araral and Mulya Amri) is
based on the institutional analysis and design framework associated with
the late Elinor Ostrom. This approach examines the manner in which
individual actors interact within institutional contexts to produce policy
choices. This represents an important blending of structural and agency
explanations for policy. The authors assess the state of the art in the use
of this approach and also raises a number of important questions about
the utility of the approach and the ways in which it can be applied.

Another of these chapters on approaches to explaining policy (8)
by Nikolaos Zahariadis, addresses bounded rationality as well as several
extensions of the study of bounded rationality by looking at "multiple
streams" approaches to policy. The argument in this strand of literature
is that policies may not be designed rationally (but see Peters 2015) but
rather represent the random confluence of several streams of action and
opportunities. Thus, policy is not so much a rational action as it is the
fortunate meeting of actors and events rather than a planned intervention.
This approach has numerous implications for the ways in which policy is
made, and the types of content that are likely to be produced.

chapter "Bounded Rationality and Garbage Can/Multiple Streams
Models of Policy-Making" adds another dimension of the explanation of
public policies by examining the role of narratives and the Narrative Policy
Framework. Rachel McGovern and Michael Jones present this addition
to the modes of explanation contained in this book, and point out what
it can add to the existing approaches. They argue that explanations for
policy choices can emerge from examining the stories surrounding the

process. This is not just description, however, but also has measurement and testing techniques analogous to other approaches to policy.

MODES OF INTERVENTION

A third major issue in policy analysis has been understanding the resources available to the public sector to produce change in the economy and society. This line of thinking usually is presented under the rubric "the tools of government" or "policy instruments" (especially after the publication of Christopher Hood's influential book in the 1980s). The instruments literature is closely linked with the study of implementation, with the tools that governments choose being related to their capacity to implement policy effectively.

But the tools of government are far from merely simple technical fixes for public problems. They are also intensely political, as is almost everything in policy-making: just as the goals of a policy intervention affect different segments of society differently, so too do the instruments used to make that intervention work (or so it is hoped). For example, student loan programs can be implemented through direct loans to students from government or through private-sector banks with the government operating as a guarantor of the loans. The latter mode of intervention makes it possible to build a political coalition between educational interests and banking interests, making the program easier to implement. As well as facilitating coalition-building, policy instruments have a range of other political effects. For example, the intrusiveness of policy instruments can influence public sentiment toward government. As the public has become more resistant to the public-policy initiatives, governments have moved toward the "New Governance," with softer and more discretionary instruments (Salomon 2001; Héritier and Rhodes 2012).

The choice of instruments may also permit government to mask some of its activities from the public. For example, choosing tax expenditures rather than direct expenditures enables governments to still move money in the direction of its desired targets without the amount of money, or even its existence, being apparent to the average citizen (Heald 2013). There are two chapters in this book that advance the study of policy instruments.

First, chapter "The Transformation of Ideas: The Origin and Evolution of Punctuated Equilibrium Theory" on interventions addresses an important development in the tools that governments utilize to affect the economy and society. Rather than attempt to coerce citizens into behaving in the manner that governments want, governments now attempt to "nudge" them to behave in the desired manner (Thalen and Sunstein 2008). Peter John discusses the original "nudge" literature and other means of intervention based more on psychology than on law or economics. This is a component of a movement to think about public policy in more behavioral terms, rather than in structural or agency terms. Although these interventions have been justified as being less intrusive than the more traditional instruments, they also may permit governments to manipulate the public in ways that may be less visible and hence less controllable.

chapter "Behavioral Approaches: How Nudges Lead to More Intelligent Policy Design" by Christopher Hood and Helen Margetts (2007) builds on the original book by Hood and a subsequent book by Hood and Margetts that examined the role of instruments in a digital age. Their chapter examines the development of policy tools as governments continue to alter their patterns for intervention in society and as the public alters their perceptions of how government should perform. They further discuss the challenges to the tools approach, and policy-making in general, presented by rapidly evolving societies. This focus on the tools themselves and their applicability in different setting does, however, to some extent exclude discussion of questions such as the politics of selecting tools.

NORMATIVE QUESTIONS IN PUBLIC POLICY

With the possible exception of attempts to define public policy, the categories of research discussed above deal with policy issues from an empirical perspective. The empirics of policy are certainly important, but policy choices also have a significant normative dimension. Most importantly, perhaps, all public policies redistribute goods—including, potentially, human rights.

and human life—and there are significant questions about the categories used in making those redistributions. We need to be able to understand why some groups are advantaged and some disadvantaged by policy choices. Fundamental normative concerns about justice, equality, and desert are all manifested in government decisions about public policies (see Sunstein 2014).

chapter "The Narrative Policy Framework: A Storied Understanding of Public Policy" is an addition to the second edition of the book. It discusses the Policy Transaction Approach understanding the policy process. Christopher Ansell, Patrick Hassenteufel and Philippe Zittoun present this novel approach which combines some elements of values with some elements of empirical analysis. It focuses in particular on the transactions that occur between State and Society as policy is made and implemented.

In the final chapter of this book Helen Ingram and Anne Schneider address the importance of democracy for public policy. Their chapter is heavily based on experiences in the USA, but increases in inequality in many industrialized democracies make their analysis more generally applicable. Their vision of democracy includes both democracy as a process and democracy as some degree of equality of the outcomes. Thus, in addition to the specific question of inequality, the more general question of how democratic participation can influence the outcomes of policy-making is crucial in both democratic and transitional regimes.

WHAT IS MISSING?

Although this volume discusses a number of the central issues in, and approaches to, the study of public policy, it inevitably has left out some of material. Perhaps most importantly it has given little or no attention to economic analysis of public policy. In the "real world" of policy-making, economics plays a central role, with techniques such as cost-benefit analysis being central to how decisions are made when adopting policies. The perspectives offered by other disciplines such as sociology, planning, and law have also been largely ignored. In addition, the increasing importance of complexity for understanding problems such as climate change is not included here.

Also, there are rich and thriving literatures on specific areas of public policy that have been touched on only in passing in this volume. Areas such as public health, social welfare, food, defense, the environment, and energy have policy specialists who apply general models of policy analysis to these fields, along with knowledge bases contained within those areas of study. Public policy is inevitably policy about something, so understanding the substance of a field can be crucial to be an effective policy scholar.

Any book is necessarily selective, and we felt it desirable to focus our attention on the research centered in political science and that situated in an area of inquiry that defines itself as policy studies. There is ample diversity within that body of research, as we believe has been indicated here. Some future attempt to map the field of policy studies more broadly (see also Peters and Pierre 2007) might well bring in a broader range of roaches and substantive policy areas, but this volume has, we believe, demonstrated that there is a rich diversity of ideas and approaches for the study of public policy.

CONCLUSION

This book will demonstrate the diversity that exists in the study of public policy, even if we focus primarily on the political science literature. For some scholars the emphasis has been on the very nature of policy, with surprisingly different ideas and methodologies applied to the same subject matter. For others the principal question is the political process, while for still others finding workable explanations for policy choices is central. Other scholars have focused on how the public sector can intervene most effectively in the economy and society, and finally others are concerned with the normative implications of policy choices.

As well as demonstrating the diversity of this field, the chapters in this book also demonstrate the continuity of the field. Most of the fundamental questions about public policy that we ask today are those that have been asked for years and even decades. This is not to say that there has been no progress—there certainly has. But this persistence of ideas and concerns does demonstrate that public policy—both as an academic exercise and as the real-world activity of governments—has persistent problems and issues that may never really be solved. In the real world of governing, those problems may be ameliorated but in academe we will have ample food for thought and for debate for the foreseeable future.

REFERENCES

Bell, S., and A. Hindmoor. 2009. *Rethinking governance: The centrality of the state in modern society.* Cambridge: Cambridge University Press.
Braybrooke, D. 1974. *Traffic congestion goes through the issue machine.* London: Routledge & Kegan Paul.
Carter, P. 2012. Policy as palimpset. *Policy & Politics* 40:423–443.

Cobb, R. W., and C. D. Elder. 1972. *Participation in American politics: The dynam-ics of agenda-building.* Boston: Allyn and Bacon.

Dery, D. 2000. Agenda-setting and problem definition. *Policy Studies* 21 (1): 37–47.

Elmore, R. F. 1985. Forward and backward mapping: Reversible logic in the analy-sis of public policy. In *Policy implementation in federal and unitary states,* ed. K. Hanf and T. A. J. Toonen, 76–98. Dordrecht: Martinus Nijhoff.

Fischer, F., and H. Gottweiss. 2012. *The argumentative turn revisited: Public policy as communicative practice.* Durham: Duke University Press.

Hayes, M. T. 2006. *Incrementalism and public policy.* Lanham: University Press of America.

Heald, D. 2013. Why is transparency about public expenditure so elusive? *International Review of Administrative Sciences* 78:130–149.

Héritier, A., and M. Rhodes, eds. 2012. *New modes of governance in Europe: Governing in the shadow of hierarchy.* Basingstoke: Palgrave.

Hood, C., and H. Margetts. 2007. *Tools of government in a digital age.* Basingstoke: Macmillan.

Jones, C. O. 1984. *An introduction to the study of public policy.* 2nd ed. Monterey: Brooks-Cole.

Jordan, A. J., and J. R. Turnpenny. 2015. *The tools of policy formulation.* Cheltenham: Edward Elgar.

Kirschen, E. S. 1964. *Economic policy in our time.* Amsterdam: North-Holland.

j, Koppenjan, and E.-H. Klijn. 2004. *Managing uncertainties in network.* New York: Routledge.

Lasswell, H. D. 1956. *The decision process; seven categories of functional analysis.* College Park: College of Business and Public Administration, University of Maryland.

Lindblom, C. E. 1965. *The intelligence of democracy: Decision making through mutual adjustment.* New York: Free Press.

Linder, S. H., and B. G. Peters. 1989. Implementation as a guide to policy formula-tion: A question of 'when' rather than 'whether'. *International Review of Administrative Sciences* 55:631–652.

Martin, L. W., and G. Vanberg. 2011. *Parliaments and coalitions: The role of legislative institutions in multiparty governance.* Oxford University Press.

May, I. V., and A. B. Wildavsky. 1978. *The policy cycle.* Sage Publications.

Payan, T. 2006. *Cops, soldiers and diplomats: Explaining agency behavior in the war on drugs.* Lanham: Lexington Books.

Peters, B. G. 2015. *An advanced introduction to public policy.* Cheltenham: Edward Elgar.

Peters, B. G., and J. Pierre. 2007. *The handbook of public policy.* London: Sage.

Peters, B. G. 2018. *Policy problems and policy design.* Cheltenham: Edward Elgar.

Rhodes, R. A. W. 1996. The new governance: Governing without government. *Political Studies* 44:652–667.

Rossi, P. H., M. W. Lipsey, and H. E. Freeman. 2014. *Evaluation: A systematic approach.* Thousand Oaks: Sage.

Sager, F., C. Mavrot and L, R. Keiser (2024) Introduction: The notion of policy implementation and why it is important, in Sager, Mavrot and Keiser, eds., Handbook of public policy implementation (Cheltenham: Edward Elgar).

Salomon, L. M. 2001. Introduction. In *Handbook of policy instruments*, ed. L. M. Salomon. New York: Oxford University Press.

Simon, H. A. 1947. *Administrative behavior.* New York: Free Press.

Sunstein, C. R. 2014. *Valuing life: Humanizing the regulatory state.* Chicago: University of Chicago Press.

Thalen, R. W., and C. R. Sunstein. 2008. *Nudge: Improving decisions about health, wealth and happiness.* New Haven: Yale University Press.

Torfing, J., B. G. Peters, J. Pierre, and E. Sørensen. 2012. *Interactive governance: Advancing the paradigm.* Oxford: Oxford University Press.

Vedung, E. 2013. Six models of evaluation. In *Routledge handbook of public policy*, ed. E. Araral, S. Fritzen, M. Howlett, M. Ramesh, and X. Wu, 387–400. London: Routledge.

Weiss, C. H. 1972. *Evaluation research: Methods for assessing program effectiveness.* Englewood Cliffs: Prentice-Hall.

Wildavsky, A., and J. L. Pressman. 1974. *Implementation.* USA: University of California Press.

Zittoun, P. 2014. *The political process of policy-making.* Basingstoke: Macmillan.

History of Public Policy Studies

Philippe Zittoun and B. Guy Peters

To better understand contemporary approaches to public policy and how these approaches fit into the dynamics of the discipline, it is essential to provide an overview of the origin and development of the field over time. This exercise is not easy, as it requires deciding not only when the policy field began but also what can be considered inside the field and what is outside. While it is very common to attribute the "origin" to Lasswell's work, with various articles discussing his contributions and history (Torgerson 2024; Deleon 1988; Dunn 2019), there is no single article or book that addresses what happened before this origin and what occurred during the preceding period and the contemporary one.

The goal of this chapter is to provide an overview of the international history of the policy field from its origins to the 1980s, when the first contemporary approaches emerged, as discussed in various books and articles mentioned in the different chapters of the book. A first roundtable

P. Zittoun (✉)
LAET-ENTPE, University of Lyon, Lyon, France

B. G. Peters
University of Pittsburgh, Pittsburgh, USA
e-mail: bgpeters@pitt.edu

© The Editor(s) (if applicable) and The Author(s), under exclusive license to Springer Nature Switzerland AG 2026
B. G. Peters and P. Zittoun (eds.), *Contemporary Approaches to Public Policy*, International Series on Public Policy,
https://doi.org/10.1007/978-3-032-06026-6_2

was held at the second International Public Policy Conference (Milan, 2015) to discuss this history, where it became apparent that there is no collective agreement about this history, but rather different stories depending on the countries and perspectives of the speakers. In 2015, the Oxford Handbook of Classics in Public Policy and Administration (Balla et al. 2015) was published, where the editors selected a relevant list of articles and books that have played a role in the public policy field. Each chapter presents the context of publication, but unfortunately, it does not provide an overview of the historical dynamic.

To engage in a history of the policy field, we have identified four periods that correspond to four ideational sequences. Defining a period is always a difficult task, well known to historians, and is necessarily a simplification that never fully covers the complex reality but allows for some guidelines. Each period corresponds to a specific moment when many articles and books seem to focus more or less on the same research questions. It is also driven by important controversies that structured the period. Additionally, it is linked to a specific political context that helps to understand the kinds of questions researchers asked.

We first begin with a broad "Pre-history" of the field. Identifying the start of this prehistory is a difficult task, and each choice can be controversial. We have chosen to focus on the origin of the concept of "policy," which has the peculiarity of existing only in English; most other languages do not have a specific word for it and use "politics"to refer to "policy." Paradoxically, the origin of the word is the old medieval French "policies," which became "police" in the eighteenth century, all derived from the ancient Greek "politeia." During this period, the concept allowed authors to discuss how to govern a society and how to develop a nation. From the nineteenth century to the first part of the twentieth century, the concept progressively disappeared, giving way to the development of knowledge about how to solve economic and social problems.

The first period in the history of the policy field emerged around the Second World War and the beginning of the Cold War in the US, with major attention given to "decision-making." Robert Dahl considered this dynamic can be considered as the result of four factors: the influence of Charles Merriam and the department of political science he managed in the 1930s producing major scholars such as Truman, Lasswell, Simon, Almond, Key, the arrival of several German Refugee scholars who insisted on the sociological dimension to understand politics, the experience of many scholars in government during the Second World War, the creation of a committee on political behavior in the Social Science Research Council, the growth of the survey methods and the financial support of foundations like Rockefeller, Rand Corporation, Ford, Carnagie, etc. (Dahl Robert 1961). This period focused on understanding individual behavior and their "bounded rationality," but also groups' behavior with the pluralist role of interest groups in the governmental decision-making process, and the search for new policy analysis methods to rationalize decisions. It also involved the development of knowledge about the content of specific policies.

The second period, starting in the 1960s, began with various controversies about the multiple biases provoked by what we call "the myth of the decision." but also the begin of empirical studies on the policy process. During this period, specific protest movements emerged in the US against government policies following the Vietnam War and issues of racism. We observed the development of multiple studies that critiqued the decision-making model based on the idea that someone chooses a "relevant" solution at a specific moment to solve a problem. The controversies began with works on the importance of the pre-decision process, including problem definition and solution formulation. It continued with numerous studies on the complex role of bureaucracy and the intricacies of implementation.

The third period, which emerged at the end of the 1960s, can also be considered the beginning of the policy field by proposing to move beyond the controversies and shift from the study of the decision-making process to the study of the policy process. This period corresponds to the end of the behavioralism and the will to propose a more meso- or macro-perspective but also a growing interest to the content of the policy. It is also the period of the development of policy schools in the US and the strategies of political scientists that allowed them to establish themselves within the field. The main idea was to transform pre-decision, decision, and implementation into a policy process and to reconcile the analysis of content with the analysis of the process. During this period, multiple textbooks and articles about the policy process emerged.

THE PRE-HISTORY OF THE POLICY STUDIES

The European "Pre-History" of the Policy Studies

The English concept of "policy" comes from the old medieval French word "policie," which was used to describe how the king should govern the kingdom and its people, with a specific focus on maintaining social order. From "Le Roman de la Rose" (thirteenth century) in France to Machiavelli in Italy, we observe the emergence of policy knowledge to advise the Prince or king on governing people, achieving peace and order, and maintaining their legitimacy. The concept evolved in the eighteenth century, becoming "police" in France and "policey" in German, referring to the development of specific knowledge about the concrete tools, modern governments should use to ensure the development of their countries. In the nineteenth century, the concept became more restricted, with "police" increasingly referring only to the administration responsible for law enforcement and sanctions.

In the medieval period, different books were published to discuss how the Prince could govern his subjects to maintain order and legitimacy. In 1405, Christine de Pizan wrote the "Livre du corps de policie" to explain how King Charles V had such a good policy that his kingdom was at peace. Her book was dedicated to the Prince and the Seigneury, offering them advice on how to govern. During the same period, Machiavelli wrote his famous "The Prince," where he also proposed giving advice to the Prince, explaining that being chosen is not enough to maintain his position; he must also win the hearts of the people by governing them effectively.

In the eighteenth century, we observed various publications in France and Germany about the "Police" or how to govern people. As Foucault observed, this period corresponds to a transformation where the issue is not limited to advising the King or The Prince to obtain the support of their people but focuses on the techniques that the government needs to use to maintain order and allow prosperity. It also corresponds to the end of the Spanish Empire's dominance and the development of competition between nations through their capacity to demonstrate their prosperity. The story began in the eighteenth century with the publication of the first books about "Police" in France ("Traité de Police," Delamare, 1706). Delamare spoke about the art of government and defined "Police" as "the noble part of public administration which includes the security and happiness of men joined in society." He addressed the bureaucrats and mentioned 13 sectors where the government has to act, which include all sectors outside finance and military issues.

In the same period, the concept also took place in Germany with a new perspective: the development of a science of "Policey." In 1756, Von Justi published an important book ("Grundsätze der Policey-Wissenschaft," Von Justi, 1756) where he proposed developing a science aimed at achieving temporal happiness for citizens by ensuring peace, security, order, abundance, health, and morality, to allow the State to be perfect. Germany became the center for the development of knowledge about policy through the first chairs of "Policey" in various universities.

In the nineteenth century, the term "police" became increasingly restricted to maintaining order, recording infractions, and sanctioning culprits. In the Napoleonic Penal Code, the term "police" was used only for "administrative police" to prevent disturbances to public order and "judicial police" to sanction those who do not respect the law. Conversely, the development of knowledge about governance took place in a new discipline, "political economy," a term that began to emerge with Adam Smith and others before becoming Economics. Political Economy also focused on happiness and prosperity but with a constant concern about the limits of State activity rather than its expansion. Some other specific policy studies also emerged during this period. One of the most famous and probably the first comparative study about Public Policy was published in 1831 by Alexis de Tocqueville and Gustave de Beaumont. They proposed comparing different prison management policies developed in various states to understand their effects on recidivism. They compared the Philadelphia policy, where prisoners are totally isolated, the Auburn policy, where isolation is limited to the night, and the French policy, where there is no isolation.

The US Pre-History of Policy Studies: The Chicago School of Political Science

When we observe the founders of Policy Studies, most of them have in common their origins from the Department of Political Science at the University of Chicago in the first half of the twentieth century. This department, managed by Charles Merriam, became the place where a new political science emerged, based on scientific knowledge, to support democracy through policy. Involved in supporting the municipality of Chicago with major problems they faced, Charles Merriam was mobilized during the crisis of 1929 to coordinate the support of social scientists from multiple disciplines to help the government develop new public policies.

Charles Merriam was recruited in 1900 to manage the small Department of Political Science and transform it within the young University of Chicago. In his first book published in 1903, he critiqued the dominance of the historical perspective in political science and defended its autonomy through the development of scientific methods (Karl 1974). He also opposed Burgess, one of the main figures in political science, by arguing that democracy is not limited by democracy and scientific progress but rather that science contributes to democracy and scientific progress. Influenced by Wallas and his work "Human Nature in Politics" (Wallas 1908), he considered that politicians do not make decisions rationally and need scientific support to make relevant decisions. This is why he defended the idea that "The real answer to this challenge of politics is the consideration and adoption of more scientific and intelligent methods in the study and practice of government" (Merriam 1931).

Charles Merriam not only wrote about the need for scientific support, he practiced it. Involved in various working groups organized by the municipality of Chicago, he began producing comparative reports on the fiscal policies of different municipalities in the US. He also worked on various other policies such as bridges and roads, criminality, and electricity policy. In his work, he was particularly attentive to the conflicts between different bureaucratic services. In 1914, he managed a commission tasked with addressing the criminality problem in Chicago. His main idea was to mobilize all the different disciplines of social sciences to better understand the problem. This included a first part on the statistics of the problem produced by Edith Abbott, an economist, a second part by Robert Gaul, a psychologist, to identify the causes, and another by experts to understand corruption. By doing so, Charles Merriam became what Lasswell later theorized as an entrepreneur who mobilizes multiple social sciences to highlight a problem. In a book published in 1929, Merriam theorized that solving problems is not a theoretical political issue but a practical one for which academics can be useful.

But one of the most fundamental experiences was in 1929 when President Hoover decided to mobilize academics to give him advice on managing the crisis. In 1929, he established a research committee on Recent Social Trends in the US, presided over by the economist Wesley Mitchell, with Charles Merriam becoming vice-president. This was followed by the National Planning Board of the Federal Emergency Administration of Public Works. These committees produced advice on public policy (Hill 1957). Robert Merton and Daniel Lerner (Merton and Lerner 1951) suggested that these committees brought together, for the first time on this scale, multiple social scientists to advise the government on how to develop public policy to solve social and economic problems.

A few years later, during the Second World War, Harold Lasswell, who was mobilized to work for the US Army in 1943, published his first report on the same topic: the need to mobilize social sciences to support the reemergence of democracy in Europe after the Second World War. Although Harold Lasswell was a student of Merriam, his early works were more comprehensive, following a Weberian tradition, and concerned with propaganda and the issue of how an elite uses propaganda and policy to maintain power. During the war, his perspective changed, and he proposed the development of intelligence departments in various ministries to provide advice based on scientific results. The project of "Policy Sciences" was born and began to be developed in the collective book he managed, "Policy Sciences: Sciences of Democracy in the US." His main goal was to develop knowledge both for and about the policy process.

STUDYING THE DECISION PROCESS

The 1950s and 1960s laid the foundation for a good deal of what has followed in the study of public policy. This was a period of significant actions, both in society and in academia. Although looked upon now as a period of tranquility, the Cold War, the beginnings of decolonization, and nascent social change were placing pressures on governments. Within the social sciences, and especially political science, behavioralism was beginning to supplant more formal, structural explanations for decisions and the growth of foundation[1] funding for research opened up opportunities for innovation in social theory and public policy.

---

[1] The RAND corporation financed by US Air Force invested a lot of money to the study of decision-making process. We can also evoked the Rockfeller foundation, the Social Sciences Research Committee funded by Charles Merriam in 1923 when he was president of APSA.

This early work focused on two fundamental questions that remain important today. The first and most basic is the linkage of decision-making and public policy. Making policy is about making a series of decisions the define that policy, and subsequent approaches to policy continue to address that question. The second major question was the role of comprehensive rationality in policymaking. While ideas of bounded rationality prevailed in the early days of policy studies, and continue to have great importance today, there is still a lingering hope to be able to address our policy challenges in a more fully rational manner.

Bounded Rationality and Incrementalism

The absence of a focus on decision-making was one of the problems that Herbert Simon identified in public administration, and in nascent public policy studies, in the late 1940s and early 1950s. The emphasis on the structures of government, and on formalized processes, seemed to ignore that what the bureaucracy was doing was making decisions, and making policies. Further, to the extent there was any emphasis on decision-making, the assumption was that public organizations and the people within them would act rationally, using all available evidence to make the best possible decisions.

Simon's now familiar argument was that making fully rational policy decisions was virtually impossible. There was always more information that could be gathered, and the capacity to process all the information that was available was limited. Further, the problems that are faced in the public sector tend to be poorly structured, making them more difficult to solve. Therefore, rather than aspiring to full rationality, decision-makers would be better advised to accept bounded rationality. Rather than seeking to optimize "administrative man"[2] should attempt to "satisfice," and make decisions that are good enough for the time being, and then continue to make additional decisions to gradually improve policy.

This basic idea of Simon's was elaborated by Charles Lindblom (1959, 1968), as he discussed incrementalism and "muddling through." Lindblom argued that incremental decision-making–making a series of small decisions to reach a larger goal–was more rational than attempting to make a single decision to attain that goal. Given the information and

---

[2] Now "administrative person" of course.

calculative challenges confronting decision-makers in the public sector, the probability of making an incorrect decision would be high for a large-scale decision. Such errors could be very costly, given their scale. Therefore, it would be more rational to make a series of smaller decisions, assessing the effects of each, and perhaps retreating when a poor decision had been made. The assumption of the incrementalists is that errors in their decision-making scenario are likely to be less costly, and potentially reversible.

It is also important to note that although the roots of bounded rationality and incrementalism were in the 1950s and 1960s, this strand of thinking has persisted in policymaking. Incrementalist scholars (Hayes 2017) have continued to analyze policymaking in the US in the way, and Simon's influence has been important for more contemporary American and European scholars such as James March and Johan P. Olsen (1983) and their version of the new institutionalism in political science (1983). These scholars have been especially interested in the bounds that organizations and institutions place on the decision-making of individuals who function within them.

Stages Models of the Decision-Making Process

Another of the foundations of policy studies also began in the 1950s. This is the "stages model" of the policy process. The basic idea is that we can describe the steps through which policies pass as they are adopted and implemented, and this provides some insights into both policymaking and the nature of the policies being adopted. These models have been heavily criticized, but they continue to provide a useful mechanism for understanding how governments address policy problems and have been central to political science teaching about public policy.

Harold Lasswell (1956) developed the first stages model of the decision. This model (see Table 1) was more analytic than most that have followed it, emphasizing the tasks that a policymaking would have to perform if s/he were to be successful in moving from the recognition of a problem in society through to the evaluation of the policy and its effects on that society. In retrospect, this model was especially interesting because it included policy termination as one of the stages, while much subsequent policy research has emphasized the persistence of policies. Lasswell's model was also notable in that he labeled it the stages of the decision process, implying that these stages would be useful for understanding any sort of decision-making. *The Beginnings of Empirical Analysis.*

The 1960s and 1970s were the beginnings of quantitative studies of policy as well. While Simon and Lindblom addressed incrementalism as a normative model of decision-making, Aaron Wildavsky approached incrementalism more empirically, albeit initially with qualitative methods. Wildavsky (1964) examined the budget process in Congress (1964), pointing out that the scale and complexity of the process led decision-makers to utilize simple incremental rules of thumb to make their decisions. That insight derived largely from interviews was supported by statistical examinations of the outcomes of the process (Davis et al. 1966) that demonstrated the persistence of incremental increases in budgets over time. While critics (Tucker 1982; See also Jones et al. 1998) demonstrated that disaggregating the budget of agencies produced less incremental results, the incremental model of budgeting became the dominant mode of thinking about budgets in the US, as well as in many other settings.

At the same time, other scholars were making attempts to explain policy choices, especially levels of public expenditure. This body of research was sparked by one article arguing that politics was largely irrelevant in such an explanation, and all that mattered was the availability of economic resources (Dawson and Robinson 1963). Other scholars of American state politics engaged in large-scale studies attempting to refute the dominance of economics, with varied results (Dye 1966; Sharkansky 1968). This type of research also began to be more comparative, and to become concerned with longitudinal versus cross sectional patterns of expenditure (Alt 1971: Peters 1972) These studies were the foundation for a large body of research investigating the causes of policy choices, as well as the consequences of those choices.

Graham Allison and Alternative Models of Choice

Although initially focused on foreign policy decisions, Graham Allison's (1971) discussion of decision-making has had a much wider influence. When examining the Cuban Missile Crisis, Allison argued that three alternative models of decision-making could be applied. The first assumed that the actors involved for both the Soviet Union and the US were fully rational, and every decision was design to advance their interests. The second model based on Simon and March's organizational perspective assumed that the decisions being made were the result of organizational processes and were routinized. The third based on Neudstadt bargaining perspective argued that the organizations involved in the process were each using the decision situation to maximize their own utility, as well as to resolve the problem.

These three models again raised issues of rationality and bounded rationality. The first and the third models assumed rationality, albeit at different levels within the decision process. The second model assumed more bounded rationality, with the existing organizational processes defining what should be done. This work is known primarily for the third model "bureaucratic politics," but is important for identifying the three alternatives for thinking about decisions. It is also important for advancing the idea of bringing multiple theories (or methodologies) to bear on a single question in order to illuminate the processes involved.

Budgeting and the Search for Rationality

As noted, Aaron Wildavsky and other scholars of the budgetary process in the 1950s and 1960s argued that the process was incremental, and should be incremental. The scale and complexity of the task of making a budget for a contemporary government did not permit the type of rational calculations that might be desirable. At the same time, however, private businesses were beginning to develop budgeting models that attempted to enhance the possibility of rationality when making these choices. Those models soon came to be tested in the public sector.

Planning-Programming-Budgeting Systems (PPBS) was the clearest example of these budgeting approaches (Padgett 1971). As well as rejecting simple incrementalism, this model rejected the fundamental assumption of making budgets on the basis on organizations, but rather sought to allocate resources to the basic programs, e.g. health, defense, economic regulation, within government, This allocation recognized that almost all programs are multi-organizational, and that almost all organizations are multi-programmatic. PPBS also moved away from the usual conception of an annual budget to link budgeting to a planning process within government.

This conception of budgeting, therefore, required integrating policy analysis into a process that had been dominated by political considerations. For that reason, in part, PPBS and other rationality based versions of budgeting helped to institutionalize more formal and economics based versions of policy analysis that were based on optimizing rather than satis-ficing. This debate over the limits of rationality in policymaking is one of the continuing themes of policymaking up to the present.

THE PRE AND POST DECISION TURN (1960'S)

The emphasis on decision-making in the 1950s and 1960s was impor-tant for the development of public policy studies, but it tended to focus just on one part of the long process of making policy. Decisions about policy made by legislatures or political executives involve decisions made both before and after those events. Those decisions made before legis-lating tend to define what information is used in the legislation, as well as the actors who have influence in the process. The decisions made after will define what the policy decisions actually mean, as implemen-tation decisions may produce policy effects rather different than what the "formators" of the policy (Lane 1972) intended.

Pluralism and Public Policy

American political science, and the study of public policy, was dominated during the 1950's (and after) by pluralist theory (Flathman 2007). The dominant assumption was that the political system was an open arena in which numerous interests competed to have their ideas adopted as law. Further, that arena is assumed to provide equal opportunities to those various interests to exert influence. In pluralism the various inter-ests are represented by groups, reflecting the history of studies of interest groups by scholars such as Arthur Bentley and David Truman. This theory provided an optimistic picture of democracy that helped legitimate the rather conservative politics of the 1950s.

In the 1960s, the pluralist approach began to attract more criticism. One of the most significant critics was E. E. Schnattschneider in his book *The Semi-sovereign People* (1960). His basic point was that the arena for pluralist contestation over ideas and policies was not as impartial and unbi-ased as assumed by the pluralists, Instead, there was a pronounced bias in favor of business and other more affluent groups. As wrote, "...the flaw in the pluralist heaven is that the heavenly chorus sings with a strong upper-class accent" (1960, 35). Schattschneider's work had a great deal of influence on other important critics of the pluralist model, such as Theodore Lowi (1969).

Agenda-Setting

The most important activity that occurs prior to the decision-making process is agenda-setting. If an issue is not on the agenda of government, then legislation concerning the problems contained within the issue will never be considered. While political scientists and policy scholars were aware that having an issue considered at all was a crucial aspect of the policy process, it had not been studies conceptualized or studies systematically. To some extent following the work of Schnattschneider and other critics of pluralism, "agenda-building" or "agenda-setting" initially focused on the question of political power and the capacity of some groups to have their issued considered while others did not.

Roger Cobb and Charles Elder (1972). See also Jones, 2016 (were central to bringing agenda-setting into a central position in the study of public policy. They argued for the importance of understanding how issues can be placed on a public agenda, as well as that the process was not unbiased and did tilt in favor of those with greater economic and political resources. Agenda-setting thus helped to make the link between democratic theory and public policymaking even stronger.

The role of power in agenda-setting became even more apparent with the use if concept of "non-decision." Peter Bachrach and Morton Baratz (1963) (see also Wolfinger 1971) argued that there was a "second face of power." Not only was power exercised when making a decision, it was exercised by preventing decisions, or even having issues finding a place on the agenda. Steven Lukes (1974) added yet a third dimension of power that is relevant for agendas and policymaking. This is an ideological dimension in which the powerful can shape the thinking of the less powerful so that they do not consider options that might undermine the dominant position of the powerful, and hence would not consider getting such options onto the agenda..

This early agenda-setting literature was important in itself, and it helped to spawn the now thriving research tradition of Punctuated Equilibrium Theory (Baumgartner and Jones 1993). Beginning with Anthony Downs (1972), this body of research examines the way in which issues move on and off the active agendas of government (see below, xx) that has led to a better understanding not only of agenda-setting but also the policy process more generally.

The End of the Process: The Bureaucracy and Implementation

After legislatures or other policymakers make policy decisions, they must be put into effect and that is the job of the public bureaucracy (along with its allies in the private sector). This was sometimes assumed to be a rather straightforward legal and administrative process, but increased examinations of the process of putting laws into action revealed that bureaucracy as an institution, and implementation as a process, are much more problematic than often assumed. Implementation is a political process in its own right, and involves substantial bargaining, and the use of power, to be effective.

The study of implementation has its roots in the study of bureaucracy, and to some extent the study of bureaucratic dysfunctions. Much of this work came out of sociology rather than political science of public administration. For example, Robert Merton (1957, 196-206) expanded on Weber's theory but also pointed out the dysfunctions that were inherent in the bureaucratic pattern of organization. For the study of implementation goal displacement is the most important of those problems, with organizations and the individuals within them becoming more concerned with their own self-interest than with the purposes of the programs being administered. In addition, Peter Blau pointed out the crucial role of informal relations in defining how organizations function, and how they can both support and subvert achievement of the official goals. Likewise, Michel Crozier (1964) pointed out how the interaction of formal elements of bureaucratic structure and power relationships among actors created numerous dysfunctions within formal organizations.

Jeffrey Pressman and Aaron Wildavsky (1974) made the principal statement about implementation, in a book of the same name. They developed the concept of "clearance points" to describe the challenges faced during implementation. The notion was that to move from legislation to outcome involved a series of decisions, and that there had to be success at each of those points for the program to go into effect as intended.[3] The rather pessimistic conclusion was that implementation is likely to fail, although critics (Bowen 1982) and later editions of the book did have more optimistic perspectives. Further, as the implementation literature evolved, alternative perspectives produced more hopeful ideas about implementation.

---

[3] This concept is similar to that of the "veto player" (Tsebelis 2002).

The implementation process has associated with the public bureaucracy, and often examines the role of one organization in making one program work. Hjern and Porter (1981), however, pointed out that implementation occurs through groups of organizations (see also Peters 2014) and argued that the "single lonely organization" was dead. They argued that most implementation was done by "implementation structures" composed of multiple public organizations, as well as private organizations (for profit and not for profit) in many cases. Implementation therefore involved a great of bargaining within the structures themselves, as well as at each clearance point.

THE INFLUENCE OF SUBSTANTIVE POLICY

To some extent theories of public policymaking developed without reference to any particular policies. The assumption for approaches such as the Advocacy-Coalition Framework and the Multiple Streams Framework is that they are relevant for almost any type of policy.[4] That assumption remains largely untested, but it also ignores the extent to which policy thinking and ideas about policymaking are influenced by the nature of specific policies. As the policy field has developed there have been three significant examples of this influence shaping research on public policy. Although every time period has specific issues that have influenced the development of policy theory, there have been three major substantive issues on the public policy field, the first beginning during and just after World War II.

Welfare State. The first example of substantive policy questions influencing public policy as an academic discipline was the development of the Welfare State. Although what we now know as the Welfare State had its roots in the late nineteenth century in Germany, that term emerged from the understanding in the United Kingdom that the country after World War II would have to be different, and would have to provide a wide range of social and health policies to support the public. The foundations of that post-war Welfare State were laid in the Beveridge Report (1942,

---

[4] Although the application of these approaches across policy domains remains largely unquestionaed, their application across areas of the world is becoming subject to a major debate. In particular, can theories developed in the "North" really be applied effectively in countries of the Global South?.

See also Greener 2022) that detailed the conditions of the British population at the time and the need for a greater public role in many aspects of the society and economy.

William Beveridge was to some extent the beginning of a tradition of Welfare State scholars in the United Kingdom. Notable examples of this tradition of scholarship were Richard Titmuss, Brian Abel-Smith and Julian Le Grand. Although each of these scholars, and others in this tradition, had his or her own particular approach, there are several things that have characterized this strand of policy research. One is a close attention to quantitative and qualitative data. The Beveridge Report itself was filled with extensive analysis of the state of the population. The other distinguishing feature has been the integration of normative and empirical analysis as typified by Richard Titmuss/s *The Gift Relationship: From Human Blood to Social Policy* (1970).

Academic studies of the Welfare State were not, of course, limited to the United Kingdom. Each country has had its own tradition of research on these policies. Notable examples, albeit not all in the same time frame, include Gunnar and Alva Myrdal in Sweden, Peter Flora in Germany, and Bruno Palier in France. Latin America also has a rich history of research on the Welfare State. Although there are national traditions, the general point that the need to understand, and reform, these social programs contributed to the development of policy studies.

Development. The second substantive policy problem that constricted to the development of policy studies emerged with the independence of many states that had been colonies. Development policies and development administration (Preston 1996) began to be a major field of research, as well as practice, in the late 1950s and early 1960s. This research tended to be based in economics, but also had some interdisciplinary elements, bringing together economic, political, and social dimensions of fostering change in these new states (see North 1990).

The studies of development had two major influences on the study of public policy. The first was to emphasize the extent to which public policy is embedded in cultural and social norms, and that it needs to be understood comparatively. There had been a few comparative studies of public policies in Western countries, but the world was now opened for a wider range of policy research. This openness was both a challenge and an opportunity that continues to this day as scholars grapple with the intellectual problems of dealing with policy in the Global South (see

Mendez et al. forthcoming)[5] Not only as substantive aspects of policy often different, but there are questions concerning the extent to which the models of policymaking developed in the North are suitable for use in the South.

The second influence of development studies on public policy was the need to think even more about policy change. Reform and change has always been an important issue for public policy scholars, but the challenges faced by developing countries raised more questions about how to understand and bring about change, and what effects government and citizens should expect from policy change. The need for new governments to respond to decolonialization and significant social changes placed the issue of reform, and associated issues such as policy learning (Dumlop and Radaelli 2020) at the heart of policy studies.

Regulation. The third impact of substantive policy issues on public policy studies has been through the increased concerns with regulation. Governments have always used regulations, but the increased importance of policy areas such as the environment have increased the centrality of regulation in public policy studies. This area of research has been especially important in bringing public policy analysis more directly in touch with legal scholarship, as well as reinforcing the links with economics.

The study of regulation has had several other influences on contemporary policy studies. One is that it has required scholars to be deeply embedded, and expert, in the details of a policy. Studies in journals such as *Regulation & Governance* contain increasingly detailed analyses of policy, revealing the complexity of the issues and their putative solutions. The other influence was that the study of regulation made the political question of how much regulation, or deregulation, was desirable more central.

Summary

These three examples of the impacts of policy are not the only cases we could mention. They do, however, make the point that public policy research is not just about alternative models of policy choice. It is also heavily influenced by what is happening in the "real world" of public policy. That connection to the environment should not at all be seen as

---

[5] The terms "South" and "North" here are in part geographical, but also refer to levels of socio-economic and political development.

a distraction from the development of academic approaches but rather represents an enrichment of those approaches, and of policy studies more generally. More recently, this can be seen in the influence of the numerous studies of the COVID epidemic on thinking about the resilience of policies.

THE POLICY TURN: THE EMERGENCE OF THE POLICY PROCESS STUDIES

In the mid-1960s, several movements emerged that helped to move beyond the 1960s controversies about decision-making by considering the pre-decision, decision and implementation phases within the same large policy process, and by integrating the study of process with the study of policy content. This marked the beginning of the study of policy as a process rather than just decision-making. This movement was the result of the collective dynamism of various political scientists who had made significant contributions to earlier debates and who proposed to take them further. It also coincided with a period of success for policy analysis and the emergence of the first policy schools in the US, dominated by economists, while political scientists sought new places.

In his presidential address in 1969, David Easton announced the "post-behaviouralist" revolution in political science. Since the 1950s, this author has always rejected the micro-perspective of behavioralism, which focuses on the decision-making process, to propose a macro-systemic perspective, in which decision-making becomes secondary and takes place in a black box of the political system, in order to highlight the importance of the complex relationship between the political system and society through the "input," which we can identify as the "demand" or the problem that stress the political system, the "output," which is the public policies that the political system produces, and the "outcome," which is their effect on society. By the way, Easton proposed a macro-processual perspective, which is becoming increasingly important in the political science literature.

Looking at the second half of the 1960s, we see for the first time an incredible proliferation of books that have in common the study of the policy process rather than the decision-making process. In response to "the number of new books, articles, and edited volumes on public policy and policy making, [which] suggests a growing awareness among social scientists" (Lowi and Olson 1970, 314), Lowi saw it as a shift from "deci-sion-making" to "policy making" that corresponded to a move beyond the behavioral revolution of the 1950s and 1960s and its interest in the "socially microscopic phenomena of interpersonal relations" (314). Bauer explains how "decision-making is an inappropriate concept for charac-terizing policy making (…) the term decision-making, when used by psychologists, decision theorists (…) implies a specific model of cognitive activity (…) assumes a single decision-making unit (…) In the process of policy making, each of these assumptions is violated."

By shifting the perspective from the decision to the policy process, the authors proposed not only to broaden the focus of observation, but also to reintegrate the content of policy into the decision-making process. This orientation was particularly emphasized by Austin Ranney, who consid-ered that "since 1945 most American political scientists have focused their professional attention mainly on the processes by which public poli-cies are made and have shown relatively little concern with their content" (Ranney 1968, p. 3). This orientation also helped to legitimize the polit-ical scientist as a "policy adviser." As Charles Jones explained, "the policy process approach offers more than just another way of looking at the same subject matter. It provides a framework within which students of politics can contribute more directly to what is going on in society"(Jones 1970, p. 5). This new activist perspective also corresponds to the context of the student protest movement in the US and around the world, including the anti-Vietnam War movement and the growing interest in policy change.

If the SSRC and its Commission on Behaviour played a central role in the 1945s, the emergence of new committees and the organiza-tion of conferences contributed greatly to the collective movement that enabled the emergence of policy process studies. In 1964, the Social Science Research Council appointed the Committee on Governmental and Legal Processes, chaired by Pendleton Herring, V.O. Key, and David B. Truman, to promote the "study of governmental and legal processes." They organized a conference in June 1965 with Robert Dahl, James March, Richard Neustadt, James Ptothro, and Aaron Wildavsky to discuss how political scientists could study, evaluate and make recommendations about the content of public policy. They continued with two subsequent conferences in June 1966 and June 1967 with other authors, such as Theodore Lowi, Thomas Dye, Ira Shalanski (etc.), to ask how the study of the governmental process and the study of policy content could be reconciled through the study of the policy process.

This period of interest in the policy process and the publication of a large number of books on the policy process also corresponds to the emergence of the first policy schools. As close Allison about the Kennedy School (Allison 2006), this movement was born in the US from the impulse of President Johnson who want to develop policy analyst and methods like PPBS in all the administration. This fascination for the rationalization of the decision in US offered a centrality to the policy analysis and to the economic perspective, but it can also create opportunity for political scientists to take a place in these schools by proposing textbooks and handbooks about the policy process and its political dimension.

This focus on the policy process rather than the decision-making process is translated by transforming some models of decision-making into the first models of the policy process. The first example is the work of Lindblom, who developed an incremental analytical model of decision-making in the 1950s, and who proposed to identify the "limits of policy analysis," which "does not fully resolve the policy question at issue"(p.12), and to broaden the perspective by integrating "defining the policy problem" (p.13).) and propose to broaden the perspective by integrating "the definition of the policy problem" (p.13), "cooperation among specialists" (p.30), "the play of power"(p.32), "the citizen as policymaker"(p.43), "voter and party competition" (p.53), "interest group leaders"(p.62), "the policymakers"(p.76). Austin Ranney has "adapted" the Easton model into a "policy process" model, where "policy process" is the response of the political system to demands and support, and "policy content" is the capacity of the response to be transformed into an output and outcome that feeds back into society (p. 9).

In this dynamic, the first two models of the policy process emerged through the transformation of a theory of decision-making. The first is the step-by-step or stage model of the policy process. This was inspired by the model of decision-making developed by Lasswell and, more precisely, the seven "functions" he identified in this process (intelligence, promotion, prescription, invocation, application, evaluation, termination) into an heuristic model of stages of the policy process. The versions of the process model that followed Lasswell (Jones 1970; Birkland 2019) have been more explicitly about public policy (Table 1). Perhaps because of that clear policy focus, they have been more political and have emphasized political components of the processes such as agenda-setting and implementation. These models do share the same linear conception of the policymaking process that was in Lasswell's version, Despite the limitations, these models also have demonstrated their more general utility through linkages with more analytic models. For example, Charles Jones adapted Lasswell's model of decision-making into a stage model of the policy process, transforming his "catalogue of functional activities" into "patterned activities can be grouped by their relationship to the central concern here: what government does to respond to public problems" (p. 11), by classifying some functions such as perception, definition, aggregation, representation in "problem to government," formulation, legitimation in "action in government," application in "government to problem"; reaction, evaluation in "policy to government."

The second model of policy process that appeared was that of Kingdon, which was inspired by the garbage can model of Cohen, March and Olsen. If their model, the three authors spoke of stream of problems to evoke the list of problems available and the stream of solutions to evoke the one of solution, Kingdon transformed them in a process. The stream of problems became the process by which the problem was created and defined, mobilizing the literature on the problem agenda of the previous period. The stream of solutions became the process of formulation driven by the policy community also developed in the previous period and the decision itself take in the garbage become the "coupling" process managed by the policy entrepreneur.

CONCLUSION

The Policy Field has a long history. Every part of its history is connected to US history and to discussions in the social sciences that influenced it. This history helps us understand how these ideas have developed and been used. The idea of "policy" has different meanings and is studied in different ways depending on the time period and the relationship between the government and society. For example, the decision issue was the main focus of academic research during the Cold War. The problem agenda was created at the same time as the protests against the government's inability to address issues like racism and discrimination in the 1960s. The Policy Turn also reflects the modernization of the state in the 1970s.

The early 1980s were also a time of change. The first is marked by crises affecting not only the economy and society, but also the welfare state model and public policy in Western countries. This is shown by the fact that people are paying more attention to how institutions are resisting change, and by the desire to better understand the challenges that change faces. This has led to discussions about institutions and the idea of "path dependency." It is also the development of a critical perspective on policy, which is important for evaluating certain kinds of reform ideas inspired by rational choice. It is also how the discipline became an official part of US institutions. This happened when the policy schools were founded in many universities and some positivist "models"were developed.

The second turn is based on the internationalization of the discipline. It was first imported to Europe in the 1970s and 1980s. It first arrived in the UK and then in some other countries, like Germany, France, and Italy. Public policy studies combined with local perspectives in these countries. In the UK, the main issue was about governance, the policy network, and the tools to understand the policy process Rose, Hood, etc.). In continental Europe, one of the main issues was the role of actors and the impact of constraints. These constraints were more influenced by other social sciences, such as sociology and planning. In France, the main issue was to focus on the importance of the bureaucracy, with its internal conflicts, and of the power of the idea in the policy process (Theonig, Jobert, Muller). In Germany, the main focus was on the interactions and conflicts among different social and political groups (Schaprf). In Italy, the topic of collective action was also a central point (Dente). The development in Latin America, Asia, and Africa by the year 2000.

Since 2010, the movement of internationalization has changed. After the Policy Field was shared in many countries, the creation of an international association and an international conference helped build an international academic community. The first international conference in Grenoble was held in 2013. It was a big success, with more than 1000 people from over 70 countries participating. The International Public Policy Association was created in 2014. It started as a small group of academics in political science. The association has grown substantially since then. In just ten years, the Association organized seven international conferences around the world. They also have started a journal and held summer schools all over the globe and have given out some awards. IPPA has helped shape international policy studies, and the nature of public policies themselves.

REFERENCES

Alt, J. E. 1971. Some social and political correlates of county borough expenditures. *British Journal of Political Science* 1:49–62.

Allison, G. 2006. Emergence of schools of public policy: Reflections by a founding dean. *The Oxford Handbook of Public Policy.*

Allison, G. T. 1971. *Essence of decision: Explaining the Cuban missile crisis.* Boston: Little, Brown.

Balla, S. J., M. Lodge, and E. C. Page. (Eds.). 2015. *The Oxford handbook of classics in public policy and administration.* OUP Oxford.

Bachrach, P., and M. S. Baratz. 1963. Decisions and nondecisions: An analytical framework. *American Political Science Review* 57 (3): 632–642.

Baumgartner, R., and B. D. Jones. 1993. *Agendas and instability in American politics.* Chicago: University of Chicago Press.

Beveridge, W. (1942) *Social Insurance and Allied Services* (London: Cmd. 6404).

Birkland, T. A. 2019. *An introduction to the policy process.* New York: Routledge.

Bowen, E. R. 1982. The Pressman-Wildavsky paradox: Four addenda or why models based on probability theory can predict implementation success and suggest useful tactical advice for implementers. *Journal of Public Policy* 2 (1): 1–21.

Cobb, R. W., and C. D. Elder. 1972. *Participation in American politics: The dynamics of agenda-building.* Boston: Allyn and Bacon.

Crozier, M. 1964. *The bureaucratic phenomenon: An examination of bureaucracy in formal organizations and it cultural setting in France.* Chicago: University of Chicago Press.

Dahl Robert, A. 1961. Who governs?: Democracy and power in an American city. New Haven, USA.

Davis, O. A., M. A. H. Dempster, and A, Wildavsky. 1966. A theory of the budgetary process. *American Political Science Review* 60:529–547.

Dawson, R. E., and J. A. Robinson. 1963. Interparty competition, economic variables, and welfare policies in the American states. *Journal of Politics* 25:265–289.

Delamare, N. 1706. *Traité de la police: Où l'on trouvera l'histoire de son établissement, les fonctions et les prérogatives de ses magistrats.* Jean et Pierre Cot.

DeLeon, P. 1988. *Advice and consent: The development of the policy sciences.* Russell Sage Foundation.

Downs, A. 1972. Up and down with ecology: The 'issue-attention cycle. *The Public Interest* 28:39–50.

Dunn, W. N. 2019. *Pragmatism and the origins of the policy sciences: rediscovering Lasswell and the Chicago school.* Cambridge University Press.

4

Dunlop, C. A., and C. M. Radaelli. 2020. Policy learning in comparative policy analysis. *Journal of Comparative Policy Analysis: Research and Practice* 24 (1): 51–72.

Dye, T. R. 1966. *Politics, economics, and the public: Policy outcomes in the American states.* Chicago: Rand McNally.

Flathman, R. E. 2007. *Pluralism and Liberal democracy.* Baltimore: Johns Hopkins University Press.

Greener, I. 2022. *The welfare state in the 21st century: The five new giants.* Cheltenham: Edward Elgar.

Hayes, M. T. 2017. Incrementalism and public policy-making. *Oxford Research Encyclopedia in Politics.* https://doi.org/10.1093/acrefore/978019 0228637.013.133.

Hjern, B., and D. O. Porter. 1981. Implementation structures: A new unit of administrative analysis. *Organization Studies* 2 (3): 211–227.

Jones, B. D. 2016. A radical idea tamed: The work of Roger Cobb and Charles Elder. In *Handbook of public policy agenda-setting*, ed. N. Zahariadis. Cheltenham: Edward Elgar.

Jones, C. O. 1970. *An introduction to the study of public policy.* Belmont, Ca: Wadsworth.

Jones, B. D., F. R. Baumgartner, and J. L. True. 1998. Policy punctuations: US budget authority, 1947–1995. *Journal of Politics.* 60:1–33.

Karl, B. D. 1974. Charles E. Merriam and the study of politics. *Political Theory* 3 (4).

Lasswell, H. D. 1956. *The decision process: Seven categories of functional analysis.* College Park, MD: Bureau of Governmental Research University of Maryland.

Lindblom, C. E. 1959. The science of muddling through. *Public Administration Review* 19:79–88.

Lindblom, C. E. 1968. *The policy making process.* Englewood Cliffs, N.J: Prentice-Hall.

Lane, J. E. 1972. The concept of implementation. *Statsvetenskapliga tidskrift* 86:17–40.

Lowi, T. J. 1969. *The end of liberalism: The Second Republic of the United States.* New York: W. W. Norton.

Lowi, T., and M. Olson. 1970. Decision making vs. policy making: Toward an antidote for technocracy. *Public Administration Review* 30 (3): 314–25. JSTOR. https://doi.org/10.2307/974053

Lukes, S. 1974. *Power: A radical view.* Basingstoke: Palgrave Macmillan.

March, J. G. And J. P. Olsen (1983) The new institutionalism: Organizational factors in political life. American Political Science Review. 78, 734–749.

Mendez, J. L., M. I Dussauge and B. G. Peters (forthcoming) *Handbook of Public Policy in the Global South* (London: Macmillan).

Merriam, C. E. 1931. *New aspects of politics.* University of Chicago Press.

Merton, R. K. 1957. *Social theory and social structure*. Glencoe, IL: The Free Press.

Merton, R. K., and D. Lerner. 1951. Social scientists and research policy. *The policy sciences: Recent developments in scope and method*, 282–307.

North, D. C. 1990. *Institutions, institutional change and economic performance*. New York: Cambridge University Press.

Padgett, E. R. 1971. Programming-planning-budgeting: Some reflections upon the American experience with PPBS. *International Review of Administrative Sciences* 37 (4): 353–362.

Peters, B. G. 1972. Economic and political effects on the development of social expenditures in France. *Sweden and the United Kingdom Midwest Journal of Political Science* 15:225–238.

Peters, B. G. 2014. Implementation structures as institutions. *Public Policy and Administration* 29 (2): 131–144.

Preston, Peter W. 1966. *Development theory: An introduction to the analysis of complex change*. London: Wiley-Blackwell.

Pressman, J. L., and A. Wildavsky. 1974. *Implementation: How great expectations in Washington*. Univ. of California Press.

Ranney, A. 1968. Political science and public policy. Markham Pub. Co.

Schattschneider, E. E. 1960. *The Semisovereign people: A realist's view of democracy in America*. New York: Holt, Rinehart and Winston.

Sharkansky, I. 1968. *Spending in the American states*. Chicago: Rand MacNally.

Torgerson, D. (2024). Harold Lasswell as distinct from his work: The method of immanent critique and its implications. *Policy Sciences*, 57: 931–947.

Titmuss, R. M. 1970. *The gift relationship: From human blood to social policy*. London: Kegan Paul.

Tsebelis, G. 2002. *Veto players: How political institutions work*. Princeton: Princeton University Press.

Tucker, H. J. 1982. Incremental budgeting: Myth or model? *Western Political Quarterly* 35 (3): 327–338.

Von Justi, J. H. G. 1756. *Grundsätze der Policey-Wissenschaft*. Vandenhoeck.

Wallas, G. 1908. *Human Nature in Politics*. Archibald Constable & Co.

Wildavsky, A. 1964. *The politics of the budgetary process*. Boston: Little, Br.

Wolfinger, R. E. 1971. Nondecisions and the study of local politics. *American Political Science Review* 65 (4): 1063–1080.

The Advocacy Coalition Framework for Comparative Analyses of Contentious Policy Issues

Christopher M. Weible and Hank C. Jenkins-Smith

INTRODUCTION

Since the emergence of public policy as a field of study in the middle of the twentieth century, a definitive challenge has been developing theoretical approaches for comparative policy processes. Such an approach would focus researchers on common questions, provide a shared vocabulary, specify similar concepts for description and explanation, and balance the need for structure in generalizing about commonalities across multiple

---

Prepared for Zittoun/Peters (ed.) *Contemporary Approaches to Public Policy* (2nd Edition)

C. M. Weible (✉)
School of Public Affairs, University of Colorado Denver, Denver, CO, USA
e-mail: Chris.Weible@ucdenver.edu

H. C. Jenkins-Smith
Institute for Public Policy Research and Analysis, University of Oklahoma, Norman, OK, USA
e-mail: hjsmith@ou.edu

© The Editor(s) (if applicable) and The Author(s), under exclusive license to Springer Nature Switzerland AG 2026
B. G. Peters and P. Zittoun (eds.), *Contemporary Approaches to Public Policy*, International Series on Public Policy,
https://doi.org/10.1007/978-3-032-06026-6_3

43

contexts with the flexibility necessary for accurately depicting the particularities of a single context.

In the US, efforts to develop theoretical approaches for the comparative study of policy processes have been ongoing for more than five decades. Examples of the early approaches were the policy-sciences framework (Lasswell 1970), systems theory (Easton 1965), a policy typology (Lowi 1964), and the funnel of causality (Hofferbert 1974). Some of these early theoretical approaches outlived their usefulness, were slowly forgotten, and sometimes subsumed by new theoretical approaches.

One theoretical approach that has endured is the Advocacy Coalition Framework (ACF). With nearly four decades of research and hundreds of applications that span the globe, the ACF is now one of the most established and widely applied approaches for studying policy processes. This chapter provides a brief overview of the ACF, covering its creation and foundation, past and recent contributions and niches, general description, three theories, development, boundaries of application, and major challenges and strategies for advancing knowledge about the policy process.

CREATION AND FOUNDATIONS

Paul Sabatier and Hank Jenkins-Smith originally developed the ACF in the 1980s and early 1990s (Jenkins-Smith 1982, 1990; Sabatier 1986, 1988; Sabatier & Jenkins-Smith 1993). It emerged from a dissatisfaction with then contemporary policy theories and, in particular, impediments associated with the policy cycle in advancing research and knowledge about the policy process. Inspiration for the framework also came from the Institutional Analysis and Development Framework (Kiser & Ostrom 1982), research on policy learning and the role of scientific and technical information in the policy process (Heclo 1974; Weiss 1977; Mazur 1981), a need to synthesize bottom-up and top-down approaches to implementation (Hjern & Porter 1981; Mazmanian & Sabatier 1983), and the idea that the best unit of analysis for studying policy processes was not a government agency or a single policy but rather a policy subsystem, which is a subset of a larger political and governing system focused on a topical area and locale (Heclo 1978).

No one knows the exact number of ACF applications in books or peer-reviewed articles in English or other languages. The estimated number of dissertations and theses that apply to the ACF is probably around

1,000. Special issues in peer-reviewed journals featuring the ACF can be found in the *Policy Sciences* (Sabatier 1988), the *Policy Studies Journal* (Weible et al. 2011), *Administration and Society* (Scott 2012), and the *Journal of Comparative Policy Analysis* (Henry et al. 2014). Applications span the globe with geographically based empirical reviews conducted in South Korea (Jang et al. 2016), in China (Li and Weible 2021), and in African countries (Osei-Kojo et al. 2023). New edited volumes include Weible et al. (2016) with applications spanning seven countries on oil and gas development, Ose-Kojo and Weible (2025) with applications in Africa, and Jenkins-Smith and Weible (2025) highlighting the distinction between textbook ACF applications and beyond. Topically, the initial applications of the ACF were on environmental or energy issues (Gabehart et al., 2022), but today the Framework is applied almost evenly across topical issues, including health, finance/economics, social welfare, disaster and crisis management, and education (Weible et al. 2009; Pierce et al. 2017; Nohrstedt et al. 2023).

PAST AND RECENT CONTRIBUTIONS AND NICHES

When it emerged in the 1980s, the ACF sought to provide an alternative to thinking about the policy process chiefly in terms of a policy cycle (Jones 1970; Brewer & deLeon 1983). The policy cycle is a linear or stage-based depiction of the policy process where issues become problems on the policy agenda; policy responses are formulated, adopted, and implemented; the outputs and outcomes are evaluated; and, occasionally, the policy is terminated.

Some of the problems with the policy cycle were its inaccurate linear characterization of policy processes, a narrow focus on a single policy rather than policies, and the dearth of causal explanations (Sabatier and Jenkins-Smith 1993). Compared to the policy cycle, the ACF provides a messier image of the policy process yet an image that is more realistic and still tractable for study.

Thirty years after the ACF emerged, many of the leading policy process textbooks are still organized by the policy cycle, force fit theories into one or more stages of the policy cycle, and promote its inaccurate linear image as the best way of organizing thinking and research on policy process. Thus, as it was 30 years ago, the ACF continues to provide an alternative to the policy cycle. Unlike the past, however, the ACF is no longer one of the few alternatives to the policy cycle (Sabatier 1999). Instead, the ACF is one of an array of policy theories that populate the field in advancing knowledge about the policy process (Weible 2023). The ACF is not in competition with these other theories. Rather, the population of theories that exist today are best imagined as a pluralistic way to help make sense of the complexity of policy processes. The ACF's utility is in helping to examine contentious politics and answering questions about coalitions, learning, and policy change.

General Description

A simplified flow diagram of the textbook ACF is shown in Fig. 3.1. On the right is the policy subsystem, wherein two coalitions and their beliefs and resources are listed. These coalitions develop and employ various strategies to influence the decisions of government, the rules governing subsystem affairs, and subsystem outcomes. Outside of the policy subsystem are relatively stable parameters, representing the context within which a policy subsystem is embedded, and external subsystem events, which are regular features outside of a policy subsystem that occasionally change. Between relatively stable parameters and external subsystem events are long-term coalition opportunity structures and short-term constraints and resources of policy subsystem actors, as well as intermediary categories that condition the effects of factors outside of a policy subsystem in shaping internal subsystem affairs. Fig. 3.1 is not meant to be comprehensive in the concepts listed in each box but instead a simplified depiction of categories of concepts and how they relate within the ACF.

Understanding and applying the ACF begins with understanding its seven foundational assumptions as a framework (Jenkins-Smith et al. 2014a, 189–193; Nohrstedt et al. 2023, 131–133).

1. *Policy subsystems are the primary unit of analysis for understanding policy processes.* A policy subsystem is a subunit of a government or political system anchored by an issue, a geographic scope, and policy actors, who are people regularly attempting to influence government decisions. Policy subsystems are nested, overlapping, and semi-autonomous (Sabatier 1998; Nohrstedt & Weible 2010; Jones & Jenkins-Smith 2009). Nested policy subsystems might occur when a subnational subsystem is embedded within a national subsystem. Overlapping policy subsystems might develop when issues overlap,

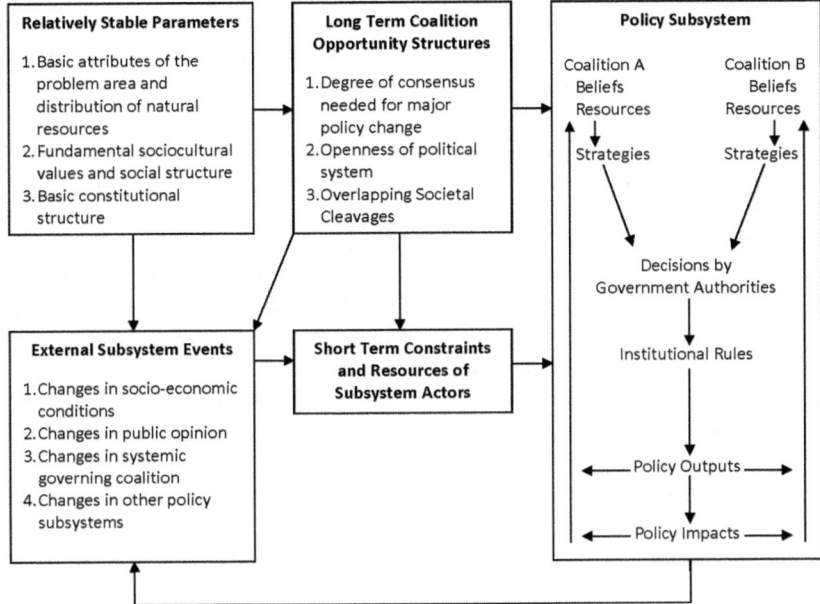

Fig. 1 Flow diagram of the advocacy coalition framework. Source: Adapted from Weible et al. (2011)

causing the actions and decisions in one subsystem to have an effect on another policy subsystem. Policy subsystems are also semi-autonomous; that is, there is some degree of independence in authority to take action and make decisions. Policy subsystems can exist at any level of government, emerge and disappear, collide with other subsystems, and are sometimes subsumed into others. Whereas policy subsystems exist in every stabilized country, their existence on a given issue will vary as will their structure. For example, a policy subsystem on a given issue might only occur at the national level in one country, be governed in several policy subsystems at the local level in another country, and might not exist at all in yet another country.

2. *The set of relevant subsystem actors include any person regularly attempting to influence subsystem affairs.* Policy subsystems emerge because of the need to focus resources in dealing with a particular

issue. The policy actors who seek to influence a policy subsystem can include, but are not limited to, officials from any level of government or government agency, representatives from nonprofit or private organizations, experts from academia, consulting firms, and think tanks, journalists working with the mainstream news media and as independent bloggers, and engaged citizens without any formal organizational affiliation. In comparative analysis, the number, intensity, and frequency of engagement by policy actors will vary across topics, locales, and time. In centralized systems, more national-level actors might be important policy actors, whereas in decentralized systems, local-level policy actors might be critically important for the same topic.

3. *Individuals are boundedly rational with limited ability to process stimuli, motivated by belief systems, and prone to experience the "devil shift."* Policy actors in the ACF are assumed to be boundedly rational with limited cognitive abilities to process information (Simon 1957, 1985). They make sense of the world through cognitive filters that lead to biases in how information is assimilated (Munro and Ditto 1997; Munro et al. 2002). The principal cognitive filter, and driver for behavior, is the policy actors' belief system. The ACF offers a three-tiered belief system.

4. At the most general level are deep core beliefs, which are normative values and ontological axioms. Deep core beliefs are not policy specific but rather span policy subsystems. Deep core beliefs are extremely difficult to change. Bounded and focused by the policy subsystem are policy core beliefs. Policy core beliefs relate to the territorial and topical scope of a policy subsystem and can be normative and empirical. Examples of policy core beliefs are basic problem definitions, causal understandings, and policy positions related to the policy subsystem. Policy core beliefs are very stable but more susceptible to change than deep core beliefs. At the most specific level are secondary beliefs. Whereas policy core beliefs entail the general policy goals of policy actors, secondary beliefs entail the means for achieving those policy goals. Secondary beliefs can also include beliefs that focus on a narrow slice of the policy subsystem. Secondary beliefs are most likely to change and are, in some situations, the focus of negotiations and compromise.

5. Finally, policy actors in the ACF are motivated by their beliefs and are prone to remember losses more than gains (Quattrone and

Tversky 1988), which create a mental state called the "devil shift" (Sabatier et al. 1987). The devil shift is the tendency for people to demonize their opponents by viewing them as more powerful and malicious than they actually are. The devil shift is one of the reasons people mobilize with like-minded allies in coalitions against a common opponent.

6. *Subsystems are simplified by aggregating actors into one or more coalitions.* The ACF is most applicable to analyzing contentious politics. In this situation, issues are under dispute, beliefs and identities are threatened, and opponents debate about whether and how government should respond. To simplify this context, the ACF views policy actors as members of coalitions based on similarities of policy core beliefs within coalitions (and differences in policy core beliefs across coalitions). Areas of inquiry that then emerge are the degree of belief and network cohesion within and between coalitions, the factors associated with learning within and between coalitions, and descriptions and explanations for policy change where one strong coalition might exploit a weak coalition or where two competitive coalitions negotiate agreements.

7. *Policies and programs incorporate implicit theories reflecting the translated beliefs of one or more coalitions.* The formulation of public policies represent the renditions of policy actors' belief systems. These renditions entail implicit theories of the causal understanding of why problems exist and how a policy solution might affect that problem. As a result, public policies are more than just what government does or does not do in relation to an issue but also a translation of the belief systems of policy actors. This is one reason why contentious politics emerge around policy issues: the content of public policy is linked to policy actors' belief systems.

8. *Scientific and technical information is important for understanding subsystem affairs.* Belief systems incorporate perceived causal patterns of the world. These patterns are informed from the day-to-day experiences of policy actors but also from scientific and technical information. The ACF, thus, puts an emphasis on the role of scientific and technical information in shaping belief systems and informing political debates. The argument is not that policy actors use such information rationally for learning and problem solving, which can sometimes be the case, but rather that policy actors use

scientific and technical information as a political resource in seeking to influence government.

9. *Researchers should adopt a long-term time perspective (e.g., 10 years or more) to understand policy processes and change.* Policy processes are ongoing and today's winners are often tomorrow's losers. Sometimes debates between coalitions can last for decades; and explanations for coalition behavior, learning, and policy change can only be understood by understanding events of the past. Researchers studying policy processes therefore must take a long-term time perspective, often spanning a decade or more. This does not imply that researchers applying the ACF must have 10 years of longitudinal data to analyze a particular situation but rather that researchers must remember that policy processes involve a temporal component where accurate description and explanation requires tracing back events and activities to the past.

Three Theories

The ACF supports three interrelated theories. The hypotheses derived from each of these theoretical emphases are listed in Appendix 1.

Theory of Advocacy Coalitions

Advocacy coalitions are defined by policy actors who have similar policy core beliefs and who coordinate their behavior in a variety of ways to influence government decisions. Scholars who analyze advocacy coalitions tend to focus on a common set of questions. A sample of these questions includes the following: Why do coalitions form? How do coalitions endure over time? What is the belief and network structure of a coalition? What resources and strategies are associated with the coalitions? How stable are coalitions over time?

Research has shown that coalitions form in part by their shared beliefs, that coalition members have common network ties, and that coalitions are relatively stable over time but not without some members defecting or joining (Jenkins-Smith et al. 1991; Zafonte and Sabatier 2004; Weible 2005; Henry 2011; Ingold 2011; Leifeld 2013; Lundmark et al. 2018; Satoh et al., 2023; Sommerville et al. 2022; Osei-Kojo, 2023). Even though evidence confirms the existence of coalitions and the importance of beliefs in forming coalitions, there has been mixed evidence concerning the relative import of policy core beliefs or secondary beliefs in forming coalitions. These mixed findings could reflect different conceptualizations of these two belief categories, different measurement methods, different context, or a faulty theoretical argument. Additionally, shared beliefs are not the only factor important in coalition formation. Other factors include interests, trust, and resources.

Research is increasingly documenting the different roles played by policy actors as coalition members, brokers, and entrepreneurs. For example, in summarizing the concept and theory of advocacy coalitions, Weible et al. (2020) highlighted central and consistent members to a coalition, called "principal" coalition actors, and those coalition members who were intermittently involved in a coalition and not central, called "auxiliary" coalition actors. Brokers are also consistently identified as important in learning and policy change. Brokers are policy actors with any organizational affiliation whose priority is to help reach agreements between opponents (Ingold and Varone 2012). Finally, policy entrepreneurs are also featured within coalitions and are likely important in leading a coalition, facilitating learning within and across coalitions, and producing policy change (Mintrom & Vergari 1996; Mintrom & Norman 2009; Petridou & Mintrom 2021).

There is no reason to expect that coalitions will have similar attributes across different policy subsystems. Work in authoritarian regimes, such as China, shows that coalitions tend to be dominant if affiliated with the government and ephemeral if in opposition to the government (Scott 2012; Li & Weible 2021). In democratic political systems with strong norms of consensus, as found in Sweden or Switzerland, there will more likely be interactions between opposing coalition members than what might be found in a pluralistic political system as in the US (Metz et al. 2021). In centralized political systems, such as South Korea, coalitions will likely involve powerful national- level policy actors who can play a decisive role in adopting policy (Jang et al. 2016). One of the next steps is to document systematic differences in coalitions across different forms of governments.

Theory Policy-Oriented Learning

One of the primary objectives of an advocacy coalition is to translate their policy core beliefs into public policy. In doing so, they adapt to their environment, adjusting to their successes and failures. The Theory of Policy-Oriented Learning refers to revisions to their belief systems and political strategies in achieving their objectives. Learning is defined as "enduring alterations of thought or behavioral intentions that result from experience and which are concerned with the attainment or revision of the precepts of the belief system of individuals or collectives" (Sabatier & Jenkins-Smith 1993, 42–56). Among the questions asked in analyzing policy-oriented learning are the following: To what extent is there learning within and between coalitions? What is the role of scientific and technical information in learning? How do belief systems change through learning? What is the role of policy brokers in learning? How do advocacy coalition members learn strategically from their successes and failures?

In the ACF's theory of learning, there are several factors that are expected to affect learning within and between coalitions (Jenkins-Smith 1990; Weible 2008). These factors include the rules structuring of the decision-making forum in which the opposing coalition members are interacting. Examples of these rules include degree of openness and norms of fair negotiations. In addition to the attributes of decision-making forums, the ACF posits that the level of conflict affects learning. Learning across coalitions is facilitated by intermediate levels of conflict and is inhibited by high or low levels of conflict. Cross-coalition learning is also inhibited with more intractable issues as the uncertainty fuels differences in interpretation and belief-based disagreements. Finally, learning is affected by the attributes of the coalition members. Coalition members with extreme beliefs are less likely to learn from opponents than coalition members with moderate beliefs.

Research on the hypotheses related to learning has produced mixed results. Learning does occur within and between coalitions, but sometimes the change is in altering policy core beliefs and secondary beliefs rather than just the latter (Sabatier and Brasher 1993; Elliott and Schlaepfer 2001). Additionally, intermediate levels of conflict, tractability of the issue, and available scientific and technical information have also been shown to facilitate learning (Larsen et al. 2006; Meijerink 2005; Funke et al. 2021; Gronow et al., 2021). Finally, evidence tends to show that most learning reinforces belief systems rather than change them, particularly in high conflict situations (Moyson, 2017; Weible 2023).

THEORY OF POLICY CHANGE

A major focus of the ACF has been in understanding the factors leading to policy change or stability. The framework makes a distinction between major and minor policy change. *Major* policy change is defined as changes in the direction or goals of the policy subsystem as they bear on the policy core and deep core beliefs of the coalitions. Minor policy change is defined as changes in the secondary aspects of the policy subsystem, such as the means by which a policy instrument is designed for achieving a particular goal. The ACF argues the following paths to policy change.

The first is external events originating outside of the policy subsystem. This includes, but is not limited to, elections, changes in socioeconomic conditions, changes in public opinion, and a crisis or disaster. These external events, by themselves, are not sufficient to lead to policy change. There must exist a coalition that exploits the opportunity associated with the event, such as heightened public attention, a favorable shift in government agendas, and a redistribution of political resources.

A second pathway is internal events that occur inside the policy subsystem. These internal events are often associated with the policies or policy actors of the policy subsystem and, thus, linked to scandals and policy failures. Internal events are different than external events in the potential for policy actors to capitalize on the opportunity to produce policy change.

A third pathway results from policy learning. Learning can lead to policy change when policy actors change their beliefs about the issue. This is most likely to occur over extended periods of time to allow for the information to accumulate and disperse across actors within the subsystem (Weiss 1977).

A fourth path to policy change is negotiated agreements when opposing coalitions reach agreement about a public policy. This is most likely to occur when there is a "hurting stalemate," which happens when opponents do not have other venues for influencing government and perceive the status quo to be unacceptable.

Fifth, the ACF argues that policy change occurs if driven by forces at a higher jurisdictional level, such as when a national government imposes change on subgovernmental units in a federally structured political system.

Lastly, policy change can happen when the power relations between advocacy coalitions change. More specifically, if a configuration of policies and programs comprising a subsystem based on the beliefs of one advocacy coalition is overcome by an opposing advocacy coalition, this new emergent coalition could impose major policy changes on the subsystem.

There has been a good deal of support for particular pathways evaluated singly (Bark 1993; Kübler 2001; Dudley & Richardson 1999; Fischer 2014; Pierce et al. 2020) and when these pathways lead to changes in the coalition controlling the policy subsystem (Ellison 1998; Olson et al. 1999; Heikkila 2014, Heinmiller 2023; Gutiérrez-Meave 2024). The challenge in understanding is that policy change is not usually the result of just one pathway but rather a combination of events that occur in a process over time (Pierce et al. 2020). For example, an instance of policy change might occur in response to multiple events within and outside the subsystem, learning within and between coalition members from those events as well as from other experiences, and negotiated agreements between two competitive coalitions—all of which might take a decade or more to transpire.

The importance of these different paths to policy change will also likely vary by the size and form of governing system embedding the policy subsystem. For example, in a centralized governing system such as that of South Korea, where there are frequent national-level elections, instances of major policy change will be frequent and led by changes in the central government (Jang et al. 2016). In decentralized systems, as found in the US, national-scale elections might not have as much of an effect on local-level policy subsystems (Pierce et al. 2020).

MAJOR CHALLENGES AND ADVANCING KNOWLEDGE

The strength of the ACF has been in its evolution in response to changing circumstances and empirical research. Yet, from Sabatier (1988) to Henry et al. (2022) and Nohrstedt et al. (2023), the basic framework of the ACF has remained nearly the same, as shown by the stability of its assumptions, scope, basic categories concepts, and general relations among concepts. While the exact number of articles published and authors contributing to this research program is currently unknown, the ACF continues to attract original thinking that advances some of its core arguments (Weible et al.,

2020; Nohrstedt & Heinmiller, 2024), innovations both conceptually and empirically (Fullerton & Weible, 2024; Heinmiller, 2023; Nowlin, 2021), methodological progress (Satoh et al., 2023), global appeal (Nwalie 2019; Asgari & Amirkhani, 2024), and research that offers practical and relevant insights (Dumet & Nelson, 2024; Haar, 2024). The ACF and its theoretical emphases have never shown such breadth or depth as currently practiced.

Part of the strength of the ACF is its compatibility with other theories. For example, Elgin and Weible (2013) borrowed the concept of policy analytical capacity (Howlett 2009) to understand better coalition resources. Heikkila et al. (2014) borrowed concepts from multiple theories, including the multiple-streams approach, in an attempt to describe a period of policy change. Jenkins-Smith et al. (2014b) and Ripberger et al. (2014) incorporate cultural theory within the ACF as a means to study deep core beliefs. Henry (2011) and Henry et al. (2010) are among many scholars that explore different rationales for the formation of networks beyond just beliefs, including resource dependence and social capital theories. There have also been recent innovations in incorporating the literature on emotions (Fullerton and Weible 2024) and collaborative governance (Koebele 2019) into the ACF. In our view, it is too often the case that scholars have limited themselves to explanations drawn from a single framework or theory at the cost of the (potentially) deeper understanding and theoretical advances that can be gleaned from comparative analyses. Hence, this growing propensity to incorporate other concepts and theories into the ACF provides a better way to test the veracity of the ACF's theories and develop knowledge about the policy process.

The textbook scope of the ACF is mature, adversarial subsystems in advanced polyarchies (Jenkins-Smith & Weible 2025; Weible & Jenkins-Smith 2025). Yet, the ACF has been usefully and regularly applied outside its textbook version. For example, the ACF has been applied to the decision-making venue level analysis in more cooperative settings. Leach and Sabatier (2005) and Leach et al. (2013) applied the ACF to multi-stakeholder partnerships involving watershed and aquaculture issues. These partnerships do not span an entire subsystem but rather represent a venue within a subsystem. This shift from subsystem to venues and from adversarial to cooperative or unitary subsystems is another way to explore the ACF outside its textbook version (Giordono 2020; Heinmiller et al. 2021).

Finding the right balance between gaining knowledge about a particular context and developing generalizable lessons has been (and will increasingly be) the fundamental challenge facing the study of policy processes. The ACF remains one of the most established platforms for the collective pursuit of knowledge about contentious policy issues across locations, topics, and time. Among the challenges in the ACF, we highlight below three areas needing the most attention and direct readers to Nohrstedt et al. (2023) for a more expansive list.

First, scholars often perceive the characterization of belief systems to be the most well-developed component of the framework. There is some validity to this observation. The three-tiered belief systems and the components therein have been subjected to numerous tests and have received broad empirical support. Nevertheless, the belief-system model in the ACF needs theoretical and conceptual refinement. One challenge is to more clearly define the distinctions among the different levels of the belief system, particularly those between policy core and secondary beliefs. Another challenge is to develop better guidelines for the specification of the general content of belief systems. One of the most promising areas is the use of cultural theory as a way to conceptual and measure deep core beliefs (Jenkins-Smith et al. 2014b; Ripberger et al. 2014). Cultural theory not only provides a common way to measure deep core beliefs but also connects the ACF to a complementary cultural theory literature (Swedlow 2014).

A second challenge is advancing the research agenda on policy-oriented learning. One of the big challenges is overcoming the myth that the ACF's concept of policy-oriented learning only includes changes (or reinforcement) of beliefs. It also includes any adjustments pertinent to advocacy coalition members' efforts to achieve their policy core goals in a subsystem. Among the next steps is a concerted effort to understand how advocacy coalitions adjust and learn to achieve their goals. Another area that needs new thinking is whether learning always coincides with belief change or whether belief reinforcement can also be conceptualized as learning (Nowlin 2021; Weible 2023). A second area needing attention is how to measure learning across different methods of data collection (Heikkila & Gerlak 2013).

The third challenge is linking factors external to the subsystem processes, outputs, and outcomes. Policy subsystems are embedded in a broader political and governing system. Yet, attention is needed in understanding how policy subsystems vary within and across such systems. For example, the degree of autonomy, the level of "nestedness," and the overlap of policy subsystems will vary depending on the form of government. The ACF currently guides researchers to analyze the relatively stable parameters, external events, and political opportunity structures, which is one way to address this challenge, but there might be others. Comparative research making these linkages has only begun to materialize (Gupta 2012, 2014; Fischer 2014; Gronow et al. 2021).

These challenges and the continued evolution of the ACF are indicative of a framework that continues to grow and mature. The progressive evolution of the ACF will continue as long as the framework continues to serve researchers interested in studying contentious politics. For the foreseeable future, the ACF will remain one of the most established tools for analyzing comparative policy processes and will, we hope, provide a theoretically sound basis from which policy analysts can understand and manage contentious politics over policy issues.

Appendix i: The ACF Hypotheses

Coalition Hypotheses

Hypothesis 1

On major controversies within a policy subsystem when policy core beliefs are in dispute, the lineup of allies and opponents tends to be rather stable over periods of a decade or so.

Hypothesis 2

Actors within an advocacy coalition will show substantial consensus on issues pertaining to the policy core, although less so on secondary aspects.

Hypothesis 3

An actor (or coalition) will give up secondary aspects of his (its) belief system before acknowledging weaknesses in the policy core.

Hypothesis 4

Within a coalition, administrative agencies will usually advocate more moderate positions than their interest-group allies.

Hypothesis 5

Actors within purposive groups are more constrained in their expression of beliefs and policy positions than actors from material groups.

Learning Hypotheses

Hypothesis 1

Policy-oriented learning across belief systems is most likely when there is an intermediate level of informed conflict between the two coalitions. This requires that (a) each have the technical resources to engage in such a debate and that (b) the conflict be between secondary aspects of one belief system and core elements of the other or, alternatively, between important secondary aspects of the two belief systems.

Hypothesis 2

Policy-oriented learning across belief systems is most likely when there exists a forum which is (a) prestigious enough to force professionals from different coalitions to participate and (b) dominated by professional norms.

Hypothesis 3

Problems for which accepted quantitative data and theory exist are more conducive to policy-oriented learning across belief systems than those in which data and theory are generally qualitative, quite subjective, or altogether lacking.

Hypothesis 4

Problems involving natural systems are more conducive to policy-oriented learning across belief systems than those involving purely social or political systems because in the former many of the critical variables are not themselves active strategists and because controlled experimentation is more feasible.

Hypothesis 5

Even when the accumulation of technical information does not change the views of the opposing coalition, it can have important impacts on policy—at least in the short run—by altering the views of policy brokers.

Policy Change Hypotheses

Hypothesis 1

Significant perturbations external to the subsystem, a significant perturbation internal to the subsystem, policy-oriented learning, negotiated agreement, or some combinations thereof are a *necessary, but not sufficient*, source of change in the policy core attributes of a governmental program.

Hypothesis 2

The policy core attributes of a government program in a specific jurisdiction will not be significantly revised as long as the subsystem advocacy coalition that instated the program remains in power within that jurisdiction—except when the change is imposed by a hierarchically superior jurisdiction.

APPENDIX 2: METHODS

There are numerous ways to apply the ACF. For instance, Henry et al. (2022) offer the first comprehensive overview of how to apply the ACF to date. Moreover, there is no easily or uniformly stated philosophical foundation of the ACF. While some categorize the ACF as a "positivist" approach to the policy process, the scientific assumptions and practices under the ACF clearly diverge from many of the classical tenets of positivism. Indeed, Paul Sabatier, co-creator of the ACF, rejected many of the assumptions of positivism, describing himself as a "presuppositionist neo-positivist" (Dudley et al; 2000, pg. 137).

This appendix does not attempt to capture the full diversity of methods and scientific arguments within the ACF research program. Instead, it highlights common patterns in practice, citations for further readings, and identifies areas where further exploration and innovation are encouraged.

Broad Strategies for Applying the ACF

1. *Applying the ACF demands a deep understanding of context.* In all ACF research, grasping the context is essential. Paul Sabatier's research practice reflected this principle, often summarized by his motto: "context-science-context." This motto emphasizes that researchers' first step is to immerse themselves in the context, employing methods such as exploratory interviews, analysis of documents, and process observation. The rationale is straightforward: understanding policy subsystems and their dynamics—such as belief systems, coalitions, learning, and policy change—cannot be achieved a priori. The ACF was not intended to be applied blindly; it requires thoughtful modifications and adjustments to fit the context. The next step, called "science," involves systematic and transparent approaches to data collection and analyses. The third step returns to context, sharing the results with the subsystem, helping interpret findings, and giving back to the subsystem that supported the research. In today's parlance, this approach to applying the ACF fits within engaged scholarship (Van de Ven 2007). We also want to emphasize that research under the ACF is sometimes heavily immersive contextually and other times less so—and this diversity is one of the sources for the ACF's resilience.

2. *Applying the ACF can target academic audiences, practical audiences, or both, depending on the goals and objectives of the researcher.* Academically, researchers might focus on developing a better measure of a concept, like learning or testing relationships between two concepts or explaining variation in policy change through instances of learning. Practically, the ACF is also regularly used to help understand policy subsystems to support the policy actors therein. For example, we have frequently used the ACF to map policy conflicts and support people involved in them. We also find that some ACF research is practically oriented first, perhaps funded by a government agency to help understand a problem and academic publications come second. In other situations, the practical and the academic work come more or less simultaneously. While the ACF's

audiences might lean more academically than practically, we know that its audiences involve both.

3. *Recognizing how a given research focus relates to ACF's textbook and non-textbook settings.* The ACF's traditional theoretical arguments are based on a textbook setting of mature policy subsystems with competitive coalitions in a political system with some degree of democratization. Not all settings come close to this description, and researchers should avoid "shoehorning" research into the textbook while not recognizing the contextual circumstances (Weible & Jenkins-Smith, 2025). At the same time, researchers should not restrict themselves to the textbook ACF and, instead, continue to develop non-textbook ACF empirical and theoretical work, such as the research found in collaborative or unitary subsystems (Koebele, 2019; Heinmiller et al., 2021).

4. *Fostering diverse relationships with research context under the ACF.* The ACF research program does not prescribe a strict orientation for researchers in relation to their research settings, leaving room for reflexivity about biases and positionality. While some researchers prefer an outsider orientation, aiming to recognize and mitigate biases through transparent methods, others adopt a more reflexive and engaged stance. Crucially, the ACF research program accommodates both orientations, allowing for methodological pluralism and diverse relationships with the context. For our research teams, we value this diversity of perspectives, welcoming some reflexivity and varied orientations, motivations, and interpretations of research questions, settings, and data. Yet, we also emphasize the importance of maintaining transparency in all aspects of the research process, ensuring rigor and accountability regardless of the methodological stance.

5. *Supporting many forms of data and analyses under the ACF.* When applying the ACF, researchers regularly use interviews (Crawford & Weible, 2024), text analyses (Garibay et al., 2024), surveys (Nowlin, 2021), and more. While listing interview protocols, textual coding procedures, and survey instruments is beyond the scope of this chapter, we recommend reaching out to the ACF community for access. In other situations, the interview protocol can be found in the application's appendix (e.g., Crawford & Weible, 2024).

6. *Working with the framework-theory distinction of the ACF.* As a framework, the ACF is best considered a platform supporting a

research program of students, scholars, and practitioners world-wide. The ACF supports three principal theories in learning, policy change, and coalitions. As a framework, the ACF is very applicable and portable across settings, as found in applications that span the globe. However, the ACF's theories and associated hypotheses are more likely to need refinement as this framework travels. For example, Nwalie (2019) and Osei-Kojo and Weible (2025) offer insights into adjusting the ACF's theories to some African states. Finally, as a framework, the ACF can also support integrating new ideas, concepts, and even other theories and frameworks to fill its gaps. For example, researchers regularly upload cultural theory to help conceptualize and measure the ACF's deep core beliefs (Ripberger et al., 2024).

7. *Practicing transparency in ACF research.* The source of the ACF's longevity lies in its commitment to transparency in its research, which fuels learning among its researchers and its adaptation over time. The best way to learn from mistakes is to be transparent. Paul Sabatier's phrase "be clear enough to be proven wrong" encapsulates this mentality. Of these seven steps in this appendix, transparency might be the most essential.

References

Bark, Richard. 1993. Managing technological change in federal communications policy: The role of industry advisory groups. In *Policy change and learning*, ed. P. Sabatier and H. Jenkins-Smith, 129–146. Boulder: Westview Press.

Brewer, Garry D., and Peter deLeon. 1983. The foundations of policy analysis, Pacific Grove: Brooks/Cole

Asgari, Hosein, and Tayebe Amirkhani. 2024. Explanation of Urmia Lake policy subsystem: Identifying active coalitions based on the advocacy coalitions framework. *Iranian Journal of Public Policy* 9 (4): 9–23.

Crawford, Anna M., and Christopher M. Weible. 2024. The political polarization over abortion: An analysis of advocacy coalition belief systems. *Policy Sciences* 57 (3): 599–620.

Dudley, Geoffrey, and Jeremy Richardson. 1999. Competing advocacy coalitions and the process of 'frame reflection': A longitudinal analysis of EU steel policy. *Journal of European Public Policy* 6 (2): 225–248.

Dudley, Geoffrey, Wayne Parsons, Claudio M. Radaelli, and Paul Sabatier. 2000. Symposium: Theories of the policy process. *Journal of European Public Policy* 7 (1): 122–140.

Dumet, Lisset, and Hal Nelson. 2024. Achieving paid family leave in Oregon, USA: Analysis of the policy process using the advocacy coalition framework.". *Journal of Public Health Policy* 45 (1): 74–85.

Easton, David. 1965. *A framework for political analysis*. Chicago: The University of Chicago Press.

Elgin, Dallas, and Christopher M. Weible. 2013. Stakeholder analysis of Colorado climate and energy issues using policy analytical capacity and the advocacy coalition framework. *Review of Policy Research* 30 (1): 116–134.

Elliott, C., and Rodolphe Schlaepfer. 2001. The advocacy coalition framework: Application to the policy process for the development of forest certification in Sweden. *Journal of European Public Policy* 8 (4): 642–661.

Ellison, Brian A. 1998. The ACF and implementation of the Endangered Species Act: A case study in western water politics. *Policy Studies Journal* 26 (1): 11–29.

Fischer, Manuel. 2014. Coalition structures and policy change in a consensus democracy. *Policy Studies Journal* 42 (3): 344–366.

Fullerton, Allegra H., and Christopher M. Weible. 2024. Examining emotional belief expressions of advocacy coalitions in Arkansas' gender identity politics. *Policy Studies Journal* 52 (2): 369–389.

Funke, Nikki, Dave Huitema, Arthur Petersen, and Shanna Nienaber. 2021. The roles of experts and expert-based information in the advocacy coalition framework: Conceptual and empirical considerations based on the acid mine drainage case study in Gauteng South Africa. *Policy Studies Journal* 49 (3): 785–810.

Gabehart, Kayla M., Aerang Nam, and Christopher M. Weible. 2022. Lessons from the advocacy coalition framework for climate change policy and politics. *Climate Action* 1 (1): 1–14.

Garibay, Kesia K., Nancy J. Burke, A. Susana Ramírez, and Denise D. Payán. 2024. Examining the role and strategies of advocacy coalitions in California's Statewide Sugar-Sweetened Beverage Tax Debate (2001–2018). *American Journal of Health Promotion* 38 (1): 101–111.

Giordono, Leanne. S. 2020. Advocacy coalitions in low salience policy subsystems: Struggles under a smooth surface. *Policy Studies Journal*, 48(4), 1135–1167.

Gronow, Antti, Maria Brockhaus, Monica Di Gregorio, Aasa Karimo, and Tuomas Ylä-Anttila. 2021. Policy learning as complex contagion: How social networks shape organizational beliefs in forest-based climate change mitigation. *Policy Sciences* 54 (3): 529–556.

Gutiérrez-Meave, Raúl. 2024. Advocacy coalitions, soft power, and policy change in Mexican electricity policy: A discourse network analysis. *Policy & Politics* 1: 1–20.

Gupta, Kuhika. 2012. Comparative public policy: Using the comparative method to advance our understanding of the policy process. *Policy Studies Journal* 40 (s1): 11–26.

Gupta, Kuhika. 2014. A comparative policy analysis of coalition strategies: Case studies of nuclear energy and forest management in India. *Journal of Comparative Policy Analysis* 16 (4): 356–372.

Haar, Roberta N. 2024. Democratic interventionists versus pragmatic realists: Employing the advocacy coalition framework to explain Obama's shift in multilateralism with European allies. *Politics & Policy*. Early view.

Heclo, Hugh. 1974. *Social policy in Britain and Sweden*. New Haven: Yale University Press.

Heclo, Hugh. 1978. Issue networks and the executive establishment. In *The new American political system*, ed. A. King, 87–124. Washington, DC: American Enterprise Institute.

Heikkila, Tanya, and Andrea K. Gerlak. 2013. Building a conceptual approach to collective learning: Lessons for public policy scholars. *Policy Studies Journal* 40 (3): 484–512.

Heikkila, Tanya, Jonathan J. Pierce, Samuel Gallaher, Jennifer Kagan, Deserai A. Crow, and Christopher M. Weible. 2014. Understanding a period of policy change: The case of hydraulic fracturing disclosure policy in Colorado. *Review of Policy Research* 31 (2): 65–87.

Heinmiller, B. Timothy. 2023. Advocacy coalitions, power and policy change. *Policy & Politics* 51 (1): 28–46.

Heinmiller, B. Timothy, Emmanuel M. Osei, and Eugene Danso. 2021. Investigating ACF policy change theory in a unitary policy subsystem: The case of Ghanaian public sector information policy. *International Review of Public Policy* 3 (1).

Henry, Adam. 2011. Power, ideology, and policy network cohesion in regional planning. *Policy Studies Journal* 39 (3): 361–383.

Henry, Adam Douglas, Mark Lubell, and Michael McCoy. 2010. Belief systems and social capital as drivers of policy network structure: The case of California regional planning. *Journal of Public Administration Research and Theory* 21 (3): 419–444.

Henry, Adam, Karin Ingold, Daniel Nohrstedt, and Christopher M. Weible. 2014. Policy change in comparative contexts: Applying the advocacy coalition framework outside of Western Europe and North America. *Journal of Comparative Policy Analysis* 16 (4): 299–312.

Henry, Adam Douglas, Karin Ingold, Daniel Nohrstedt, and Christopher M. Weible. 2022. Advocacy coalition framework: Advice on applications and methods. In *Methods of the policy process*, eds. Christopher M. Weible and Samuel Workman. Routledge.

Hjern, Benny, and David Porter. 1981. Implementation structures: A new unit of administrative analysis. *Organization Studies* 2: 211–227.

Hofferbert, Richard I. 1974. *The study of public policy*. Indianapolis: Bobbs-Merrill.

Howlett, Michael. 2009. Policy analytical capacity and evidence-based policy-making: Lessons from Canada. *Canadian Public Administration* 52 (2): 153–175.

Ingold, Karin. 2011. Network structures within policy processes: Coalitions, power, and brokerage in Swiss climate policy. *Policy Studies Journal* 39 (3): 435–459.

Ingold, Karin, and Federic Varone. 2012. Treating policy brokers seriously: Evidence from the climate policy. *Journal of Public Administration Research and Theory* 22 (2): 319–346.

Jang, Sojin, Christopher M. Weible, and Kyudong Park. 2016. Policy processes in South Korea through the lens of the advocacy coalition framework. *Journal of Asian Public Policy* 9 (3): 274–290.

Jenkins-Smith, Hank. 1982. Professional roles for policy analysts: A critical assessment. *Journal of Policy Analysis and Management* 2 (1): 88–100.

Jenkins-Smith, Hank. 1990. *Democratic politics and policy analysis*. Pacific Grove: Brooks/Cole.

Jenkins-Smith, Hank, Gilbert St. Clair, and Brian Woods. 1991. Explaining change in policy subsystems: Analysis of coalition stability and defection over time. *American Journal of Political Science* 35 (November): 851–872.

Jenkins-Smith, Hank C, Daniel Nohrstedt, Christopher M. Weible, and Paul A. Sabatier. 2014a. The advocacy coalition framework: Foundations, evolution, and ongoing research. In *Theories of the policy process*, eds. Paul A. Sabatier and Christopher M. Weible. 3rd ed. Boulder: Westview Press.

Jenkins-Smith, Hank C., Carol L. Silva, Kuhika Gupta, and Joseph T. Ripberger. 2014b. Belief system continuity and change in policy advocacy coalitions: Using cultural theory to specify belief systems, coalitions, and sources of change. *Policy Studies Journal* 42 (4): 484–508.

Jenkins-Smith, Hank C., and Christopher M. Weible. 2025. The advocacy coalition framework: Origins theories, and the textbook version. In *The advocacy coalition framework*, eds. Hank Jenkins-Smith and Christopher M. Weible. Palgrave. Forthcoming.

Jenkins-Smith, and Christopher M. Weible. (ed.) *The advocacy coalition framework*. Palgrave. Forthcoming.

Jones, Charles. 1970. *An introduction to the study of public policy*. Belmont: Wadsworth Publishing Company.

Jones, Michael, and Hank Jenkins-Smith. 2009. Trans-subsystem dynamics: Policy topography, mass opinion, and policy change. *Policy Studies Journal* 37 (1): 37–58.

Kiser, Larry L., and Elinor Ostrom. 1982. The three worlds of action: A met theoretical synthesis of institutional arrangements. In *Strategies of political inquiry*, ed. E. Ostrom, 179–222. Beverly Hills: Sage.

Koebele, Elizabeth A. 2019. Integrating collaborative governance theory with the advocacy coalition framework. *Journal of Public Policy* 39 (1): 35–64.

Kübler, Daniel. 2001. Understanding policy change with the advocacy coalition framework: An application to Swiss drug policy. *Journal of European Public Policy* 8 (4): 623–641.

Larsen, Jakob Bjerg, Karsten Vrangbaek, and Janine M. Traulsen. 2006. Advocacy coalitions and pharmacy policy in Denmark. *Social Science and Medicine* 63 (1): 212–224.

Lasswell, Harold. 1970. The emerging conception of the policy sciences. *Policy Sciences* 1 (1): 3–14.

Leach, William D., and Paul A. Sabatier. 2005. To trust an adversary: Integrating rational and psychological models of collaborative policymaking. *American Political Science Review* 99 (4): 491–503.

Leach, William D., Christopher M. Weible, Scott R. Vince, Saba N. Siddiki, and John Calanni. 2013. Fostering learning in collaborative partnerships: Evidence from marine aquaculture in the United States. *Journal of Public Administration Research and Theory*. 24 (3): 591–622.

Leifeld, Philip. 2013. Reconceptualizing major policy change in the advocacy coalition framework: A discourse network analysis of German Pension Politics. *Policy Studies Journal* 41 (1): 169–198.

Li, Wei, and Christopher M. Weible. 2021. China's policy processes and the advocacy coalition framework. *Policy Studies Journal* 49 (3): 703–730.

Lowi, Theodore J. 1964. American Business, public policy, case studies, and political theory. *World Politics* 16 (4): 677–715.

Lundmark, Carina, Simon Matti, and Annica Sandström. 2018. The transforming capacity of collaborative institutions: Belief change and coalition reformation in conflicted wildlife management. *Journal of Environmental Management* 226: 226–240.

Mazmanian, Daniel, and Paul Sabatier. 1983. *Implementation and public policy*. Lanham: University Press of America.

Mazur, Allan. 1981. *The dynamics of technical controversy*. Washington, DC: Communications Press.

Meijerink, Sander. 2005. Understanding policy stability and change: The interplay of advocacy coalitions and epistemic communities, windows of opportunity, and Dutch coastal flooding policy 1945–2003. *Journal of European Public Policy* 12 (6): 1060–1077.

Metz, Florence, Eva Lieberherr, Aline Schmucki, and Robert Huber. 2021. Policy change through negotiated agreements: The case of greening Swiss agricultural policy. *Policy Studies Journal* 49 (3): 731–756.

Mintrom, Michael, and Phillipa Norman. 2009. Policy entrepreneurship and policy change. *Policy Studies Journal* 37 (4): 649–667.

Mintrom, Michael, and Sandra Vergari. 1996. Advocacy coalitions, policy entrepreneurs, and policy change. *Policy Studies Journal* 24 (Fall): 420–434.

Moyson, Stéphane. 2017. Cognition and policy change: The consistency of policy learning in the advocacy coalition framework. *Policy and Society* 36 (2): 320–344.

Munro, Geoffrey D., and Peter H. Ditto. 1997. Biased assimilation, attitude polarization, and affect in reactions to stereotype-relevant scientific information. *Personality and Social Psychology Bulletin* 23 (6): 636–653.

Munro, Geoffrey D., Peter H. Ditto, Lisa K. Lockhart, Angela Fagerlin, Mitchell Gready, and Elizabeth Peterson. 2002. Biased assimilation of sociopolitical arguments: Evaluating the 1996 U.S. Presidential debate. *Basic and Applied Social Psychology* 24(1): 15–26.

Nohrstedt, Daniel, and Christopher M. Weible. 2010. The logic of policy change after crisis: Proximity and subsystem interaction. *Risks, Hazards, and Crisis in Public Policy* 1 (2): 1–32.

Nohrstedt, Daniel, Karin Ingold, Christopher M. Weible, Elizabeth A. Koebele, Kristin L. Olofsson, Keiichi Satoh, and Hank C. Jenkins-Smith. 2023. The advocacy coalition framework: Progress and emerging areas. In *Theories of the policy process*, ed. Christopher M. Weible 5th ed. Routledge.

Nohrstedt, Daniel, and Tim Heinmiller. 2024. Advocacy coalitions as political organizations. *Policy and Society* 43 (3): 304–316.

Nowlin, Matthew C. 2021. Policy learning and information processing. *Policy Studies Journal* 49 (4): 1019–1039.

Nwalie, Martin Ike. 2019. Advocacy coalition framework and policy changes in a third-world country. *Politics & Policy* 47 (3): 545–568.

Olson, Richard Stuart, Robert A. Olson, and Vincent T. Grawronski. 1999. *Some buildings just can't dance: Politics, life safety, and disasters*. Standford: Jai Press.

Osei-Kojo, Alex, Karin Ingold, and Christopher M. Weible. 2023. The advocacy coalition framework: Lessons from applications in African countries. *Politische Vierteljahresschrift* 63 (2): 181–201.

Osei-Kojo, Alex. 2023. Analysing the stability of advocacy coalitions and policy frames in Ghana's oil and gas governance. *Policy & Politics* 51 (1): 71–90.

Osei-Kojo, Alex, and Christopher M. Weible. eds. 2025. *Advocacy coalitions and policy change in Africa*. Oxford University Press. Forthcoming.

Petridou, Evangelia, and Michael Mintrom. 2021. A research agenda for the study of policy entrepreneurs. *Policy Studies Journal* 49 (4): 943–967.

Pierce, Jonathan J., Holly L. Peterson, Michael D. Jones, Samantha P. Garrard, and Theresa Vu. 2017. There and back again: A tale of the advocacy coalition framework. *Policy Studies Journal* 45 (S1): S13–S46.

Pierce, Jonathan J., Holly L. Peterson, and Katherine C. Hicks. 2020. Policy change: An advocacy coalition framework perspective. *Policy Studies Journal* 48 (1): 64–86.

Quattrone, George A., and Amos Tversky. 1988. Contrasting rational and psychological analysis of political choice. *American Political Science Review* 82: 719–736.

Ripberger, Joseph T., Kuhika Gupta, Caral L. Silva, and Hank C. Jenkins-Smith. 2014. Cultural theory and the measurement of deep core beliefs within the advocacy coalition framework. *Policy Studies Journal* 42 (4): 509–527.

Sabatier, Paul A. 1986. Top-down and bottom-up models of policy implementation: A critical analysis and suggested synthesis. *Journal of Public Policy* 6 (January): 21–48.

Sabatier, Paul A. 1988. An advocacy coalition model of policy change and the role of policy-oriented learning therein. *Policy Sciences* 21 (fall): 129–168.

Sabatier, Paul A. 1998. The advocacy coalition framework: Revisions and relevance for Europe. *Journal of European Public Policy* 5 (March): 98–130.

Sabatier, Paul A. 1999. *Theories of the policy process*. Boulder, CO: Westview Press.

Sabatier, Paul A., and Anne M. Brasher. 1993. From vague consensus to clearly differentiated coalitions: Environmental policy at Lake Tahoe, 1964–1985. In *Policy change and learning*, ed. P. Sabatier and H. Jenkins-Smith, 177–208. Boulder: Westview Press.

Sabatier, Paul A., and Hank C. Jenkins-Smith. 1993. *Policy change and learning: An advocacy coalition approach*. Boulder: Westview Press.

Sabatier, Paul A., Susan Hunter, and Susan McLaughlin. 1987. The devil shift: Perceptions and misperceptions of opponents. *Western Political Quarterly* 40: 51–73.

Satoh, Keiichi, Antti Gronow, and Tuomas Ylä-Anttila. 2023. The advocacy coalition index: A new approach for identifying advocacy coalitions. *Policy Studies Journal* 51 (1): 187–207.

Scott, Ian. 2012. Analyzing advocacy issues in Asia. *Administration & Society* 44 (6s): 4–12.

Simon, Herbert A. 1957. *Models of man: Social and rational*. New York: Wiley.

Simon, Herbert A. 1985. Human nature in politics: The dialogue of psychology with political science. *American Political Science Review* 79 (June): 293–304.

Sommerville, Kylie, Alison Ritter, and Niamh Stephenson. 2022. Pill testing policy: A comparative analysis using the advocacy coalition framework. *Drug and Alcohol Review* 41 (1): 275–284.

Swedlow, Brendon. 2014. Advancing policy theory with cultural theory: An introduction to the special issue. *Policy Studies Journal* 41 (4): 465–483.

Van de Ven, Andrew H. 2007. *Engaged scholarship: A guide for organizational and social research*. Oxford University Press.

Weible, Christopher M. 2005. Beliefs and policy influence: An advocacy coalition approach to policy networks. *Political Research Quarterly* 58 (3): 461–477.

Weible, Christopher M., Paul A. Sabatier, and Kelly McQueen. 2009. Themes and variations: Taking stock of the advocacy coalition framework. *Policy Studies Journal* 37 (1): 121–140.

Weible, Christopher M., Paul A. Sabatier, Hank C. Jenkins-Smith, Daniel Nohrstedt, and Adam Douglas Henry. 2011. A quarter century of the advocacy coalition framework: An introduction to the special issue. *Policy Studies Journal* 39 (3): 349–360.

Weible, Christopher M., Tanya Heikkila, Karin Ingold, and Manuel Fischer, eds. 2016. *Policy debates on hydraulic fracturing: Comparing coalition politics in North America and Europe*. Springer.

Weible, Christopher M., Karin Ingold, Daniel Nohrstedt, Adam Douglas Henry, and Hank C. Jenkins-Smith. 2020. Sharpening advocacy coalitions. *Policy Studies Journal* 48 (4): 1054–1081.

Weible, Christopher M., ed. 2023. *Theories of the policy process*. Taylor & Francis.

Weible, Christopher M., and Hank C. Jenkins-Smith. 2025. The advocacy coalition framework—Advancing scholarship in the textbook and beyond. In *The advocacy coalition framework*, eds. Hank Jenkins-Smith and Christopher M. Weible. Palgrave. Forthcoming.

Weiss, Carol. 1977. Research for policy's sake: The enlightenment function of social research. *Policy Analysis* 3 (Fall): 531–545.

Zafonte, Matthew, and Paul A. Sabatier. 2004. Short-term versus long-term coalitions in the policy process: Automotive pollution control, 1963–1989. *The Policy Studies Journal* 32 (1): 75–107.

Institutionalism and Public Policy

B. Guy Peters

The social sciences have had a continuing debate over the explanation of phenomena by structure or by agency. Most contemporary social science is based on agency, with the behavior of individuals (whether assumed to be driven by social or psychological attributes, or by utility maximization) dominating theoretical development (Hay 2002). That said, the resurgence of institutional explanations has forced greater consideration of structural factors and the role that organizations and institutions play in shaping decisions.

This debate about structure and agency has existed within the social science in general and has been no less apparent in the study of public policy. Public policies represent the choices made by governments and their allies—interest groups, not-for-profit organizations, etc.—and therefore are the products of decisions made by numerous individuals. But those individuals interact within formal structures, and they interact according to the rules that govern those structures. Indeed, those rules may be used to define the institution (Rowe 1997). And structures also

B. G. Peters (✉)
University of Pittsburgh, Pittsburgh, USA
e-mail: bgpeters@pitt.edu

B. G. Peters and P. Zittoun (eds.), *Contemporary Approaches to Public Policy*, International Series on Public Policy,
https://doi.org/10.1007/978-3-032-06026-6_4

engage in systematic interactions in the process of making policy and must be assumed to have some influence over policy.

In an institutionalist perspective on policymaking, or other aspects of political behavior, individuals are not atomistic but rather are embedded in a number of institutions. The individuals acquire the meanings for their political behaviors from those institutional connections, and they also acquire cues for their behavior. Those cues may come in the form of incentives or disincentives, or they may be more normative, but the institutions provide guides for action and may also provide sanctions for individuals who do not conform to the expectations of the institutions. And, being formal structures, their rules may make certain actions possible and others impossible.

Also, in this analysis, I will at times shift between talking about institutions and talking about organizations. While the literature does differentiate between institutions and organizations (see North 1990) in practice making that differentiation may be difficult. For example, while the public bureaucracy can be considered an institution, it is composed on multiple organizations, and when making policies, the institution may not act so much as a single entity as through the multiple organizations (see Genieys 2010). Each of these organization will be functioning with its own values and its own interests.[1] Thus, institutions and organizations tend to overlap, both in reality and in theory, but must still be considered separately.

Also, by way of preface to this chapter, I will be arguing that institutions can be defined by their policies. These are not two elements that are only tangentially linked, but the public sector institution and its attempts to influence the economy and society are closely bound up with each other. We can think of institutions being defined at least in part by what they do, and when there is a disjuncture between action and the fundamental logic of the institution there will be a need to modify one or the other, or both. Thus, to say public sector institutions make or influence public policy is to some extent the same as saying institutions *are*.

This linkage between policies and institutions is perhaps most obvious in the historical institutionalism literature (see below). Indeed, the institutions that are the focus of this mode of institutionalism are in reality

---

[1] There are instances in which the bureaucracy may act as a single institution, e.g. the pursuit of higher civil service salaries, but there are generally analytic dangers in considering the institution as a unitary actor.

policies, and the path dependency central to the approach is defined by the stability of policies rather than structures. Those policies may be associated with structures such as agencies that deliver the policies, but the path, and any changes that occur, are focused on the policy itself.

This chapter will first briefly discuss the varieties of institutional theories that are being utilized in political science, and to some extent in the other social sciences (see, for example, Brinton and Nee 1998). It will then proceed to discuss a number of specific points about the role of institutions in explaining policy choice, and also the role of that policy choices may have in defining institutions. The paper will conclude with some assessment of the challenges that institutional theory faces when attempting to explain policy choices, and some possibilities for addressing those challenges.

THE VARIETIES OF INSTITUTIONAL THEORY

There are numerous discussions of the variety of institutional theory in the literature, and I will not belabor this point here (see Peters 2019; Hall and Taylor 1996; Lowndes and Roberts 2011). That said, however, it is important for anyone attempting to understand the role that institutions play in explaining policy choices to understand that institutionalism has substantial internal diversity. Indeed, one of the principal questions in contemporary institutional analysis is whether there is enough of a common core among the approaches to justify the assumption that there is *an* institutional approach (see Peters 2025). Or are there really multiple approaches all relying on a limited number of institutional factors for their explanations?

I will not attempt to explicate the various approaches to Institutionalism that are available at any great length. But a brief precis of each may be necessary to enable understanding of the remainder of this paper for those who are not embedded in the institutionalist literature. Although the list could be expanded, I will focus on four principal versions of institutional theory in political science: Normative institutionalism, rational choice institutionalism, historical institutionalism and discursive institutionalism.

(1) Normative Institutionalism

The original call to the discipline to reassert the role of institutions and organizations in explaining political life came from what can now we called normative institutionalism. As implied by this label, this version of institutional defines institutions through the values, symbols and even myths that are used to guide behavior. This version of institutionalism has close linkages with sociological organization theory, especially the approach of Selznick (1996), and has been called sociological institutionalism by some scholars classifying these several approaches (Hall and Taylor 1996).

The significance of values in the normative approach has a clear relationship with public policy. If values essentially define the institution then they will also define the policies being made by that institution. Some of the values within an institution may be procedural, e.g., how are decisions made, but many also are substantive. These substantive and procedural values are inculcated to individuals who become members of the institution and become guidelines for their actions while members of the institution. Thus, actors in this approach are guided by a "logic of appropriateness" and behave according to the values they have learned are suitable for their membership in the institution. That logic of appropriateness also defines what sorts of policy choices are acceptable to the institution and to its members.

The normative institutionalism can be connected with the study of institutional logics in sociology (Thornton et al. 2012). This approach argues that institutions, and the behavior if their members, can be understood through the various internal ideas and values that are defined as "logics." Each institution will contain a number of different logics, e.g., the basis of legitimacy, and of internal authority. For policies, these logics define the mission of the institution, the appropriate strategies and policy instruments, and relations with other institutions (Haveman and Gualtieri 2017).

(2) Rational Choice Institutionalism

The second version of institutional theory in political science is usually labeled called rational choice institutionalism, being based as it is on the utilitarian logic of rational choice theory within the discipline. The fundamental assumption of this approach is that individuals pursue their self-interest and do so using rational calculations. This is what March and Olsen refer to as the "logic of consequentiality," with members making decisions based on the assumed outcomes of the decisions, rather than on what is considered appropriate and normatively correct within the institution.

In the rational choice version of institutionalism the preferences of the actors are considered exogenous to the institution; the actors come into the institution seeking to maximize their utilities and that fundamental value is not altered by membership in the institution. With that individualistic logic, institutions become structures designed to produce certain outcomes by utilizing those motivations. For example, Ostrom's (1990) approach utilized rules to create incentives and disincentives for behavior by the members of institutions. And principal-agent models of institutions assume that there is a need to design the institutions to monitor compliance by the agents (Waterman and Meijer 2004).

Given the above, one of the virtues of the rational choice approach to institutionalism is that institutions are relatively easy to change. All the would-be designer of the institution must do is to alter the rules or incentives and s/he can expect the behavior of the members of the institution to be changed as well. This is in contrast to the normative approach above in which changing the institution would require changing the values held by its members. While a simplistic conception of rational choice institutionalism might make such a strong assumption, this perspective has itself been adapting to critiques and has begun to add assumptions about learning and values to the strictly utilitarian conceptions of behavior that have been at its center.

(3) *Historical Institutionalism*

In many ways, the most simplistic conception of institutions and their relationship to public policies is provided by historical institutionalism (Steinmo 2008). The basic assumption is that once an institution embarks on a path, often meaning once it selects a policy, it is likely to persist on that path unless there are strong pressures—a punctuation in the equilibrium that will divert it from that path. This builds on a common perception about government that it tends to be bureaucratic in the pejorative sense of the term and does not react effectively to changing conditions in its environment.

Advocates of the historical institutionalism have attempted to respond to the numerous critiques of the approach, notably the excessive stability of policy choices and the absence of change except through major punctuations. In particular, Kathleen Thelen and her colleagues (Streek and Thelen 2005; Mahoney and Thelen 2010) have argued for the existence of four types of more gradual change in policies and institutions: layering, drift, displacement and conversion. These can be seen as ways in which to describe and analyze more general processes of incremental change within institutions and public policies (Hayes 2006).

(4) *Discursive Institutionalism*

The discursive version of institutionalism (Schmidt 2010; see also Hay 2006 on constructivist institutionalism) defines institutions in terms of the discourses that are being carried on within the institution. Like the normative institutionalism, this approach is defined primarily through ideas. The difference between the two is in part that they come from different intellectual traditions and also that they assume different degrees of agreement on ideas within the institution.

In this approach to institutionalism, there are assumed to be (at least) two types of discourses within the institution. One is the *coordinative discourse*, or the discourse used more internally among the members to define what they consider the institution to be. The other, the *communicative discourse* is used externally to define to outsiders what the institution is and what it intends to do. The coordinative discourse within the institution is more contested than in the normative approach, and hence there is greater likelihood of change within the discursive version of institutionalism.

(5) *Empirical institutionalism*

Finally, there is a long literature on empirical institutionalism. This was the foundation of comparative political science and continues to address fundamental questions about the impact of structures on politics and policy. Although the dualism associated with much of this literature, e.g., presidential vs. parliamentary systems, or federal versus unitary systems, is

perhaps too simple (Cheibub et al. 2014), examining the empirical consequences of institutional formats does help to understand how institutions
function, and how they impact policy choices.

While much of institutional theory is interested in the effects abstract
variables on the formation and performance of institutions, this approach
utilizes a more common sense definition of institutions and seeks to
understand how institutions such as legislatures, bureaucracies and courts
make and enforce decisions. The fundamental question is "do institutions
matter," and the answer usually is yes (Weaver and Rockman 1983).

(6) *Common Dimensions in Institutional Approaches*

If we assume that there is a relatively common institutional perspective
operating in political science and policy studies, then we need to identify
those common elements and see how they create a common perspective. The most obvious of those common elements in institutional theory
is the capacity of institutions to create predictability. If institutions are
functioning well, then they generate predictable behaviors on the part of
their members as well as predictable outcomes—the public policies that
are the concerns of this chapter. While some institutions—the military
for example—may demand greater conformity and greater regularities of
behavior, all institutions demand some predictability.

Associated with predictability is the capacity of institutions to reproduce themselves across time. Institutions may change gradually and
almost without notice but they also tend to reproduce patterns of
behavior among their members. That persistence, in turn, tends to
produce persistence in the decisions made by the institutions and therefore in the policies being implemented. Of course, viewing institutions
from alternative perspectives may lead to greater or less emphasis on
the reproduction of behaviors, with the historical institutionalism being
defined largely through that continuity of action, but in all versions the
reproduction of behavioral patterns is a crucial element of the institutional
approach. This reproduction of behaviors is, rather obviously, associated
with the standard critique that institutionalism cannot deal effectively with
change.

Thirdly, all versions of institutionalism assume some separation of the
institution from its environment. Although institutions are dependent on
their environment for energy (personnel, financial resources, etc.) they

also must maintain their autonomy and be capable of acting to pursue their own goals.[2] Further, we should think of the environment of any institution as being dominated by other institutions. For the institutions of government, for example, law and the market are significant institutions that frame the capacity of government to function (see Dimaggio and Powell 1983). Governments depend upon the market for resources but also regulate the manner in which the market functions and perhaps more fundamentally create effective markets through the rule of law and the enforcement of those laws.

HOW INSTITUTIONS AFFECT POLICY

Taking the above descriptions of the various approaches to institutionalism, and the common threads within the approach, I will now proceed to discuss the links between institutional analysis and public policy. This discussion will focus more on some common influences of instructions on policy, rather than on the relationships of individual approaches to policy choices. But inevitably some versions of institutionalism will be more relevant for some of the points being made about policy and must therefore be emphasized.

(1) Institutions Create Stability

One of the fundamental characteristics of institutions is that they create stability, even if the underlying conflicts in society appear likely to produce instability. This analysis has been made about the capacity of institutions to produce equilibrium outcomes even in the face of fundamental political differences (Shepsle 1986, and much the same can be said for their influence of policies. Attempting to make policies without clearly defined institutional rules, e.g., through policy networks or other informal structures, will be substantially less stable and predictable than when working through institutions.

The stability that one finds in policy within an institutional context arises from several sources, to some extent dependent upon the theoretical

---

[2] This argument is analogous to the open-systems approach to organization theory. See Katz and Kahn (1978).

perspective being applied to those institutions. For example, the normative approach creates stability through the socialization of the members of the institution so that they will behave in predictable manners. And other ways of understanding institutions, especially the historical institutionalism, also assume that stability will be maintained through a range of mechanisms such as positive feedback (Pierson 2000), habit (Sarigil 2023); or mere inertia (Rose and Karran 1984).

The danger with strong institutions is that they will be too successful in maintaining stability, both for themselves and for the policies which they implement. Huntington (1968) argued that the institutionalization of public sector organizations involved creating the capacity for adaption, but most considerations of institutions and institutionalization emphasize stability over adaptation. Newer approaches to public organizations and institutions, e.g., resilience and robustness (Ansell et al. 2023).

(2) Institutions Have Ideas, or At Least Propagate Ideas

There is some tendency to think of institutions in formal and structural terms. As discussed above, however, institutions may also be defined by ideas and by the commitment of their members to those ideas (see Beland). Individuals may join institutions because they agree with the ideas, or they may be socialized to those ideas once they become members, but in either case, institutional ideas shape the manner in which decisions get made within the institution,. This role of ideas may be evident in social institutions, but it is also important for shaping public policies.

The role of ideas in shaping public policies may see most clearly in the public bureaucracy. Charles Goodsell, for example, has argued (2011) that organizations within the public sector can be defined by their missions, or the ideas that they utilize to shape their own internal policy making. These ideas are also utilized to engage in political battles over budgets and the control of policy with other parts of government. Any structural understanding of an institution would-be insufficient to explain how institutions formulate policies and then diffuse them throughout the political process.

It is also crucial to understand that policy ideas are not just relevant in the upper echelons of institutions and organizations. The policy ideas may be developed and propagate by the top of the organization, but also will permeate the institution. That said, there is substantial evidence that ideas for public policies may well be initiated at the middle, or even the bottom of public organizations (Page 2010) and then percolate upward. Thus, there continues to be some interaction within the institution or organization about policies and the ideas that can be used to shape, or at least justify, the policy choices.

(3) *Institutions Channel Political Pressures*

There is some tendency to think of institutions within the public sector as being almost apolitical, and making their decisions according to their own values and rules.[3] That argument has been made especially concerning the public bureaucracy but has been made more implicitly for other institutions. It is, however, impossible for any institution within the public sector to function without considering political pressures and political values. As well as having their own policy perspectives institutions in the public sector channel political pressures from the society, privileging some and tending to deter others.

The rational choice version of institutionalism, and perhaps especially the approach based on veto points and veto players (Tsebelis 2000; but see) is particularly useful for understanding the channeling of political pressures. The structural design of an institution can make it more or less open to political pressures, with more veto points and players limiting the range of options that may be considered. If then we add more normative perspectives that would privilege certain types of political ideas and actors over others then it becomes clear that institutions do shape the influence of external actors.

In addition, if we consider some of the classic distinctions in comparative politics among types of political structures, that more common-sense conceptualization of institutions may also help explain the channeling of political pressures. For example, what difference does the choice of a parliamentary versus presidential form of government make (Weaver and Rockman 1986) or perhaps differences among types of presidential systems (Shugart and Haggard 2001). Further, differences between unitary and federal systems, or perhaps more generally centralized and

---

[3] That is, of course, somewhat the opposite of the perspective of March and Olsen in their seminal work on the New Institutionalism (1984). In that view, institutions were fundamentally political, and politics was fundamentally institutional.

decentralized systems, may also have significant policy implications. In all of these structures, the design of the institution creates or removes opportunities for political influence over policy and thus helps to shape the policy choices.

(4) *Institutions Constitute the Environment for other Frameworks of Policymaking*

This volume contains chapters on a number of frameworks for understanding policy choices, e.g., the Advocacy = Coalition Framework (ACF) and the Multiple Streams Framework (MSF). These frameworks provide descriptions of policy processes that in turn can be used to explain policy choices, and the ways in which they function are shaped to some extent by the institutional settings within which they are located. For example, the availability of policy windows in the MSF can be affected by the nature of the institutions involved.

This claim is not intended to be imperialistic relative to other approaches to policy, but it does reflect the pervasiveness of institutions in governing, Differences among institutions can alter factors such as the openness of the system to external actors, the role of the bureaucracy, the number of veto points within the decision-making process, and a host of other factors. So, for example, an institutional arrangement that allows easier entry for challengers may make it more difficult to maintain the coalitions central to the ACF logic.

(5) *Informal Institutions Matter as Well as Do Formal Institutions*

Although the concept of an informal institution may appear to be an oxymoron, in reality informal structures in society, and those linking society to the political system, are important for governing and for policymaking. Further, these structures often have the characteristics of institutions, such as replication, described above. In making and implementing public policies informal structures appear to be increasingly important actors that can contribute to the success or failure of policies. In particular, networks of social actors can play a major role in policy and governance (Torfing et al. 2011).

The relationship between formal and informal institutions may take on a variety of forms. For example, Helmke and Levistsky (2004) argue that the relationship between the formal and the informal depends upon the extent to which their goals are similar and the effectiveness of the formal institutions. For example, if there are reasonably common goals and the formal institutions are effective then the two actors complement each other. On the other hand, if the formal institution is ineffective then the informal may substitute for the formal. When goals are more divergent the interactions will be less harmonious but the two sets of actors can still be significant players in policymaking and will exert reciprocal influences. Zeki Sarigil (2023) developed a more extensive typology of forms of informal institutions and has related them to policy choices in Turkey.

How Policy Affects Institutions

Another of the common assumptions about institutions is that they are stable and almost immutable, but although they are sources of stability institutions do change. The public policies that they choose and implement can be one of the sources of change in institutions. That feedback from earlier choices is often not considered when examining the nature of institutions in political science, but these interactions may generate institutional change more effectively than other assumed drivers.

Policy failure may be one of the more significant sources of institutional change, especially when the policy in question is closely linked with the values of the institution. If a policy does not perform as intended, or even has negative unintended consequences, then we should expect the institution to alter its behavior. For example, the failures of the Federal Emergency Management Agency after Hurricane Katrina hit New Orleans produced significant changes within that organization and the set of institutions responsible for emergency response in the United States.

And even if policies do not fail abjectly, feedback from their implementation may affect the institutions and its policy approaches. Just as there is a tendency to consider institutions as virtually immutable, so too is there some tendency to consider that policies tend to be relatively stable, except for relatively major transformations. There is, of course, a continuing incremental process of adaptation of policies, both by design and by accretion, with a continuing interaction of institution and the environment occurring largely through the policies being adopted and implemented by the institution.

The above having been said, institutions also display a remarkable ability to persist in their old patterns of behavior even in the face of abject policy failure (see Peters and Nagel 2022; see also Boswell 2023). And the more institutionalized the structure involved may be, having success-fully inculcated a particular set of institutional and policy values into their members, the more likely that institution will be to persist in its old poli-cies and to continue with its established patterns. For example, military organizations tend to persist in outdated tactics and strategy long after it has become apparent that they are no longer successful.[4]

Thus, policy success may be very dangerous for an organization or institution responsible for that policy. If the institution is successful then the policy may become locked in, and challenges to the policy become more difficult. Given that the environment being affected by policies changes generally more rapidly than do the policies being implemented, the capacity of the seemingly successful institution to maintain that success may be more limited in cases of clear success than in cases of more questionable success. From a more analytic perspective, that questionable success may be a clear opportunity for alternative policy discourses to be debated within the institution and for adaptation to occur.

In a somewhat related manner, Brunsson and Olsen (1992) have argued that institutions will change when their actions do not conform to their espoused values. In the public sector institutions—especially the public bureaucracy—may be expected by their political masters to imple-ment policies that do not necessarily conform to their values.[5] This disjuncture may lead to institutional change, either is altering the values or through those socialized into a particular set of values deciding to leave the institution. Demands to implement the policies of illiberal polit-ical leaders have led to internal opposition, as well as exit, in public bureaucracies, but seemingly little value change (Yesilkagit et al. 2024).

---

[4] The continuing belief that the cavalry could produce breakthroughs in World War I, even when confronted by increasingly lethal weapons, is but one example of the persistence of ideas in the face of negative outcomes (Ellis 1976).

[5] For example, environmental agencies may find themselves opposed to the policy agendaof conservative governments that may generate internal conflicts and perhaps more fundamental change within the institution.

THE METHODOLOGY
OF INSTITUTIONAL ANALYSIS OF POLICY

Although some scholars have argued that institutionalism is a method in itself (Diermeier and Krehbiel 2003), the diversity of institutional theories leads to a diversity of methodologies for research on policy when employing that theoretical perspective. The empirical institutionalists have the clearest methodological approach, depending largely on standard empirical methodologies to attempt answers to the question raised by Weaver and Rockman (1983)—Do Institutions Matter? There are any number of studies assessing the differences between presidential and parliamentary systems, federal and unitary systems, corporatist and pluralist systems. These studies utilize the standard armamentarium of the social sciences to identify whether institutions do matter.

As well as understanding the effects studying institutions also involves understanding the internal dynamics of the institutions involved in making policy. Methods such as surveys, structured observations are more important for internal studies of institutions than are statistics methods. In these analyses of institutions, the approach to institutions being used also determines to some extent the methodology. Normative institutionalism emphasizes uncovering the "logics of appropriateness," and hence uses interviews or documentary analysis to identify those logics. Historical institutionalism may document changes in policy, or the lack thereof, and use case studies to determine how policies are maintained, or changed.

WHAT INSTITUTIONS DO NOT DO?

I have been making a case above about the importance of institutions for explaining policy choices. Although I can easily argue that institutions are important in explaining some aspects of policy, they also have significant weaknesses in providing those explanations. These weaknesses are to some extent a function of the strengths of the approach. In particular, the emphasis on stability within institutionalism tends to undermine the capacity to explain policy change, and change is essential to the understanding of public policy (Carter 2012). Likewise, the emphasis on structure tends to weaken agency-based explanations, or may make those explanations anthropomorphize institutions more than is appropriate.

Institutions tend to be stable and also tend to be associated with stable public policies. Therefore, an emphasis on institutions may make policy change more difficult to understand and to explain. As already noted, some versions of Institutionalism have been built on a logic of persistence, even in the face of pressures for change. In such a perspective change appears unlikely. The one major exception to that view of institutions comes from the discursive institutionalism, with its assumptions of existence of multiple discourses competing for dominance within an institution, and the relative fleeting nature of the dominance of any one of those discourses. Like the normative institutionalism, this perspective in institutions emphasizes the role of ideas, but unlike that perspective there is no assumption that the ideas within an institution can perpetuate themselves effectively.[6]

The second concern about institutionalism as an explanation for public policies is the emphasis on structures versus agency in the theoretical analysis. As noted in the introduction to this paper, there is a tendency in institutional analysis to emphasize the nature and importance of structures rather than the role of individuals within those structures in making decisions (see Knill et al. 2024). That structural emphasis, is turn, leads to a tendency to anthropomorphize institutions and to assume that those structures somehow function as the decision-makers. Thus, the original arguments of March and Olsen (1984) about the need of the social sciences to abandon, or at least supplement, the methodological individualism of both behavioralism and rational choice approaches to politics comes full circle, and there may some need to include more of that individual analysis in institutional analysis.

Institutional theories therefore need to consider ways in which individuals and the institutions in which they function interact. The logic for some approaches, especially the normative institutionalism, is that institutions shape individuals—that endogenous source of preferences is indeed the underlying logic of normative Institutionalism. Others assume that individuals are largely unaffected by their membership in the institution, and that indeed individuals affect institutions more than vice versa. For rational choice institutionalism, for example, individual preferences are largely unaffected by their involvement with the institution, but individuals can and do design institutions to perform in certain ways (Calvert

---

[6] As we argued for historical institutionalism (Peters et al. 2005) change may come about only when there is a new idea that is capable of replacing the ideas that have been dominating policies within the institution.

1996). And except for the work on change in historical institution-alism (Mahoney and Thelen 2010), this approach seems to undervalue significantly the role of individuals.[7]

The emphasis on stability and the associated emphasis on structure in institutional theory combine to produce significant limitations on the dynamic element in any explanations of public policy generated through this approach. While ideas by themselves can be useful in formulating policies (Beland and Cox 2011), institutionalism cannot always identify how those ideas are actually translated from concepts into action and how they can influence the policies chosen. Institutionalism may, for example, be combined with other approaches to provide a more comprehensive explanation of how policies and form, and especially how they change.

For example, the normative perspective on institutions, and to some extent the discursive perspective, provide more useful explanations of how individuals become involved in the institution than they do of how decisions are made within those institutions. These approaches may, however, be combined usefully with the Advocacy-Coalition Framework (ACF, see Weible, this volume) to help understand how those ideas come are put into effect in the policy process. The ACF contains a clear political dynamic that is especially useful for understanding how policies change, if not necessarily how they are formed initially. The emphasis on the advocacy of alternative policy perspectives demonstrates how ideas can be used to motivate policy choices.

One of the more important exceptions to the generalization above is the "Institutional Analysis and Development Framework." Although there is a separate chapter on this framework in this volume (see Araral, Chapter x), it has a clear foundation in the institutional literature. This framework evolved from Elinor Ostrom's earlier work on institutional theory (1990; Crawford and Ostrom 1996). Her initial analysis empha-sized the use of rules to shape actions within institutions, and this more extensive framework linked individual and collective actions at a variety of levels within an institution. This framework includes agency to a much greater extent than is true for most institutional analysis. Thus, this

---

[7] That statement is perhaps somewhat unfair to this strand of literature. Pierson's expla-nations for the maintenance of paths (2000), for example, do depend on the reinforcement coming to individuals through positive feedback, as do explanations of path dependency based on habituation (Sarigil 2017).

version of institutionalism contains more of its own dynamic than do the other approaches.

SUMMARY AND CONCLUSIONS

The central argument of this chapter is that institutions do affect policy choices. This is certainly true in the real world of policymaking, and the academic analysis of public policy also has a great deal to gain from careful attention to the literature on institutional theory. Institutions, both the formal ones within government and the social actors that work with (or at times against) the formal institutions play a major role in advancing policy ideas and in shaping the policy choices that governments make.

Although institutions are important in making policy, we must always remember that institutions are composed of individuals and it is those individuals, and the interactions among them, that actually make the policy. Therefore, thinking about institutional analysis in policy requires thinking about the ways in which individuals shape institutions and institutions shape individuals. Further, it is important to think about individuals as a source of change for institutions and for the policies they make, given that institutions are often more static than might be desirable for successful adaptation to changing circumstances. Institutions are important, but they are functioning in a complex policymaking systems with other institutions, individuals and socio-economic pressures that may be difficult for even the most powerful institution to control.

REFERENCES

Ansell, C., E. Sørensen, and J. Torfing. 2023. Public administration and politics meet turbulence: the search for robust governance responses. *Public Administration* 101 (1): 3–22.

Béland, Daniel, and Robert Henry Cox. 2011. *Ideas and politics in social science research*. Oxford: Oxford University Press.

Boswell, J. 2023. *Magical thinking in public policy: why Naïve ideas about policymaking persist in cynical times*. Oxford: Oxford University Press.

Brinton, M. C., and V. Nee. 1998. *The new institutionalism in sociology*. Palo Alto: Stanford University Press.

Calvert, R.L. 1996. The rational choice theory of institutions: implications for design. In *Institutional Design*, ed. D. L. Weimer. Newell, MA: Kluwer.

Carter, P. 2012. Policy as Palimpset. *Policy & Politics* 40: 423–443.

Cheibub, J., Z. Elkins, and T. Ginsburg. 2014. Beyond presidentialism and parliamentarism. *British Journal of Political Science* 44: 515–544.

Crawford, S. E. S., and E. Ostrom. 1996. A grammar of institutions. *American Political Science Review* 89: 582–600.

Diermeier, D., and K. Krehbiel. 2003. Institutionalism as a methodology. *Journal of Theoretical Politics* 15: 123–144.

Dimaggio, P. J., and W. W. Powell. 1983. The iron cage revisited: institutional isomorphism and collective rationality in organizational fields. *American Sociological Review* 48: 147–160.

Ellis, J. 1976. *The social history of the machine gun*. New York: Pantheon.

Genieys, W. 2010. *The new custodians of the state: programmatic elites in French society*. New Brunswick, NJ: Transaction.

Hall, P.A., and R. Taylor. 1996. Political science and the three institutionalisms. *Political Studies* 44: 936–957.

Haveman, H.A., and G. Gualtieri. 2017. Institutional logics. In *Oxford research encyclopedia, business and management*. https://oxfordre.com/business/display/10.1093/acrefore/9780190224851.001.0001/acrefore-978019022 4851-e-137

Hay, C. 2002. *Political analysis: a critical introduction*. Basingstoke: Palgrave.

Hay, C. 2006. Constructivist institutionalism. In *Oxford handbook of political institutions*, ed. R. A. W Rhodes, S. Binder, and B. A Rockman. Oxford: Oxford University Press.

Hayes, M.T. 2006. *Incrementalism and public policy*. Lanham, MD: University Press of America.

Helmke, G., and S. Levitsky. 2004. Informal institutions and comparative politics: a research agenda. *Perspectives on Politics* 2: 725–740.

Huntington, S. P. 1968. *Political order in changing societies*. New Haven: Yale University Press.

Katz, D., and R. L. Kahn. 1978. *The social psychology of organizations*. New York: Wiley.

Knill, C., Y. Steinebach, and X. Fernandez-i-Marin. 2024. Political institutions and public policy. In *Handbook of political institutions*, ed. A. Vatter and R. Freibershaus. Cheltenham: Edward Elgar.

Lowndes, V., and M. Roberts. 2011. *Why institutions matter: new institutionalism in political science*. Basingstoke: Macmillan.

Mahoney, J., and K. Thelen. 2010. *Explaining institutional change: ambiguity, agency and power*. Cambridge: Cambridge University Press.

March, J. G., and J. P. Olsen. 1984. The new institutionalism: organizational factors in political life. *American Political Science Review* 78: 738–749.

North, D. C. 1990. *Institutions, institutional change and economic performance*. Cambridge: Cambridge University Press.

Ostrom, E. 1990. *Governing the commons: the evolution of institutions for collective action*. Cambridge; Cambridge University Press.

Page, E. C. 2010. *Policy without politicians: bureaucratic influence in comparative perspective*. Oxford: Oxford University Press.

Peters, B. G. 2019. *Institutional theory in political science: the new institutionalism*, 4th ed. Cheltenham: Edward Elgar.

Peters, B.G. 2025. Is there an institutional theory of comparative politics? Can there be?. In *Handbook of political institutions*, ed. A. Vatter and R. Freibergbaus. Cheltenham: Edward Elgar.

Peters, B. G., J. Pierre, and D. S. King. 2005. The politics of path dependency: political conflict in historical institutionalism. *Journal of Politics* 63: 1275–1300.

Peters, B. G., and M. L. Nagel. 2022. *Zombie ideas in public policy*. Cambridge: Cambridge University Press.

Pierson, P. 2000. Increasing return, path dependence and the study of politics. *American Political Science Review* 94: 251–267.

Rose, R., and P.L. Davies. 1984. *Inheritance in public policy: change without choice in Britain*. New Haven, CT: Yale University Press.

Rowe, N. 1997. *Rules and institutions*. Ann Arbor: University of Michigan Press.

Sarigil, Z. 2009. Paths are what actors make of them. *Critical Policy Studies* 3: 121–140.

Sarigil, Z. 2023. *How informal institutions matter: evidence from Turkish social and political spheres*. Ann Arbor: University of Michigan Press.

Schmidt, V. A. 2010. Taking ideas and discourse seriously: explaining change through discursive institutionalism as the fourth new institutionalism. *European Political Science Review* 2: 1–25.

Selznick, P. A. 1996. Institutionalism "Old" and "New." *Administrative Science Quarterly* 41: 270–277.

Shepsle, K.A. 1986. Institutional equilibrium and equilibrium institutions. In *Political science: the science of politics*, ed. H.F. Weisberg. New York: Agathon.

Shugart, M.S., and S. Haggard. 2001. Institutions and public policy in presidential systems. In *Presidents, parliaments and policy*, ed. Haggard and M. D. McCubbins. Cambridge: Cambridge University Press.

Steinmo, S. 2008. Historical institutionalism. In *Approaches and methodologies in the social sciences: a pluralist approach*, ed. D. Della Porta and M. Keating. Cambridge: Cambridge University Press.

Streeck, Wolfgang, and Kathleen Thelen, eds. 2005. *Beyond continuity: institutional change in advanced political economies*. Oxford: Oxford University Press.

Thornton, P.H., W. Ocasio, and M. Lounsbury. 2012. *The institutional logics perspective: a new approach to culture, structure and process*. Oxford: Oxford University Press.

Torfing, J., B. G. Peters, J. Pierre, and E. Sørensen. 2011. *Interactive governance: advancing the paradigm*. Oxford: Oxford University Press.

Tsebelis, G. 2000. *Veto players: how political institutions work*. Princeton, NJ: Princeton University Press.

Waterman, R.W., and K.J. Meijer. 2004. Principal-agent models: a theoretical Cul-de-Sac. In *Bureaucrats, politics and the environment*, ed. R.K. Waterman, A.A. Rouse and R. Wright, 19–42. Pittsburgh: University of Pittsburgh Press.

Weaver. R.K., and B.A. Rockman. 1983. *Do institutions matter?: Government capabilities in the United States and abroad*. Washington, DC: The Brookings Institution.

Yesilkagit, K., B.G. Peters, and J. Pierre. 2024. The guardian state: strengthening the public service against democratic backsliding. *Public Administration Review* 84: 414–25.

Meaning in Public Policy Approaches: Discursive Practices, Emotions, and Political Power

Anna Durnova, Frank Fischer, and Philippe Zittoun

INTRODUCTION

Over the last few decades, different policy approaches have emerged that analyze policy and grasp policy processes differently by focusing on the meaning dimension. These approaches reject the dominance of rational choice theory for policy analysis and the positivist perspective for policy processes. They reject the illusion of objective knowledge *for* and *on* policy and take the construction of policy knowledge, the subjectivity of policymakers, and the role of their discursive practices seriously. They therefore produce meanings to help grasp the world and interact with

A. Durnova
Department of Sociology, University of Vienna, Wien, Austria
e-mail: anna.durnova@univie.ac.at

F. Fischer
Albrecht Daniel Thaer Institute, Humboldt Universität, Berlin, Germany
e-mail: ffischer@gmx.com

P. Zittoun (✉)
LAET-ENTPE, University of Lyon, Lyon, France
e-mail: pzittoun@gmail.com

© The Editor(s) (if applicable) and The Author(s), under exclusive
license to Springer Nature Switzerland AG 2026
B. G. Peters and P. Zittoun (eds.), *Contemporary Approaches to Public
Policy*, International Series on Public Policy,
https://doi.org/10.1007/978-3-032-06026-6_5

others. Drawing inspiration from the "linguistic turn" in philosophy and the social sciences, these approaches grasp how meaning is produced, analyze the processes through which this meaning shapes actions and institutions, and identifies the contexts in which these meanings evolve (Bevir and Rhodes 2010).

These approaches, which are characterized by their focus on social meaning, underscore the pivotal role of language in comprehending public policy and the policy process. As Majone explains, they all consider that "as politicians know only too well but social scientists too often forget, public policy is made of language." (Majone 1989, p. 1). The primary focus of this research is to examine how public problems and public policy are defined, argued, and implemented, both individually and collectively. Additionally, it explores how these concepts are transformed by and through discourse. Rather than approaching concepts such as "interest," "ideas," "instruments," or even "value" as objective and independent variables that explain policy processes in the same positivist manner physical science explains object movement through independent variables, a different approach is taken here. Each of these concepts is viewed as a social construct that depends on how meaning is produced and used by actors during the process. The process of defining a public problem, analyzing a policy, formulating a policy solution, coupling a problem with a solution, arguing and persuading about the relevance of public policy, building a network or a coalition, and struggling with other policy aspects are all considered social and political constructions that policymakers undertake *by* and *through* their social activities.

The theoretical underpinnings of these approaches are rooted in divergent social science traditions, which all reject the positivist methodologies espoused by Comte, Saint-Simon, and Durkheim. These traditions also share a common focus on examining how subjective meaning influences individual and collective human behavior. The first of these approaches draws inspiration from the theories of Max Weber, who posited that an individual's behavior can be comprehended only through the subjective meaning they ascribe to their actions and society as the voluntary or involuntary result of the aggregation of their subjective rationality. The second approach draws inspiration from the works of Georg Simmel and Herbert Mead. These scholars rejected individual/society dualism, preferring instead to understand individual behavior as structured by relational dynamics of differentiation within individuals' social interactions.. In both cases, the focus is on meaning practices used by individuals to understand the social world around them, the importance of language in grasping and interacting with the world, and how this reflexivity influences their behavior.

A close examination of these approaches reveals that they stem from a variety of theoretical orientations, including hermeneutic, constructivist, ethnomethodological, and pragmatist perspectives. Additionally, these approaches draw upon a range of concepts such as discourse, argument, narrative, statement, framing, discursive practices, emotion, and persuasion. Rather than proposing a catalog of these approaches, we would like to categorize this diversity based on their understanding of how policy meaning addresses the central issue of political power. Breaking with the longstanding tradition of examining the various aspects of power without taking discourses and meanings into account, these policy approaches all have in common a strong interest in how issues of meaning and power intertwine in three very different ways.

The first and oldest tradition focused on the discourse of power. From this perspective, power is associated with a policy elite that occupies a dominant position in society, a specific sector, or a specific domain. Discourse is the weapon that this elite uses to maintain its domination. In contrast, the second tradition posits that power is inherent in policy discourse itself and its capacity to influence and constrain individual behavior. The third tradition is characterized by a rejection of classical epistemological dualism, which is the theoretical framework that posits the separation of the object and the subject, discourses, and practices. Instead, it emphasizes the collaborative construction of the power of policy argument and the policy argument of power.

Common Foundations of Meaning in Policy Approaches

Although there is a wide range of approaches that emphasize meaning to understand the policy process, they share a commonality. As Wittgenstein would say, they have "un air de famille." These approaches recognize that meaning is not merely an added element in understanding policy activities within the policy process but also a crucial driver of individual and collective action. It is this aspect that motivates individuals to commit to, agree to, and, at times, engage in conflict over a particular policy within the policy process.

(1) The Quest for Meaning to Understand Policy Individuals' Behavior and Collective Action

The policy work that addresses the question of meaning seriously returns to the concerns of the classical authors of the social sciences. It also takes place in old controversies opposing Durkheim, who proposed to develop the social sciences as a "positivist science" based on the study of social phenomena considered as a "fact" without specific attention to the subjective meaning, and Max Weber, who considered that the subjective meaning is the key to understanding social and collective action. This part of Weberian social science was taken further by Clifford Geertz who grounded social science in a comprehensive interpretive tradition (Geertz 1973). At the same time, in his later work on religion, Durkheim has built a foundation for the interpretive tradition of cultural sociology, known also as the Strong program or the structural hermeneutics (Alexander and Smith 2001). This return to the classic works of social science shows, the juxtaposition of diverse theoretical approaches. These approaches include functionalism, structuralism, and rational choice, which have been contrasted with interpretivism, constructivism, and interactionism, among others. The crux of this debate lies in the question of whether social phenomena should be regarded as "facts" devoid of any contextual or subjective interpretation, or if they should be viewed as inherently multifaceted and open to interpretation.

In the longstanding controversy between determinism and agency, the question of meaning takes on a particular dimension. According to Durkheim, social activities are driven by "objective" constraints that have coercive power over human activities and which can be grasped through rigorous scientific methods. This approach requires separating subjective meaning from scientific explanation. In contrast, Weber emphasized that social action is meaningful behavior, shaped by individuals' interpretations, not just external causes. Simmel, similarly, highlighted meaning in dynamic, reciprocal interactions, challenging Durkheim's linear causality by suggesting that causes and effects are multiple and interwoven. Although meaning was central to early social science—e.g., symbolic interactionism, phenomenology, and ethnomethodology—it was downplayed with the rise of behavioralism in the 1950s and paradigms like rational choice, functionalism, and structuralism. Yet, critics within these traditions, such as Herbert Simon, questioned assumptions of "objective rationality." Simon (1997) argued that real behavior is bounded by cognitive limits and shaped by the environment. Drawing on Dewey, he proposed concepts like "valuation" to show that means and ends are interdependent, and facts cannot be neatly separated from values (pp. 82–85, 93, 121). Functionalism, while less focused on meaning, incorporated it in Merton's distinction between "manifest" and "latent" functions, and in his emphasis on "subjective disposition".

The question of meaning returns to the forefront of the social sciences with linguistic turn. While it is not possible to summarize such a diverse and multifaceted intellectual movement here, we will focus on some central issues for public policy scholarship. From Husserl to Gadamer, passing through Heidegger on one side, and from Dewey to Wittgenstein to Apel and Habermas on another side, the relationship between language and thought became the center of the discussion. They all rejected the positivist view of the social sciences arguing that no language is truly neutral, logical, or independent from historical and contextual influences. On one side, Gadamer and later Ricoeur renewed the old hermeneutic tradition which focus on interpreting religious and philosophical texts. They redefined interpretation as an essential ontological activity through which individuals make sense to the world within a historical context rejecting any idea that a transcendental language could place itself above these interpretation. On the other side, Apel and Habermas developed a critical theory that treated interpretation differently. They consider interpretation as an epistemological activity which can be criticized from an external posture that also uses language. When Habermas published "technology and science as "ideology"," he offered a critical perspective on the role of the language using the "technical" rationality" to impose the only interpretation.[1]

---

[1] Following this philosophical linguistic turn, some authors brought this issue into the social sciences. Inspired by Shütz's social phenomenology, Berger and Luckmann's book about the social construction of reality proposed reconciling Weberian subjectivity and Durkheimian objectivity through their research question: How does the subjective capacity of human beings contribute to the perception of reality as "objective"? (Luckmann and Berger 1991). They emphasized the importance of the ability to produce meaning linked to the definition of situations in which individuals participate and their capacity to share intersubjective meaning in concrete situations. More fundamentally, they highlighted the capacity of human beings to not only follow routines, but also to problematize situations that cannot be grasped by established meanings. From this perspective, Blumer emphasized the discursive and non-discursive interactions individuals use to understand each other and build collective action, while Garfinkel worked on the world of meaning to grasp how to objectify individual subjectivity.

Based on the centrality of meaning in understanding individual and collective behavior, the linguistic turn in the social sciences proposed a new perspective to grasp human activities, focused on their linguistic activity to produce meaning, define the world around them through the game of language, and interact with others through discussion. In response to critiques of the Weberian approach regarding its difficulty in grasping the "intentionality" of individuals, the linguistic turn proposed focusing on their concrete speech and argumentation to grasp their subjective and communicative rationality, as well as their discussions and negotiations to understand their collective actions. In response to critiques of the Durkheimian approach regarding the problem of grasping "objectively" the institutional constraints, the approach proposed focusing on the legitimacy of institutions through the reflexive meaning individuals have about these institutions.

(2) Grasping Meaning Through Policy Discursive Practices

If there are many different approaches to addressing issues of meaning seriously, they all share the goal of grasping this meaning through the multiple forms of discourse, both individual and collective, used in and for the policy process. These forms can be written or spoken discourse, speeches, discussion, argumentation, deliberation, negotiation, enunciation, etc. The study of these discourses "in action" is based on three main characteristics.

First, it takes seriously into account the language and practical forms of enunciation that individuals use to define the world in the situation in which they are involved. Rather than impose a definition or rationality on their speech, the main idea is to observe how individuals put words together to form sentences and sentences together to give meaning to their purpose. Wittgenstein called this a game of language, including all practical activities such as defining, describing, justifying, analyzing, comparing, etc. As Berger and Luckmann (1966) explain, "These definitions, explanations, and assertions are constructed to help us make sense of those things and events that we experience and to help us to decide how to respond to those experiences." There are many forms of communication, from narratives to statements, argumentation, and justification. All these forms correspond to the same meaning process, which involves adding words and sentences and chaining them together in a specific arrangement.

This definitional perspective has become important in the sociological and policy literature about public problems. Rejecting the previous tradition of defining social problems as the "result of an intrinsic malfunctioning of a society," Blumer argued that "social problems are fundamentally products of a process of collective action instead of existing independently as a set of objective social arrangements with an intrinsic methods". Rejecting the "value-conflict" approach to social problems which considered both its objective and subjective elements, Spector and Kitsuse proposed focusing on defining the problem "as the activities of groups making assertions of grievances and claims to organizations, agencies, and institutions about some putative conditions". Further, they argued that group activities are "attempts to transform private troubles into public issues (...) complaints about the condition are raised and the strategies used to press the claims, gain publicity, and arouse controversy" (p. 147). Cobb and Rochefort also explained that "Language is essential to understanding, argument, and individual and group expression, which all figure into the definition of social problem for public attention" and suggested observing "some statement about its origins," "the question of culpability," the "impersonal causes," "blaming," and "severity". Stone explained that "problem definition is a process of image making where the image have to do fundamentally with attributing cause, blame and responsibility". Gusfield also emphasized the dramatization on which these definitional activities are based. This understanding of problems through definitional activities can also be used for policy analysis (Majone 1989) and policy formulation.

The second important characteristic is the centrality of the different forms of communication as relational activities that contribute to building collective action. If Truman considered that "any mutual interest (...) and shared attitude is a potential group", Olson argued against considering collective action as a natural phenomenon resulting from people sharing the same interests or values. Instead, he proposed viewing it as a constructed phenomenon involving negotiation and coercion. The issue of collective action becomes particularly salient in policy process studies when all policy activities involve collective action (Lindblom 1968), but it is also very controversial. There are two opposing views: an institutional perspective in which collective action takes place beyond the organization affiliations of "corporate actors", and a "policy community" perspective which, proposes to go beyond the institutional affiliation and focus on networking activities. These proposed meaning perspectives go beyond the controversies by opening the black box of collective action through the construction of collective statements, arguments, or narratives. As Ostrom explained, one of the main questions excluded by game theory is the discursive practice of "face-to-face" communication, in which individuals try to convince each other to share a common claim. By studying discursive practices that occur during interactions, meaning approaches propose understanding the relationship between problem/ policy definition and the making of collective action.

The main idea is to consider the definition of a problem and how the formulation of a policy enable discussion, and discussion enables them. Following this perspective, discussions between policymakers can produce an agreement to collectively define a problem or policy, and the resulting collective definition can stabilize relationships between individuals. This process of agreement-making can appear as a deliberation in which individuals need to redefine the problem or policy to transform it into a collective definition through communicative and deliberative rationality (Habermas 1987), argumentation (Fischer 2003), and emotions. Gusfield discussed the ownership process to explain the glue which links the problem definition and the problem "owner". In this process, the definition of the problem encompasses more than just a problematic situation; it also includes the definition of the interests and the identities of the various collective actors. This perspective was largely developed by Bruno Latour in his "actor-network" theory to highlight the formation of "collectives" and the mediation and translation that attach different individual and collective actors together. Meaning approaches are more closely tied to the concepts of "discursive," "narrative," and "statement" coalitions to highlight this process (Hajer and Wagenaar 2003; Durnova and Zittoun 2013a, b).

The third important dimension is the struggles dimension of the interpretation developed by the meaning approaches. The question of political struggles is generally associated with two opposing traditions. The first is the American pluralism perspective which considers democracy to be the result of interest groups' efforts to influence government policy. The second tradition is associated with elitism, viewing conflict as opposition between a dominant group and minority groups. In meaning approaches, struggles generally concern the "multiplication" of meaning but also echo these two perspectives. Meaning struggles can be seen as the competition among different collective actors to impose their perspectives in different arenas. For example, Hajer spoke about the struggles between different discursive coalitions. A critical tradition observes the rhetoric of the dominant position to criticize them as one meaning between others. This is the logic developed by Habermas about technology and science as "ideology" and what he referred to as "strategic communication." It is also the logic developed by Edelman (1988) to criticize the power of the dominant group and by Fischer to criticize the dominant rational choice argument.

(3) The Origin of the Linguistic Turn in Policy Analysis and Policy Process Theories

If it is always difficult to pinpoint the exact moment when specific interest in the meaning and language activities in the policy process emerged, we want to begin by evoking the debate that took place in the 1960s and 1970s in sociology and political science, specifically, regarding the definition of the problem that influenced most of the theories on the policy process. Without going into detail, we can mention the influence of William James and John Dewey's pragmatism, which largely influenced the Chicago School of Political Science, and more specifically Lasswell. One of the founding scholars of policy sciences, Lasswell played an important role in this debate about the definition of public problems in the 1960s and 1970s. Without detailing this period, we would like to suggest that the linguistic turn was more widely accepted in policy studies in the 1980s and 1990s through three main research dimensions that often overlapped.

The first dimension focuses on public policy and proposes considering it as a political construction. Following Edelman's perspective, which views political discourse as mystification in a political spectacle, different authors proposed grasping public policy itself as a political discourse. This perspective is more well-known in sociology than in policy studies, but it has been quoted by numerous important authors, such as Stone, Majone, and Cobb and Rochefort. In 1981, Gusfield published a book about "The culture of Public Problems" in which he focuses not only on problem definition but also on public policy. He argues that one should understand "public policies as theatrical to emphasize the ritual, ceremonial, and dramatic qualities of actions. It is possible to see public actions, like plays, as artistic, as constructed within conventional understandings between audience and performer" (Gusfield 1981, 22). In 1989, Deborah Stone published an article in which she took a "social constructionist view of policy problems," considering that "real situations are always mediated by ideas [which] are created, changed and fought over in politics." Stone proposes observing "how political actors used narrative story lines and symbolic devices to manipulate so-called issue characteristics". In 1987, Jobert and Muller published a book explaining how public policy can be considered a meaningful activity that drives the dominant interpretation of society supported by the government (Jobert and Muller 1987). In 1993, Schneider and Ingram argued that studying public policy is a political phenomenon containing the social construction of the target population. In their view, "Constructions become embedded in policy as messages that are absorbed by citizens and affect their orientations and participation". Similarly, Dvora Yanow proposes considering how various policy interpretations can affect policy implementation.

A second dimension focuses primarily on policy analysis, policy design, and all methods of problem solving. In 1989, Majone published an important book called "Evidence, Argument, and Persuasion in the Policy Process" in which he proposed "to develop a single idea: the notion that in a system of government by discussion, analysis—even professional analysis—has less to do with formal techniques of problem solving than with the process of argument" (Majone 1989, 7). In 1990, Fischer published a book discussing how technocracy could use rational choice as an authoritarian argument rather than an argument like any other. In 1993, Fischer and Forester published the "Argumentative Turn in Policy Analysis and Planning" to highlight the "argumentative character of policy analysis." These early efforts by Forester and Fischer (1993) set out a new perspective, moving away from the mainstream approach to problem-solving inherent in policy analysis from the outset. Fundamentally, this was achieved by introducing language and argumentation as basic elements of policy inquiry. As an alternative orientation, the "argumentative turn" incorporated developments in post-positivist epistemology with critical political and social theory in an attempt to propose a socially relevant policy methodology. At the outset, this perspective emphasized practical argumentation, policy judgment, rhetorical analysis, frame analysis, and narrative storylines (Gottweis 2006). Maturing in the first half of the

1990s, argumentative policy analysis developed into a significant orientation within policy studies. As Peters (2004) put it, the argumentative approach to policy had evolved into one of the main competing theories

The final dimension concerns the policy process itself and the role of meaning within it. Several authors have already considered the link between the meaning of policy, policy analysis, and the policy process. According to Shneider and Ingram, "the theory contends that social constructions influence the policy agenda and the selection of policy tools". Fischer also considered that "the argumentative turn focused on the fact that policymakers work and communicate contextually in the medium of ordinary language and argumentation" (Fischer 2015). Majone proposed considering argumentation as the "key process focus through which citizens and policymakers arrive at moral judgment and public choices" (p. 2) and emphasized observing the argument of feasibility as a way in which "they all limit the freedom of choice of the policymaker" (p. 70). Other authors focus more precisely on discursive and relational practices to understand how policymakers define problems, formulate policy, and argue to persuade other policymakers to join them in collective action in support of their definition. Vivien Schmidt proposed focusing on the role of discourse in the policy process by emphasizing "the interactive processes of discourse implicit as they discuss the ideas generated, deliberated, and legitimated by public actors, the carriers of ideas (...) address explicitly the representation of ideas (how agents say what they are thinking of doing) and the discursive interactions through which actors generate and communicate ideas (to whom they say it) within given institutional contexts (where and when they say it)." (Schmidt 2008). Maarten Hajer developed the concept of "discourse coalition" to highlight "a group of actors who share a social construct" (p. 44, 1993) (Hajer 2003). Zittoun proposed opening the "black box" of collective action by observing how policymakers mobilized their definitions and arguments to enroll other policymakers and fight those who supported different positions in various government arenas (Zittoun 2013a, b).

(4) Approaching Policy Processes Through the Lens of Emotions

The recognition of the centrality of the interpretation of meanings has brought forward the interpretive inquiry of emotions. The question of emotions is usually associated with psychological works in studying political behavior, including deliberation and collective action (Jasper 2006). Inside public policy scholarship, the approach through social movements was the first one to look at emotions—not as disturbances of political rationality- but as elements that initiate action, created groups and identities. Interpretive works started at this point, asking what these identities and groups mean, and how emotions become interpretive filter of political rationality and political legitimacy. growing number of interpretive works began to emerge to show that studying emotions means to study meanings of emotions, the role of the context in which these emotions emerge, or be understood as such. In the past two decades, large number of works has emerged to show how emotions frame policy designs, and how they mobilize actors in a policy conflict.

We can distinguish two sorts of attention paid to emotions in policy processes that these studies have brought to the analysis of policy processes through the discursive paradigm. On the one hand, emotions enter policy processes as discursive parts of fear, hope or compassion related to particular policy issues. This aspect has mainly been investigated in the analysis of women's issues as (Ahmed 2004; Fonow and Cook 1991; Martin 2001), or in analysis on health, risk and marginalization caused by particular illnesses (see, e.g., Orsini and Wiebe 2014). On the other hand, emotions refer to the evaluative judgments in which actors are entitled to participate or are seen as relevant to policy negotiation around a particular issue. Some research has been undertaken in that respect in the area of policy planning (see, e.g., Sullivan and Skelcher 2002) and studies on strategies of policy workers have also contributed (see, e.g., Newman 2012).

The emotional approach to policy process goes beyond the specificities of particular policy issues and seeks to question the nature of policy processes traditionally framed as "rational." To highlight limits of such a notion of rationality this approach turns the analytical attention to how we frame the categories through which we analyze and think of policies. The approach builds, in this regard, on some of the premises of the argumentative turn, which can be seen here as providing a substantial basis for such study, providing grounds for analyzing arguments and interactions of actors. However, the emotional approach argues that the argumentative turn tended to see arguments and discourses as themselves also a sort of rationalizing structure, as if we could think of an argument purified of emotions (Durnova 2015).

Indeed, both emotions and discourses reveal to us the tension between the individual part of knowledge (for example, moment, feeling, point of view) and its collective validation (the cultural context, the habitus, the established practice). Thus, we can treat emotions analytically as elements that reveal to us the prioritization of values. One such example is the study on smoking bans by Lars Larsen (2010), in which he shows that the decisive moment in the succession of smoking bans all around the world cannot be explained by the simple fact that smoking is unhealthy, since this scientific evidence had been circulating in public debates for over twenty years. He argues, among other things, that framing the problem as a potential threat for workers ultimately fused this scientific evidence with the idea of a ban in public spaces. However, and this is crucial for the role of emotions in the analysis of policy processes, this happens in concert with pointing out that smoking by patrons constitutes "shameful" treatment of "poor" workers in bars who cannot escape this while working, implying that it would be even more "shameful" to deny these people a hygienic work environment. Larsen does not frame these moments through emotions, but the arguments he uses appeal to the emotion of shame and the meaning of smoking as a threat becomes prioritized over the meaning of smoking as a freedom, giving a more important role to the discourse in favor of a smoking ban.

As values are collectively validated through the policy process the same tension between individual experience and its collective understanding can be followed in the case of the classification of actors as legitimized to take part in respective policy negotiations. In that sense, emotions clarify why some values are prioritized and reveal social relationships among actors; especially why some values are qualified as trustworthy and others as disturbing. To come back to the initial example of the controversy over the location of the railway station we can see that the actors gathered in respective groups through two different ways of sharing values on "citizen engagement" and "politics." The group around the public officials that had been advocating for the relocation of the railway station explained this relocation through the narrative of "modernity," relying on effective decision-making, trust in politicians and a restrictive notion of citizen engagement. The protest group was marked by the opposite: to stay in the current location was seen as an attempt to deal carefully with both the environment and the citizen—because the latter was seen as the main user of the location and therefore was framed as the main user of the policy proposed.

For these reasons, the emotional perspective is interested in the tension between the individual and the collective dimension of emotional experience, which becomes reflected both in how knowledge is produced and in what qualifies this knowledge as relevant. This enables us to reflect how policy processes are designed, why they are designed in that particular way and, beyond that, enables us to question the apparent claim of "rationality" upon which the policy process as such seems to stand. Integrating emotions into study of public policy—and combining it with the power of discourse and argumentation—has therefore evolved into a vibrant field allowing to better understand how policy conflict emerge and develop over time how they give rise to new forms of policy designs, as well as coproduce legitimacy of expert knowledge.

The Multiple Faces of the Discourse-Power

The question of power has been of particular importance from the earliest authors of the linguistic turn to leading policy scholars focusing on meaning and discourse and their complex, mutually constitutive relationship. Habermas, Edelman, Foucault, and Bourdieu all address the central question of this complex relationship between power and discourse. Majone, Stone, Fischer, Hajer, Schmidt, Bacchi, Dryzeck, Roe, Rose, Durnova, Howarth, Dodge, and Zittoun, among others, have explored this issue in order to gain a better understanding of the intricate relationship between policy and politics.

All policy approaches that consider the dimension of meaning seriously are interested in how discourses engage with the question of power. However, they do not understand the relationship between power and discourse in the same way. Rather than being limited to three faces, the concept of power has multiple dimensions that extend through, within, or beyond discourse. Some authors define power as the capacity of a group to be dominant, viewing language as a weapon to maintain this domination. Others argue that power lies in the capacity of discourses to shape and control people. Still others consider that the power of discourse lies in its ability to persuade and build collective action through argumentation. Finally, this dualism between the individual and their argument is rejected in order to interrogate the power of the Individual-Discourse. Among these multiple ways of understanding the relationship between power and discourse, some authors consider the contradiction between the power of discourse and the discourse of power, while many others have used and proposed ways to reconcile the different faces of this relationship to study public policy.

(1) The Policy Discourse of Power to Shape Public Consent, Maintain the Domination of the Policy Elite, and Legitimize the Government

A first perspective proposes to analyze the relationship between power and discourse by examining the discourse used by the dominant group. This group may operate at a global level, such as a government or an elite, or at an intermediate level, such as a group of policy experts. Its discourse is understood as a means by which those already in power influence public opinion. From Walter Lippmann and Harold Lasswell to Habermas, Bourdieu, and Chomsky, many scholars have emphasized the importance of analyzing the speeches of governments or influential groups as tools for legitimizing their rule. However, their understanding of power is complex. On the one hand, they associate the source of power with the system and the unequal positions of individuals, independent of language. On the other hand, they attribute power to language itself, arguing that systemic position alone is insufficient to maintain domination; legitimacy also requires the ability to be accepted.

To understand the complexity of this perspective, it is important to revisit the distinction proposed by Max Weber between Power (*Macht*) and Domination (*Herrschaft*). Weber considers power as the ability to impose a decision through coercion or force, without the consent of the people, whereas domination is understood as a relational concept that involves not only those in power but also the capacity of the dominated to consent to their own subjugation. The concept of domination thus encompasses both an unequal relationship between the dominant and the dominated and the necessity for the dominant to secure the consent of the dominated to maintain their position. In Weber's view, domination is more stable than power and is primarily sustained by institutions that foster the consent of the dominated.

Although Max Weber did not focus on discourse, various authors have understood "rhetoric" and later "propaganda" as means by which governments shape the consent necessary to maintain their domination over the people. From the Greek sophists to post-World War I thinkers like Lippmann and Lasswell, and through a long tradition of authors such as Gramsci, the role of language as a political tool for shaping public consent and preserving dominance has been a recurring topic of analysis. Thrasymachus, for example, argues in *The Republic* that laws and rhetoric serve as instruments for governments to maintain their power. Gramsci, meanwhile, emphasizes the capacity of language to shape perception and sustain the hegemony of the elite. This longstanding interest was significantly renewed after World War I, with growing concerns about the development of mass media, public opinion measurement through surveys, and the increasing role of governmental speeches. In his 1922 book *Public Opinion*, Walter Lippmann highlighted the role of leaders as propagandists, writing: "Every leader is in some degree a propagandist (...) deciding more and more consciously what facts, in what setting, in what guise he shall permit the public to know. That the manufacture of consent is capable of great refinements no one, I think, denies. The process by which public opinion arises is certainly no less intricate than it has appeared in these pages and the opportunities for manipulation open to anyone who understands the process are plain enough. (...) Persuasion has become a self-conscious art and a regular organ of popular government".

Influenced by Lippmann, Harold Lasswell was also one of the major scholars who studied how elites use propaganda to manipulate symbols and influence public opinion. In *Propaganda Technique in the World War* (1927), he explains that "propaganda is the management of collective attitudes by the use of significant symbols (...) the elite must rely on propaganda as a means of securing consent among the governed (....) In democratic societies, the governance of opinion is the key to power." In his famous book *Politics: Who Gets What, When, and How*, Lasswell theorizes that "the study of politics is the study of influence and the influential" (Lasswell 1950). He emphasizes how elites use propaganda to manipulate symbols in their discourse, including words and emotions, to shape public perception: "Propaganda is conducted with symbols, which are utilized as far as possible by elite and counter-elite."

After the linguistic turn, the interest in language as a tool of government to shape consent was revitalized. Murray Edelman, for example, published a book in 1964 in which he analyzed how governments, through the "forms and meaning of political language (...), win the acquiescence" of the public and emphasized the role of "needs and emotions in men". The *political spectacle* relies on the elite's ability to manipulate the public through their speeches, allowing them not only to legitimize their power but also to distinguish themselves from others. This focus on the discourse of the dominant class was also developed by Pierre Bourdieu, who criticized Saussure, Habermas, and Austin for seeking the power of language within words themselves. Instead, Bourdieu highlighted that the power of language is a *delegated power* granted to spokespersons. He explained "To seek in language the principle of the logic and efficiency of institutional language is to forget that authority comes to the language from outside, as is clearly shown by the scepter that Homer holds out to the speaker about to take the floor. This authority represents language at most".

This perspective of discourse as an instrument of power and domination plays a crucial role in various policy approaches that take meaning-making seriously. When Cobb and Elder published their article on the politics of agenda-building, they emphasized the legitimacy of a group as a key factor in determining its success or failure in placing an issue on the agenda. In his book, Joseph Gusfield introduced the concept of *the ownership of public problems* to highlight that "the recognition that in the arenas of public opinion and debates all groups do not have equal power, influence, and authority to define the reality of the problem" (Gusfield 1981, 10). He stressed the centrality of "the ability to create and influence the public definition of a problem (...); the metaphor of property ownership is chosen to emphasize the attributes of control." Rochefort and Cobb later extended Gusfield's concept to develop *The Struggle for Problem Ownership*, describing it as a conflict over "the domination of the way a social concern is thought of and acted upon in the public arena". In her article *Causal Stories and the Formation of Policy Agendas*, Deborah Stone expanded on the perspectives of Cobb, Elder, and Gusfield by demonstrating "how political actors use narrative storylines and symbolic devices to manipulate the so-called issue characteristics (...) a systematic process with fairly clear rules of the game by which political actors struggle to control interpretations and images of difficulties.". Following Habermas' perspective on *strategic communication*, Frank Fischer explored how some experts mobilized rational choice theory as a means to maintain their dominant expert position in the policy process (Fischer 2003). Finally, Zittoun developed the idea that policymaking itself is the manufacture of a discourse of legitimation, shaping how governments present themselves as capable of solving problems and transforming society (Zittoun 2014).

Using Austin's distinction, the power of policy discourse can be seen as *illocutionary*, in the sense that consent is assumed to be obtained through the elite's ability to *say something* ("by saying something"). The concrete enunciation of policy discourse constitutes an act of relational power between the dominant and the dominated. Most studies focus on the elite's position and the content of the discourse rather than on its effects—specifically, the impact generated by the very act of speaking.

(2) The Performative Power of Policy Discourse to Shape Public Behavior

Contrary to the first perspective, which focuses on the power of the elite and the capacity of policy discourse to secure public consent and maintain domination, the second perspective emphasizes the consequences of policy discourse enunciation, particularly its role in shaping public behavior. In this view, power is not concentrated solely in the hands of the elite but is distributed throughout society, embedded in discursive relationships that establish a balance of power. From Saussure to Foucault, Barthes, and Derrida, this perspective has influenced various policy studies, including those of David Howarth, Ingram and Schneider, and Yanow, among others. The central idea is that discourse itself has the power to influence and constrain public behavior through its *performative effects*.

Although Saussure did not directly study the question of power in discourse, he highlighted the influence of the structure of language *"in itself and for itself*," shaping the way we think and act. This structural perspective contributed to redefining the understanding of language, which was initially seen primarily as a system of grammar. It also influenced Wittgenstein, who introduced the concept of *language games*, associating meaning with the use of words. In linguistic philosophy, Austin was one of the first to explore the performativity of language and how words can be used to *do things*. Rejecting the strict opposition between constative and performative statements, he proposed a distinction between *illocutionary acts*, which are embedded within discourse and reveal the speaker's intention, and *perlocutionary acts*, which concern the expected and unexpected effects of discourse on its audience.

Foucault went much further in his analysis of the power of discourse. He argued that power is not "a set of institutions and apparatuses that guarantee the subjection of citizens in a given state" or "a general system of domination exercised by one element or group over another", but rather "the multiplicity of power relations that are immanent in the domain in which they are exercised, and are constitutive of their organization." For him, the key question is not what kind of discourse is developed by the state or dominant groups, but what kind of power relationships are at play in the concrete, situated discursive practices that people either engage in or reject, and how individual struggles occur both through and for these discourses. He argued that "discourse is simultaneously the instrument and the effect of power" (p. 133). Foucault, interested in the archaeology of knowledge-discourse, explained how, for example, the development of discourse-knowledge about homosexuality in the nineteenth century simultaneously served as a means to better control it, but paradoxically also allowed the emergence of a discourse aimed at its liberation. The power of discourses, according to Foucault, is primarily based on their ability to establish an order that separates what is madness and what is not, what practices are possible and what are forbidden, and so on.

While Foucault primarily explored the power of language at a level different from that of government, he later discussed the issue of governance and what he termed *governmentality*. He explained that the power to govern is inseparable from the power of knowing and shaping populations through discourse. For him, *governmentality* refers to "institutions, procedures, analyses and reflections, calculations and tactics, which allow this very specific form of power to be exercised, targeting the population". Foucault emphasized the capacity of knowledge-discourses to control individuals. Referring to the old French word *police*—from which the English term *policy* is derived—he argued that "the goal of *police* (policy) is to control and manage individual activities, as these activities can constitute a differential element in the development of the state (...) First, policy must address the number of people (...) the necessities of life (...) health problems (...) their activities (...) and their circulation" (p. 331).

Following the interest in the power of policy discourse, a large number of policy studies focus on the performative dimension of policy definitions themselves, and the way they establish specific social orders. Schneider and Ingram, for example, proposed focusing on "the social construction of target populations (...) embedded in policy as messages that are absorbed by citizens and affect their orientations and participation". In their perspective "Target population (...) attempts to achieve goals by changing people's behavior (...) and become part of the reelection calculus." This question of definition, classification, and typification as a means to shape collective action has also been developed in various ways. It can concern different types of classification, such as the classification of migrants, for example. Deborah Stone also discussed the importance of categorization and highlighted the significance of numbers. James Scott explored how classification and categorization are central instruments of governmental power. Judith Butler emphasized gender classification in discourse, while Sheila Jasanoff studied the role of science in the social construction of policy categorization (Jasanoff 2006). David Howarth examined how "the power (…) consists of radical acts of decision and institutions which involve the drawing of political frontiers via the creation of multiple lines of inclusion and exclusion".

(3) The Power of Policy Discourse to Shape Collective Action

In various policy studies, some authors focus specifically on the power of discourse to persuade others and build collective action. Discourse is seen as a means of establishing a relational activity that allows participants to reach an agreement and coordinate collective action. Discourse resembles a discussion more than a speech, in which people debate their definitions of the problems to be solved, the relevant policies to mobilize, and the policy narratives. During these discussions, participants argue to persuade others, but also to negotiate through their definitions and arguments. As Majone mentions, argumentation is a central activity in the policy process, mobilized at every stage that researchers need to study. However, its relationship with power is not easy to clarify.

The issue of argumentation is an old, classical question. In his book, Chaim Perelman renews Aristotle's legacy by defining argumentation as a discursive practice aimed at winning the support of listeners and the audience, highlighting that this practice also includes a definition of who needs to be convinced. In this sense, argumentation is a situated practice built by individuals to persuade an audience. Perelman distinguishes between a small audience, where argumentation develops during a discussion, and a large audience, where argumentation is more embedded in a speech. Although Perelman did not directly address the question of power, he considered that persuasion occurs within the content of the discourse rather than through the authority of the speaker. Habermas similarly argued that discursive practices, particularly argumentation and deliberation, contribute to creating agreement among individuals. He maintained that the question of power resides in the capacity of communicative rationality rather than in the authority of the speakers. Similarly, Hannah Arendt contrasts persuasion and argumentation with authority, explaining that "authority is incompatible with persuasion, which presupposes equality and operates through a process of argumentation. Where arguments are used, authority is left out. Faced with the egalitarian order of persuasion is the authoritarian order, which is always hierarchical."

The question of the power of argument was initially studied in terms of "influence." Simon distinguished between "suggestion" and "persuasion" by defining suggestion as a "social transfer of statements (...) without arguments," generally linked to the recognition of the social status of the speaker, and persuasion as the process through which someone mobilizes arguments to convince their interlocutors (Herbert Alexander Simon 1948). In the 1960s, Banfield proposed studying what he called "political influence." Considering the fragmentation of the state and the many disagreements among people, he suggested understanding influence as the capacity to persuade and negotiate in the policymaking process in order to coordinate such a fragmented population. He explained that "to concert activity for any purpose, a more or less elaborate system of influence must be created. Any cooperative activity may be viewed as a system of influence" (Banfield 1961, 4). He proposed studying government as "patterns of influence" and emphasized that influence operates through a system of persuasion.

In his book (Majone 1989), Majone made an important contribution to the discussion on the importance of persuasion through argumentation in the policy process. While he initially considered the role of the analyst to be that of providing arguments and evidence for public debate, he also examined the role of policy advisers in advising policymakers and overseeing the policymaking process through the "multiple advocacy [which] is a process of debate and persuasion designed to expose the policymakers systematically to competing arguments made by the advocates themselves" (p. 40). He emphasized the persuasive dimension of the feasibility argument, as well as the technical, economical, and political constraints which "restrict our freedom of choice by eliminating certain courses of action" (p. 92). Furthermore, the power of discourse is evident in its ability to shape our understanding of the situation. Vivien Schmidt uses the concept of "coordinative discourse" to highlight "the capacity of actors to persuade other actors of the cognitive validity and/or normative value of their views" which contribute to coordinate policy actors. Maarten Hajer expands on the coordination issue, referring to it as a "discourse coalition" which he defines as "a group of actors who share a social construct". Zittoun extends this line of thinking by questioning how such coalitions are formed and the role that persuasion plays in the construction of a shared definition of the alternatives they wish to support.

(5) The Dialectic Between Power and Discourse Through Meaning Struggles

The final dimension we wish to highlight regarding the complex relationship between power and discourse is how policy actors fight each other with and through their discourse, as well as through them. From this perspective, the issue is not merely an opposition between dominant and dominated groups, where discourse is seen as the weapon of the dominant, nor just a matter of persuasion between policy actors. Rather, it is a competition between two or more groups to impose their definition of the problem and/or the policy proposal they advocate. This focus on struggles with uncertain outcomes makes it difficult, from an epistemological standpoint, to distinguish between the discourse of power and the power of discourse.

The conflictual dimension of the policy process has long been emphasized, including in relation to discourse. David Truman, who published a pluralist perspective on the governmental process in which group interests compete, referred at various points to the role of discourse. He suggests that one of the main tactics of influence developed by competing interest groups involves propaganda, which aims "to guide and to control opinion". From a more elitist perspective, Schattschneider develops the idea that competing groups also engage in definitional struggles to impose their own interpretation of the problem. He argues that "political conflict is not like an intercollegiate debate in which opponents agree in advance on a definition of the issues. As a matter of fact, the definition of alternatives is the supreme instrument of power; the antagonists can rarely agree on what the issues are." He contends that "power is involved in the definition (...) the definition of alternatives is the choice of conflicts, and the choice of conflicts allocates power". Moreover, he sees the dialectic between power and language, asserting that power resides in language ("in the definition"), and that groups fight to gain power through the power of language they impose.

The main idea is to highlight that different groups defend different discourses and fight to impose their own policy definitions, statements, or narratives while simultaneously asserting their dominance. In the same vein, Gusfield emphasized the competition among various groups to impose their own definition of the problem they want the government to address. Following Schattschneider, he also underscored the importance of denying public problems and the struggles for control over problem definitions (Gusfield 1981). Banfield focused on struggles for influence, where multiple groups attempt to assert their power, with particular attention to the fragmentation of the bureaucracy that contributes to these struggles. Rochefort and Cobb expanded on Gusfield's concept to develop the idea of "The Struggle for Problem Ownership," framing it as a conflict to understand the "domination of how a social concern is conceived and discussed in the public arena." (Rochefort and Cobb 1994) In Hajer's perspective, each discourse coalition has its own definition and strives to impose it on the governmental agenda.

For Foucault, however, meaning struggles are not about conflicts between different definitions supported by various groups, but rather about discursive struggles over the very conditions that make definition possible. Foucault focuses on the struggles over meaning, particularly in terms of exclusion, classification, and the establishment of the truth conditions for these definitions (Foucault 1971). In his view, different groups attempt to control and organize the power of discourse. The "order of discourse" involves struggling to control the conditions under which discourses are produced, such as excluding certain words, imposing specific categorizations, or shaping the truth conditions. Struggling over forbidden words is not only about fighting for a particular discourse; it is also about fighting through discourse by controlling how people produce and engage with it. Similarly, Foucault emphasized that meaning struggles include debates about the conditions of truth, which should be understood as a practice of exclusion. Foucault referred to this as the "regime of truth."

While this perspective considers that coalitions fight to impose their own discourse, other authors focus more on the discursive struggles themselves. They argue that the definition of policy is not just the result of a power struggle between two coalitions with competing discourses, but also a complex negotiation or transaction where the conflict itself affects the final definition. In his work, Luc Boltanski emphasizes the role of justification and critique in social relationships. He developed the idea that critique, even if it does not impose a new point of view, impacts the dominant discourse, which is always required to produce justifications in order to resist critique. For example, he argued that capitalism's best allies were its critiques, which contributed to the creation of new discourses and practices designed to resist those critiques. Latour views meaning struggles and controversies as the key moments in the production of scientific truth, where scientists test their discourses but also transform them in order to withstand the regime of scientificity. Similarly, Chailleux and Zittoun developed the concept of the "transilience of the definition of policy solutions" to describe how the groups supporting a policy solution must adapt and transform their own definition to resist critiques (Chailleux and Zittoun 2023a).

These approaches suggest that there is continuity between the identity of actors and the characteristics of their discourses, making it impossible to separate meaning struggles from human struggles. While Foucault initially focused on epistemic struggles, which are essentially discursive, he expanded his perspective with the concept of the "dispositive," which links words, things, and individuals, and contrasts different arrangements. With his network theory, Latour argues that statements link not only their owners but also all the human and non-human elements to which the discourse refers. Scientific controversies, in his view, are struggles that oppose and merge both the discourses and their owners. Chailleux and Zittoun have shown how the "coupling" between problems and solutions also involves a coupling between the two owning groups, and how the transformation of policy statements reconfigures coalitions. Ansell, Hassenteufel, and Zittoun developed the concept of "policy transaction" to highlight the inseparability of definitions and definition-makers. They argue that collective action simultaneously links definitions and identities, considering meaning struggles as a transaction involving the identities of policymakers.

CONCLUSION

This chapter summarizes key strands of thought in policymaking that have challenged positivist approaches to politics since the 1970s by placing meaning at the center of analysis. Over the past decades, several such policy approaches have emerged, placing the dimension of meaning at their core. Rejecting the dominance of rational choice and positivist perspectives, these approaches underscore the importance of language, discourse, and interpretive practices in understanding public policy processes. They argue that policy is socially constructed through discursive practices, shaped by subjective meanings actors attribute to problems, policies, and instruments. Inspired by the linguistic turn, these frameworks emphasize that meaning is not an additional component but a crucial element driving individual and collective actions within policy processes. They examine how policymakers define problems, create narratives, and employ arguments to legitimize and build support for their positions, highlighting the central role of discursive interaction in policymaking.

It began by highlighting the need to unpack the political implications of policies and policy analysis. It then turned to two recent research areas that have advanced our understanding of policy processes: the argumentative turn, the importance of policy narrative and statement, and the growing focus on emotion—both of which open promising avenues for future research. The fact that discursive approaches Themselces can no longer be treated as a single, unified tradition reflects the richness of the paradigm and its growing influence in public policy research.

Moreover, these interpretive policy approaches explore the intricate relationship between discourse and power. This relationship is analyzed here through four dimensions: the discourses used by elites to maintain domination; the performative power of discourse to shape behavior and social structures; discourse as a persuasive tool for collective action; and the struggles over meanings between competing groups. The authors highlight how power is embedded in the capacity of discourse to persuade, influence, and mobilize actors, thus shaping political outcomes. Furthermore, contemporary studies integrating emotions reveal additional layers of complexity, show how emotional discourses influence the legitimacy, prioritization, and dynamics of policy issues and conflicts, challenging traditional notions of purely rational policy processes.

In recent years, contentious policy areas such as environmental policy, urban planning, and migration have increasingly drawn on discursive perspectives for their ability to capture the diversity of public discourse and structure it around how knowledge is constructed, presented as expertise, and translated into policy. The ongoing challenge to mainstream policy analysis—through the lenses of politics, argumentation, and emotion—shows no sign of slowing down.

REFERENCES

Ahmed, S. 2004. *The cultural politics of emotion*. New York, NY: Routledge.
Bachrach, Peter S., and Morton S. Baratz. 1963. Decisions and non-decisions: an analytical framework. *American Political Science Review* 57 (3): 641–651.
Barnes, Marianne. 2008. Passionate participation: emotional experiences and expressions in deliberative forums. *Critical Social Policy* 28 (4): 461–481. https://doi.org/10.1177/0261018308095280.
Bevir, M., and R. A. Rhodes. 2010. The state as cultural practice. OUP Oxford.
Clemons, R. S., and M. K. McBeth. 2001. *Public policy praxis: theory and pragmatism, a case approach*. Prentice-Hall.
Crozier, Michel, and Erhard Friedberg. 1977. *L'acteur et le Système*. Paris: Seuil.
Dryzek, J. S. 2001. Legitimacy and economy in deliberative democracy. *Political Theory* 29 (5): 651–669.
Durnová, A. 2013a. A tale of 'Fat Cats' and 'Stupid Activists': contested values, governance and reflexivity in the Brno Railway Station controversy. *Journal of Environmental Policy & Planning* 1–17.
Durnová, A. 2013b. Governing through intimacy: Explaining care policies through 'sharing a meaning.' *Critical Social Policy* 33 (3): 494–513. https://doi.org/10.1177/0261018312468305.
Durnová, A. 2015. Lost in translation: expressing emotions in policy deliberation. In *Handbook of critical policy studies*, ed. F. Fischer, D. Torgerson, A. Durnová, and M. Orsini. Cheltenham: Edward Elgar Publishing.
Fischer, F. 1980. *Politics, values, and public policy: the problem of methodology*. Westview Press.
Fischer, F. 2003. *Reframing public policy: discursive politics and deliberative practices*. Oxford: Oxford University Press.
Fischer, F. 2009. *Democracy and expertise: reorienting policy inquiry*. Oxford: Oxford University Press.
Fischer, F. 2012. Debating the head start program: the westinghouse reading scores in normative perspective. In *Public policy*, vol. 1, ed. Hupe Peter and Hil Michael. Los Angeles: Sage Publications.
Fischer, F. 2015. In pursuit of usable knowledge: critical policy analysis and the argumentative turn. In *Handbook of critical policy studies*, ed. Frank Fischer, Douglas Torgerson, Anna Durnova, Michael Orsinin. Edgar Elgar.
Fischer, F., and J. Forester. 1993. *The argumentative turn in policy analysis and planning*. Durham: Duke University Press.

Fischer, F., and H. Gottweis. 2012. *The argumentative turn revisited: public policy as communicative practice*. Durham: Duke University Press.

Fishkin, James S. 1991. *Democracy and deliberation: new directions for democratic reform*, vol. 217. Cambridge: Cambridge Univ Press.

Fonow, M.M., and J.A. Cook. 1991. *Beyond methodology: feminist scholarship as lived research*. Indiana University Press.

John, Forester, ed. 1985. *Critical theory and political life*. Cambridge: MIT Press.

Foucault, Michel. 1963. *Naissance de La Clinique; Une Archéologie Du Regard Médical*. Galien Histoire et Philosophie de La Biologie et de La Médecine. Paris: Presses universitaires de France.

Foucault, Michel. 1966. *Les Mots et Les Choses Une Archéologie Des Sciences Humaines*. Bibliothèque Des Sciences Humaines. Paris: Gallimard.

Foucault, Michel. 1971. *L'ordre du discours*. Editions Flammarion.

Foucault, Michel. 1975. *Surveiller et Punir: Naissance de La Prison*. Bibliothèque Des Histoires. Paris: Gallimard.

Freund, J. 1986. *L'essence du politique*. Paris: Dalloz.

Fung, A., and E.O. 2003. *Deepening democracy: institutional innovations in empowered participatory governance*, vol. 4. Verso.

Goodwin, J. 2001. *Passionate politics, emotions and social movements*. Chicago: University of Chicago Press.

Gottweis, H. 2006. Argumentative policy analysis. In *Handbook of public policy*, ed. J. Pierre and B. G. Peters, 461–480. Thousand Oaks: Sage.

Gottweis, H. 1998. *Governing molecules: the discursive politics of genetic engineering in Europe and the United States*. MIT Press.

Gottweis, H. 2003. Theoretical strategies of poststructuralist policy analysis: towards an analytics of government. In *Deliberative policy analysis. Understanding governance in the network society*, 247–265

Gottweis, Herbert. 2007. Rhetoric in policy making: between logos, ethos, and pathos. In *Handbook of public policy analysis. Theory, politics, and methods*, ed. Frank Fischer and G.J. Miller. Boca Raton: Taylor & Francis.

Gusfield, Joseph. 1981. *The culture of public problem*. Chicago: Chicago University of Chicago Press.

Habermas, Jürgen. 1987. *Théorie de L'agir Communicationnel*. Vol. L'espace du politique. Tome 1: Rationalité de L'agir et Rationalisation de La Société. Paris: Fayard.

Hajer, M. A., and H. Wagenaar. 2003. *Deliberative policy analysis: understanding governance in the network society*. Cambridge: University Press.

Hallin, D.C. 1985. The American news media: a critical theory perspective. In *Critical theory and public life*, ed. Forester John, 121–46. MIT Press.

Hawkesworth, M.E. 1988). *Theoretical issues in policy analysis*. SUNY Press.

Jann, W., and K. Wegrich. 2003. Phasenmodelle und Politikprozesse: Der policy cycle. *Lehrbuch der Politikfeldanalyse* 2: 106.

Jasanoff, S. 2006. Ordering knowledge, ordering society. In *States of knowledge. The co-production of science and social order*, ed. S. Sheila Jasanoff, 13–45. London: Routledge.

Jasper, J.M. 2006. Emotions and the microfoundations of politics: rethinking and means. In *Emotion, politics and society*, ed. S. Clarke, P. Hoggett and Thompson, 14–30. Basingstoke: Palgrave Macmillan.

Jasper, James M. 2011. Emotions and social movements: twenty years of theory and research. *Annual Review of Sociology* 37 (1): 285–303. https://doi.org/10.1146/annurev-soc-081309-150015.

Jobert, Bruno. 1994. *Le Tournant Néo-Libéral En Europe*. Paris: L'Harmattan.

Jobert and Muller. 1987. L'Etat en action, Paris, PUF, 1987.

Jones, Brian D., and Frank R. Baumgartner. 2005. *The politics of attention. how government prioritizes problems*. Chicago: University of Chicago Press.

Kingdon, John. 1995. *Agendas, alternatives and public policies*. New York: Longman.

Larsen, Lars T. 2010. Framing knowledge and innocent victims. Europe bans smoking in public places. *Critical Discourse Studies* 7 (1): 1–17.

Lasswell, Harold. 1942. The relation of ideological intelligence to public policy. *Ethics* 53 (1): 25–34.

Lasswell, H. 1951. The policy orientation. In *The policy sciences*, ed. H. Lasswell, and D. Lerner. Stanford: Stanford University Press.

Lasswell, Harold D. 1971. *A pre-view of policy sciences*. Houston: Elsevier.

Lindblom, Charles. 1958. The science of muddling through. *Public Administration Review* 19 (2): 78–88.

Lindblom, Charles. 1965. *The intelligence of democracy: decision making through mutual adjustment*. New York: Free Press.

Lindblom, Charles. 1968. *The policy-making process*. Englewood Cliffs: Prentice-Hall.

Lindblom, Charles. 1979. Still muddling, not yet through. *Public Administration Review* 39 (6): 517–526.

Lindblom, C. E., and D. Cohen. 1978. *Usable knowledge: social science and social problem solving*. New Haven: Yale University Press.

Majone, Giandomenico. 1989. *Evidence, argument and persuasion in the policy process*. New Haven: Yale University Press.

Martin, Emily. 2001. *The woman in the body: a cultural analysis of reproduction*. Boston: Beacon Press.

Mayntz, Renate. 1993. Policy Netzwerke und die Logik von Verhandlungssystemen. Policy Analyse. Kritik und Neuorientierung". *Politische Vierteljahresschrift* 34: 39–56.

Newman, Janette. 2012. Beyond the deliberative subject? Problems of theory, method and critique in the turn to emotion and affect. *Critical Policy Studies* 6 (4): 465–479. https://doi.org/10.1080/19460171.2012.730799.

Ney, S. 2009. *Resolving messy problems: Handling conflict in environment, transport, health and aging policy.* London: Earthscan.

Orsini, M., and S.M. Wiebe. 2014. Between hope and fear. Comparing Canada: methods and perspectives on Canadian Politics, 147.

Parsons, Wayne. 2003. *Public policy: an introduction to the theory and practice of policy analysis.* Northampton: Edward Elgard Publishing.

Peters, B. G. 2004. Review of "Reframing public policy: discursive politics and deliberative practices." *Poltiical Science Quarterly* 119 (3): 566–567.

Rein, M. 1976. *Social science and public policy.* New York: Penguin Books.

Schmidt, V. A. 2008. Discursive institutionalism: the explanatory power of ideas and discourse. *Annual Review of Political. Science* 11: 303–326.

Schram, S., and P. T. Neisser, eds. 1997. *Tales of state: narrative in contemporary U.S politics and public policy.* New York: Rowman and Littlefield.

Schubert, K., and N. Bandelow. 2003. *Lehrbuch der Politikfeldanalyse.* Oldenbourg: Oldenburg Verlag.

Scriven, M. 1987. Probative logic. In *Argumentation across the linerw of discipline*, ed. F.H. Van Eemeren et al. Amsterdam: Foris.

Simon, Herbert A. 1945. *Administration behavior.* New York: Free Press.

Stenner, P., and D. Taylor. 2008. Psychosocial welfare: reflections on an emerging field. *Critical Social Policy* 28 (4): 415–437.

Stone, D.A. 1988. *Policy paradox and political reason.* Addison-Wesley Longman.

Sullivan, Helen, and Chris Skelcher. 2002. *Working across boundaries: collaboration in public services.* Palgrave.

Toulmin, S. 1958. *The uses of argument.* Cambridge: Cambridge University Press.

Wittgenstein, L. 1958. *Schriften: Suhrkamp.*

Wittgenstein, *Philosophische Untersuchungen*, Suhrkamp Verlag KG, 2003.

Yanow, D. 1996. *How does a policy mean?: Interpreting policy and organizational actions.* Washington, DC: Georgetown University Press.

Zittoun, P. 2009. Understanding policy change as a discursive problem. *Journal of Comparative Policy Analysis* 11 (1): 65–82.

Zittoun, P. 2013a. Entre définition et propagation des énoncés de solution. *Revue Française De Science Politique* 63 (3): 625–646.

Zittoun, P. 2013b. *La fabrique des politiques publiques.* Paris: Presses de Science Po.

Zittoun, P. 2014. *The political process of policymaking: a pragmatic approach to public policy.* New York: Palgrave-McMillan.

The Transformation of Ideas: The Origin and Evolution of Punctuated Equilibrium Theory

Rebecca Eissler and Bryan D. Jones

In 2001, Orrin Hatch (R-UT) introduced the DREAM Act. In his speech on the floor of the Senate, Hatch outlined the key components of the bill: aid for undocumented children to help with the affordability of higher education and providing a path to permanent residency for undocumented children who graduate from college (Hatch 2001). His speech emphasized the need for hope and opportunity, extending the American dream to many more. The legislation was expected to pass with bipartisan support, with a vote and celebration scheduled for September 12th, at which Tereza Lee, a Brazilian-born Korean American music student,

---

Many thanks to Annelise Russell, who was a co-author on the first edition of this chapter. Her thoughts are present in this revised version.

R. Eissler (✉)
San Francisco State University, San Francisco, USA
e-mail: reissler@sfsu.edu

B. D. Jones
University of Austin, Austin, USA
e-mail: bdjones@austin.utexas.edu

was going to perform as a symbol of the contributions of undocumented minors to American society (Hong 2023; Levere 2020). The attacks on September 11th disrupted the planned vote, and despite several attempts to revive the legislation over the successive decade, it wasn't until President Obama's executive action which created the Deferred Action for Childhood Arrivals (DACA) program that there was any real movement on the issue. In 2012, the immediate response from Republican legislators was anger over what was viewed as presidential overreach (Preston and Cushman 2012), but that anger soon settled into opposition to the policy itself. By January 2018, not only had President Trump announced his intention to end the DACA program (Romo et al. 2017), but Congress's ongoing gridlock and inability to come to an agreement about a path for undocumented minors was seen as one of the significant contributors to the government shut down (Stolberg and Kaplan 2018). How did this dynamic shift so drastically, from one of bipartisan support to extreme contention, and what was the process of policy change? This process of episodic or disjointed change and periods of stability is the foundation of Bryan Jones and Frank Baumgartner's argument for how we should understand policy change, Punctuated Equilibrium Theory.

Punctuated Equilibrium Theory (PET) characterizes the policy process as made up of two dynamics: abrupt policy shifts interspersed with periods of stability or incremental change between the sizable shifts. This model of policy change describes a process that is less predictable than the theories of incrementalism that came before; however, it was seen to be a better explanation for real world dynamics as it also accounted for transformative change (Jones and Baumgartner 2012). Punctuated equilibrium began as a theory by which to study agenda change in the U.S. federal government, but authors soon discovered the framework also applied to the underlying mechanisms of agenda setting (Baumgartner and Jones 2009). PET has evolved significantly over the years, well beyond its origins in *Agendas and Instability in American Politics* to address numerous facets of the policy process across a range of institutions (2009). Scholars studying measures of attention utilized the PET framework to understand shifts in how and when policy is defined, establishing the general punctuation thesis (Jones and Baumgartner 2005). This core component of PET was pushed even further as studies moved beyond attention into understanding the underlying concept of information processing (Workman, Jones, and Jochim 2009). Information makes up the building blocks of the policy process, and it is foundational to higher-order studies of framing and agenda setting. This has led to a deeper consideration of policy dynamics outside the United States, in both democratic and non-democratic settings, allowing us to understand the way in which the governmental systems affect agenda setting, attention, and information processing.

The applicability of PET, and the theorizing that came out of it, across the public policy literature is not only due to its generalizability and wide adoption, but more importantly to scholars' efforts to better refine and understand the foundations of PET, which is the decision-making process. Punctuated equilibrium theory is not a synonym for agenda setting, but rather a theory that applies to numerous facets of the policy process that when taken individually, are only partial explanations for agenda change. By deconstructing traditional agenda setting components—such as attention, framing, and policy feedback—and studying the role of information processing and attention allocation, we get a fuller picture of how policy change occurs across institutions worldwide.

A Prequel to Punctuated Equilibrium Theory

Punctuated Equilibrium Theory began as a response to policy models that emphasized incremental adjustments but gave little to no consideration to periods of high levels of attention that resulted in large policy changes. Baumgartner and Jones saw policy change as oftentimes disjoint, episodic, and unpredictable (2009). Early policy process models in the 1950s and 1960s characterized decision making as incremental and the political order as stable. The status quo bias reigned as preferences were believed to remain largely unchanged and minor adjustments were achieved by shifting norms or rules (Wildavsky 1964) and via "mutual partisan adjustments" (Lindblom 1959) agreed to by the participants. The incremental approach seemed normatively beneficial because it meant that policymakers were operating within the range of alternatives based upon previous actions that had been deemed allowable and incremental adjustments could always be easily reversed. Interest group theorists also emphasized a sense of balance, in which preferences were weighted by the intensity of those involved.

The first generation of rational choice models in political science also emphasized the need to explain equilibrium and scholars acknowledged the constrained conditions under which equilibrium between policies and the preferences of participants in a political system could be maintained (Jones and Baumgartner 2012). Kenneth Arrow (1951) and Duncan Black (1958) assessed the problem of preference cycling, highlighting how complex and unpredictable the political process could be. But the uncertainty resulting from that complexity was eased by analysts' assumptions that the preferences of publics and policymakers were stable and ordered along a simple left-right dimension. The popular median voter theorem predicted convergence to a stable and central position along this single dimension. Changes from this pivot point were assumed to be incremental, or at least mostly predictable. These models seemed comforting to many but were inadequate to describe the mechanisms of policy change. While they got the story mostly right, the part that they missed, the large changes in policy, was far too important to simply ignore.

Newer models of agenda setting began to challenge the preference-based, incremental, and rational choice approaches to policy change. E.E. Schattschneider (1960) had long advocated the role of political parties as mechanisms capable of disrupting the pluralist interest group system by expanding the scope of conflict and including new political actors in the decision-making process. Cobb and Elder (1983) detailed how participants bring in new groups—and, as a result, new policy ideas—into the policymaking arena. John Kingdon (1984), building off Cohen, March, and Olsen (1972), argued that change was a function of attention-based choices and the simultaneous coupling of problems and solutions. These foundational studies, which were already highlighting the underlying mechanisms of spurious attention and information, laid the groundwork for punctuated equilibrium theory.

PUNCTUATED EQUILIBRIUM THEORY ORIGINS: AGENDA SETTING

Baumgartner and Jones laid out their principal argument for PET in *Agendas and Instability in American Politics*, arguing that change in public policy in the United States is not simply gradual and incremental, but rather disjointed and episodic (2009). Periods of stability are interrupted by shocks, which can occur when policy images are reframed, and conflict is expanded. Punctuated equilibrium is at its core a dynamic theory of public policy focusing on the mechanisms and boundedly rational decision makers that lead to policy change. Alternative models of policy change too often point to change coming from electoral turnover. Elections are one of many institutional mechanisms for change, most obviously in so-called mandate elections. For example, Grossback, Peterson, and Stimson (2006) show the long-term policy consequences of the mandate or critical elections in 1964, 1980, and 1994. But Baumgartner and Jones emphasize that elections and ideology only paint a partial picture of policy shifts. They draw on foundational works by E.E. Schattschneider and Herbert Simon to present a theory of how elite actors, driven to maintain benefits and stable political outcomes, may occasionally feel an intense sense of urgency to redirect attention to new issues or new policy dimensions. This collective sense of urgency may stem from a variety of mechanisms, including exogenous events, political mobilization, and contagion. Underlying all these mechanisms is the fundamental mechanism of *disproportionate information processing*, the idea that systems of policymakers tend to over- or under-react to signals that indicate potential problems (Jones 2001; Jones and Baumgartner 2005). Disproportionate information processing stems from the cognitive and emotional architectures of the human mind, namely the principle of bounded or behavioral rationality, which highlights the intended, but imperfect, rationality of decision making.

Herbert Simon (1957, 1983, 1986) introduced the concept of bounded rationality to further detail how individuals and human-design organizations operate. A departure from classical economic rationality, he argued that individual and group decision-making was executed through a combination of serial processing and parallel processing. A single actor can devote conscious attention to just one thing at a time, serial processing, but organizations—such as governments or businesses—are more tractable, capable of handling multiple issues at a time in parallel. To do this, political institutions set up institutional frameworks, such as policy subsystems, to serve as a mechanism for parallel processing, as like individuals, they cannot simultaneously consider all the issues that face them (Jones 1994). The idea of the boundedly rational elite actor is not a new concept, as previous works by Kingdon (1984) and Wildavsky (1964) assume actors are cognitively limited, adaptable, and possess some level of uncertainty, but bounded rationality is a key underpinning of PET.

Boundedly rational individuals are unable to perfectly tally up costs and benefits from a potential decision and to choose the best option, otherwise known as maximizing the scenario's potential returns. Instead, their decision-making procedures are incomplete and driven by cognitive and emotional limitations on their ability to pay attention to all possibilities. This limited processing power and attention shapes the decisions over which issues make their way onto the agenda, and more importantly, the way that agenda change occurs. Political systems, like people, can focus intensely only on a limited number of public policies, which is one major reason that policymaking is invariably assigned to policy subsystems. These principles contribute to a political system that is not based on complete updating and gradual shifts from the status quo, but rather people who rely on heuristics and norms, and processing mechanisms where uncertainty and limited attention lead to larger shifts in the policy agenda.

Baumgartner and Jones posit that individual policies can look chaotic and conflictual or stable and consensual at a single point in time, but that this only paints a partial picture. PET analysis is best applied to longer-run policy development, to incorporate both short- and long-run temporal changes. Appreciating policy complexity requires systematic and compatible measures of policy over time. The U.S. Policy Agendas Project began as a solution to this need by offering comparable policy measures. The Policy Agendas Project collects and categorizes government data from various US institutions to monitor and assess changes in public policy over time. The project's original dataset—congressional hearings—was used to provide empirical tests for theories of the policy process at the agenda-setting stage. The project continues to provide a quantitative foundation for punctuated equilibrium studies and additional datasets offer indicators of institutional attention over time and throughout the policy process. The project also continues to provide a venue for assessing the episodic or incremental nature of policy change across issues.

Some of the early applications of data from the Policy Agendas Project extended PET to include an explanation for changes in national budgeting (Jones, Baumgartner, and True 1996; Jones, Sulkin and Larsen 2003; Jones and Baumgartner 2005). Federal budget actions are characterized by the same boundedly rational patterns as other policymaking decisions. Budgets quantify collective political decisions made in response to incoming information, the preferences of decision makers, and institutional structure (Jones et al. 2009). Decision-makers in a political system—given their limited processing abilities—set up a framework for parallel processing of information via collective attention—whether they are characterized as subsystems, policy monopolies, iron triangles, or issue networks. Policy subsystems enable budgets to change incrementally, but sometimes issues move from subsystem politics to the macro political environment, which can be spurred by national attention in Congress, actions by the President, a change in policy image, or a change in policy learning (Baumgartner and Jones 2009, Sabatier and Weible 2007).

When attention draws additional actors or special interests into the decision-making process, policies and programs can make radical or disjointed departures from previous actions, causing policy to lurch, producing large changes. If members of a given policy subsystem advocate for additional economic stimulus that simultaneously has negative or controversial environmental consequences, the most prominent of those competing values will be reflected in decision-makers' attention and potentially in policy actions, which often show up in budgetary allocations. If attentiveness to these two dimensions were to shift dramatically—due to an exogenous shock or changes in the underlying members of the subsystem—then the budgeting policy may mimic that shock.

PUNCTUATED EQUILIBRIUM EVOLVES: INFORMATION PROCESSING

Punctuated equilibrium theory began as a study of agenda change, but over time scholars began to better understand the micro-foundations behind those changes. One opportunity for policy entrepreneurs to alter the policy agenda or to introduce new uncertainty is through shifting the way we conceptualize or define a problem, which is known as framing. Jones (1994) showed that shifting the framing of an issue was equivalent to changing the weights in a multi-dimensional model of decisions, such that the overall level of attention to an issue is maintained, but the issue is redefined to match the goals and preferences of additional actors. For example, Baumgartner and his colleagues examined capital punishment, finding that despite the War on Terror, G.W. Bush's presidential policies, and religious evangelicals, incidences of capital sentences decreased by more than 60 percent due to a reframing of the issue from morality to a focus on error, inefficiency, cost, and possible wrongful death (Baumgartner et al. 2008). By shifting the frame, and thus shifting attention, they demonstrated how policy change is not necessarily incremental nor due to electoral change. This work highlights how PET's perspective of policy change is evident not only in the more general notion of agenda setting, but in the critical components of attention and framing. Mechanisms of positive feedback and rapid response show how the stars can align, and surprising policy shifts can come about.

Yet, policy shifts can also provoke a response of their own. Just as issue framing can lead to a punctuation in attention, the rise of an issue on to the agenda through redefinition can prompt a backlash, in which a countermobilization arises prompting a subsequent punctuation as competing sides of an issue battle over the policy area (Patashnik 2023). Policy backlashes occur when a change in policy, or even just an attempt to change policy, produces widely noticed resistance (Patashnik 2022). That resistance, whether among voters, grassroots movements, or elites, can prompt a punctuation in attention in the same way that the initial issue redefinition brought the potential change on to the agenda. Policy backlashes form a kind of negative feedback dynamic that doesn't just maintain the status quo but can reverse enacted policy change. This dynamic is critical, as the range of policy areas in which governments are active has grown substantially (Jones, Theriault and Whyman 2019), with those expansions providing opportunities for backlash. Eric Patashnik's work on policy backlash highlights several potential motivations for backlashes, namely policies that produce concentrated costs on particular communities, highly salient costs that affect everyone, policies that affect groups who feel strongly attached to the status quo, and policies that provide benefits to the "undeserving" (Patashnik 2023). All of these are motivations that may produce a particularly strong countermobilization to policy change that produce a response far beyond what theories of incrementalism would have predicted. Just as it is important to understand the way in which issues are defined, it is important to understand the nature of the information that is being supplied or manipulated in the decision-making process. A competent and informed society is a fundamental feature of political decision making and political or policy information enables individuals—both inside and outside of government—to perform various roles in law and policy making (Delli Carpini & Keeter 1996). Information and signals are imperfectly supplied to the electorate and policymakers via media outlets (Boydstun 2013, Baumgartner and Jones 2009, Sabatier and Weible 2007), political parties (Snyder and Ting 2002, Downs 1957), advertising (Lupia and McCubbins 1998, Jamieson 1992, Freedman and Goldstein 1999), and communities (Campbell et al. 1960; Green et al. 2002; Jennings and Niemi 1968).

But while information matters, not all information is equal, accurate, or readily accepted given the variety of values, preferences, and constraints within society. Policy advocates and government officials can distort information to support their positions and there is no guarantee that all aspects of a relevant issue will enter the political debate. Differences in information supply and attentiveness will often lead to inequalities in representation and policy implementation within mass publics, and elite-centered information processing within political institutions is not free from the problems associated with information supply and prioritization. After all, decision-makers face uncertainty and ambiguity in the face of new information, in addition to holding various established policy preferences and values that act as filters on the world around them.

In a modern political climate where uncertainty and ambiguity continue to dominate, there is now, more than ever, a need to understand how the dynamics of information, actors, and institutions contribute to the pressure or friction in political systems. Baumgartner and Jones demonstrated that this incremental change was only part of the picture (2009). Punctuations are the direct result of the increased pressure in the system, but the micro-foundations and critical components of the process that produces such punctuations have remained unclear. The dynamic principles of information, attention, and disproportionate information processing within the system have motivated scholars to try and better understand how these components characterize both policy change and stasis. By understanding how we process information—and the distribution of attention and policy images that result—we can better understand the policy process.

Information processing is the "collecting, assembling, interpreting, and prioritization [of] signals from the environment" (Jones and Baumgartner 2005, p.7). In order to be useful to a decision maker, information must be processed because its exact meaning can be uncertain and subject to multiple interpretations (Jones and Baumgartner 2012). Policy decisions require individuals to assign meanings to the signals they receive, and devise solutions based on those meanings. Political entrepreneurs often use political manipulation and frames as a mechanism for supplying information and signals that maximize the temporal constraints of policy actors (Kingdon 1984).

Policymakers' ability to consume an abundant supply of information from a variety of sources, as well as decisions regarding how to understand the information that one is receiving, are dictated by the cognitive and emotional limitations of the individual, which are critical components of a bounded rationality perspective of choice (Jones et al. 2006; Workman et al. 2009). Despite their ability to adapt to the task environment, individuals and groups may find it very difficult to adequately update and adjust their choices based on new information (Jones 2001). The short-term memory, which is involved in a great deal of decision-making, is only able to include a small number of considerations at any given time (Baumgartner & Jones 2015, Kahneman 2011). These cognitive limitations contribute to individual cognitive friction, where the process of attending to new information and assimilating it into the cognitive architecture leads to delays followed by over corrections (Jones, Sulkin, and Larsen 2003). These characteristics of cognition are critical to understanding the dynamics of information processing and the effect that they have on policy, especially at the systems level.

Just as it is critical to understand the cognitive processes within individuals, it is important to understand the information environment in which they exist. Information in the political system is characterized by two conditions: the information supply and information processing (Workman, Jones, & Jochim 2009). Theories of information supply vary across disciplines. Some political scientists envision the political environment as one where information is costly and thus scarce (e.g., Krehbiel 1992), while others see the political environment being characterized by information oversupply (Jones 2001, Workman, Jones, & Jochim 2009). The information processing theory is based on the view that in an open, democratic system information is oversupplied as actors vie for the attention of decision makers.

Yet, because of those cognitive limits, attention must be prioritized, which leads actors to pay attention to some issues and not others. And those priorities may change. Those issues that are not prioritized at time T_1 have the potential to be the center of later policy punctuation at time $T+n$ when they finally receive attention, due to policy makers' overcorrecting for past neglect. Political institutions can assist with prioritization because they allow for individuals, who are by nature serial processors, to engage in parallel processing (Jones 1994, Simon 1983). Individual attention is characterized by serial processing as individuals can only contend with one issue at a time. Consequently, many other issues, both pressing and not, get ignored. Parallel processing is the ability of organizations, which through division of labor are able to deal with many diverse issues simultaneously (Workman, Jones, & Jochim 2009). Parallel processing enables institutions to cope with the oversupply of information, lowering the costs associated with processing information for each individual by delegating search and the assimilation of information to individual units, who then direct attention to relevant attributes. Parallel processing can still fail to address the oversupply of information when those smaller units prioritize some aspect of an issue over another, magnifying the error in attention across the whole political system. Whether occurring at the individual or institutional level, the need to prioritize can result in imperfect outcomes.

This imperfect prioritization leads to friction within the political system, as the choice to deal with some issues rather than others results in accumulated errors within the system. When information is ignored, whether because of information oversupply or systemic bias toward particular interpretations over others, it can accumulate to the point where it demands policymakers' attention, leading to a large amount of attention to the issue in order to correct for the earlier inattention and ensuing problems (Jones and Baumgartner 2005). The limited ability of policymakers to efficiently respond to the oversupply of policy information—and the various images, frames, and definitions associated within those domains—suggests the theory of punctuated equilibrium that dominates the policy process is actually a theory of disproportionate information processing.

PUNCTUATED EQUILIBRIUM THEORY IN NON-DEMOCRACIES: LESSONS IN INSTITUTIONAL DESIGN

Initial studies of PET focused primarily on American federal institutions, but over time, scholars tested its generalizability by considering the dynamics of multiple levels of government and political systems. Baumgartner and Jones initially thought that the punctuated dynamics they observed were a product of federalism and the pluralist system in the United States, which provides many opportunities for disruption in the political system (Jones and Baumgartner 2012; Eissler and Russell 2016). However, many studies suggest that policy punctuations and limited attention are global phenomenon across political systems, a product of human nature that is shaped by the type of regime and the particular institutional design in a government, rather than something that exists in some governments and not in others (Baumgartner et al. 2017; Jones et al 2019).

Traditionally, international theories of policy change within institutions focused on elections as a mechanism for substantial policy change (Jones and Baumgartner 2012), but punctuated equilibrium theory and much of the work growing out of the Comparative Agenda Projects has proved that to be incomplete. While not all of the work coming out of the Comparative Agendas Project is based on PET or the general punctuation hypothesis (Baumgartner et al 2019), this collective effort of political scientists from 20 countries (plus the US States of Florida and Pennsylvania, as well as the European Union) and counting demonstrates the universality of the theories of the policy process across disparate political systems (Baumgartner et al. 2009).

Yet, perhaps one of the greatest contributions to the scholarship of punctuated equilibrium theory in the past decade or so has been the push to explore punctuated equilibrium theory and information processing outside of the context of Western democracies. It is this work, which has examined the dynamics of punctuations in contexts such as China, Turkey, Brazil, and Hong Kong, among others, that has demonstrated the universality of these policy process dynamics. The early work of the Comparative Agendas Project demonstrated the similarities across western democracies, for example, demonstrating that changes in public budgets across many western countries follow a similar non-Gaussian distribution (Jones et al. 2009). This work was important as they confirmed the generalizability of many of the findings regarding punctuated equilibrium and the theories of information processing. Many of these works have advanced our understanding of agenda setting, framing, attention, and information processing, such as John and Bevan's work to better understand the types of policy punctuations (2012). In their work, they advance the idea of punctuations in attention by creating a typology of punctuations, differentiating between large, highly salient punctuations and small, low salience punctuations. This is but one example of the contributions that have been made in the punctuated equilibrium theory because of the work across levels of government and disparate political systems.

With the expansion of research into non-democracies and countries that have switched between democracies and autocracies, we have gained a new appreciation for the impact of institutional design on two key components of the information processing perspective: information acquisition and institutional friction. The precise structure and design of governing institutions directly shapes the policy dynamics at play. Work by van den Dool and Li (2022), which conducts a systematic review of Chinese-language PET journal articles, highlights aspects of the Chinese political system that they believe contribute to the punctuated nature of attention in China, specifically identifying the effect of centralized institutions, the single party system, and strict hierarchy of information transmission. These features of the institutional design contribute to the dynamics of policy attention, which has been shown by Chan and Zhao (2016) to be more punctuated than many democratic systems. Sebok and Berki (2018) also find similar attention dynamics in their study of Hungary from 1868 to 2013, which covers periods in which Hungary was under both authoritarian and democratic regimes, dividing the time period into "free," "partially free," and "not free" regimes. They find that periods in which the political system was understood to be "free" saw fewer punctuations than when the government was "not free" or "partially free." This article reinforces the importance of understanding the influence that regime type has on the structure of institutions and consequently on the processing of information and institutional friction.

The work on the role of information in decision making in authoritarian regimes highlights some curious dynamics worthy of further exploration. Chan and Zhao highlight the way that minority groups in democracies can obstruct political change, and in doing so, provide important information to governments and decision makers about policy problems and public preferences. They theorize that there are even greater levels of policy punctuations in China than in democratic systems because authoritarianism shuts off these sources of information, resulting in a decision-making system which lacks independent sources of information (2016). Jones and Liu also explore the role of information in the Chinese political system, focusing on the way the New China News Agency (Xinhua) does, or does not, provide information about policy (2018). They highlight a feature of the Chinese information environment, in which Xinhua, by virtue of its monopoly over the news granted by the government, does not necessarily play the same role that the media plays in many democratic countries, which is to provide the government with information about policy problems. Because the New Chinese News Agency does not provide the full range of information, focusing instead on news that is supportive of the governing regime, they play a role in undermining the ability for the public to gain access to information, particularly related to the scope of problems. For Jones and Liu, this suggests an ambivalence in the Chinese political system around creating the capacity to process information about policy problems (2018). Additionally, work on policy disasters highlights the role that information plays in the rate of disasters across different political systems. Fagan, in a comparative study across 70 countries, both democratic and authoritarian, finds that democratic systems with stronger flows of information from diverse sources experience fewer policy disasters (2021).

This expansion outside western democracies has also expanded our understanding of friction in the policy process. Friction can be understood as the structures that introduce costs to decision-making, which makes them less efficient, but potentially more democratically responsive (Baumgartner et al. 2009). Often this friction comes from the design of institutions and decision-making processes which make action costly by forcing actors to work together to make policy happen. One important aspect of the relationship between punctuated equilibrium theory and friction is that, generally, lower institutional friction corresponds to lower levels of punctuations (Jones, Larsen-Price, and Wilkerson 2009). This led scholars of punctuated equilibrium in authoritarian regimes to test the theory that the centralized nature of decision making might allow for an environment with lower levels of institutional friction, and consequently fewer punctuations (Baumgartner et al. 2017). However, Chan and Fan find that sometimes the government will create friction in the system to try to ensure control by the central government (2020). In the Chinese bureaucracy, the central government introduces friction by sending bureaucrats to work outside their home provinces and to regularly move them to prevent bureaucratic cooperation that might operate independently from the central party's control (Chan and Fan 2020). This finding illustrates the complexity of policy dynamics across political systems and highlights the importance of studying policy making and punctuated equilibrium theory beyond western democracies.

CONCLUSION

In a modern political climate characterized by uncertainty, institutional constraints, and abundant information, how do we understand policy change as part of a dynamic policy process? For years, scholars described a policy process characterized by incremental shifts interrupted by elections, and by rational actors seeking to maximize preferences and seek re-election. A look at the data on punctuations in budgetary and other areas of policymaking show definitively that this is far too narrow an approach. Most punctuations in policy occur in the inter-election period and are not correlated with changes wrought by elections. Baumgartner and Jones developed a theory to explain a more complex policy process by reassessing information processing, emphasizing the principles of bounded rationality and the limited attention of actors and institutions. Punctuated Equilibrium Theory describes a less predictable policy process; one which is characterized by long periods of stability with incremental changes, regardless of election changes, interrupted by episodic changes that may be externally or internally initiated. The key is not where the stimulus for the change come from; the key lies in the disproportionate information processing that causes policymakers to ignore important signals of problems for long periods of time before taking action. In at least some cases, this action morphs into a strong overreaction, as was the case for crime policy in the United States (Jones, Thomas, and Wolfe 2014) or in policy disasters more broadly (Fagan 2021). PET emerged out of a need to understand the agenda-setting stage of the political process, in which new alternatives are strategically considered—and ignored—within a disjointed policy process. But it has evolved beyond its agenda setting origins to explain underlying components of change throughout the policy process.

These underlying mechanisms of policy change, such as framing and information processing, are more than just independent variables in models of agenda setting. Baumgartner and Jones, along with a number of scholars across the policy field, have used PET as a way to gain leverage to understand how information is supplied and how it is processed. The drastic changes to immigration policy in the twenty-first century were not just due to changes in preferences or electoral cycling; go-to explanations from pre-PET policy frameworks. Even the punctuated equilibrium theory framework has grown and evolved to better explain the changes we see in immigration, as the change in the policy area is a product of more complexity than mere shifts in salience or policy images. Instead, it is critical to understand how, undergirding the PET framework, is an understanding of information processing, specifically focusing on how sources of information shift and how political entrepreneurs manipulate policy narratives. In the case of immigration, those dynamics produced a policy backlash triggering a complete re-prioritization of the information available, which led to an abrupt shift in attention and the ensuing backlash and change in perspective about the issue, particularly among Republican members of Congress. These changes then become entrenched, in large part because institutional friction made changing positions for those that were part of the policy backlash, or are politically aligned with those actors, extremely costly. These individual components of policy change contribute to an agenda building process that looks less like the theories of incremental shifts from the past and more like the disproportionate and dynamic information processing system that punctuated equilibrium theory has evaluated and advanced.

REFERENCES

Arrow, Kenneth. 1951. *Social Choice and Individual Values*. New York: John Wiley and Sons.

Baumgartner, Frank R., and Bryan D. Jones. 2009a. *Agendas and Instability in American Politics*. 2nd ed. Chicago: University of Chicago Press.

Baumgartner, Frank R., Christian Breunig, Christoffer Green-Pedersen, Bryan D. Jones, Peter B. Mortensen, Michiel Nuytemans, and Stefaan Walgrave. 2009. Punctuated Equilibrium in Comparative Perspective. *American Journal of Political Science* 53 (3): 603–620.

Baumgartner, Frank R., Marcello Carammia, Derek A. Epp, Ben Noble, Beatriz Rey, and Tevfik Murat Yildirim. 2017. Budgetary Change in Authoritarian and Democratic Regimes. *Journal of European Public Policy* 24 (6): 792–808.

Baumgartner, Frank R., Suzanna L. De Boef, and Amber E. Boydstun. 2008. *The Decline of the Death Penalty and the Discovery of Innocence*. New York: Cambridge University Press.

Baumgartner, Frank R., and Bryan D. Jones. 2009b. *Agendas and Instability in American Politics*. 2nd ed. Chicago: University of Chicago Press.

Black, Duncan. 1958. *The Theory of Committees and Elections*. Cambridge: Cambridge University Press.

Campbell, Angus, Philip E. Converse, Warren E. Miller, and Donald E. Stokes. 1960. *The American Voter*. New York: John Wiley & Sons.

Cobb, Roger, and Charles D. Elder. 1972 (1983). Participation in American Politics. Baltimore: Johns Hopkins University Press.

Cohen, Michael, James March, and Johan Olsen. 1972. A Garbage Can Model of Organizational Choice. *Administrative Science Quarterly* 17:1–25.

Carpini, Delli, X. Michael, and Scott Keeter. 1996. *What Americans Know about Politics and Why It Matters*. New Haven, CT: Yale University Press.

Downs, Anthony. 1957. A Theory of Political Action in a Democracy. *Journal of Political Economy* 65:135–160.

Eissler, Rebecca, and Annelise Russell. 2016. The Policy Agendas Project. In *American Governance*, ed. S. Schechter, 50–51. New York: Macmillan.

Fagan, Edward J. 2023. Political institutions, punctuated equilibrium theory, and policy disasters. *Policy Studies Journal* 51, no. 2: 243–263.

Freedman, P., and K. Goldstein. 1999. Measuring media exposure and the effects of negative campaign ads. *American Journal of Political Science* 43 (4): 1189–1208.

Hong, Jane. 2023. The Surprisingly Bipartisan History of Pathway to Citizenship Policies. PRRI. February 3. https://www.prri.org/spotlight/the-surprisingly-bipartisan-history-of-pathway-to-citizenship-policies/.

Jamieson, Kathleen. 1992. The Paradox of Political Ads: Reform Depends on Voter Savvy.

Jennings, M. Kent, and Richard G. Niemi. 1968. The Transmission of Political Values from Parent to Child. *American Political Science Review* 62:169–184.

John, Peter, and Shaun Bevan. 2012. What Are Policy Punctuations? Large Changes in the Legislative Agenda of the UK Government, 1911–2008. *Policy Studies Journal* 40 (1): 89–107.

Jones, Bryan, and Xinsheng Liu. 2018. Designing Political Institutions to Foster Problem Solving. *Peking University Political Science Review* 2:16–26.

Jones, Bryan D., and Frank R. Baumgartner. 2005. *The Politics of Attention.* Chicago: University of Chicago Press.

Jones, Bryan D., and Frank R. Baumgartner. 2012. From There to Here: Punctuated Equilibrium to the General Punctuation Thesis to a Theory of Government Information Processing. *The Policy Studies Journal* 40:1–18.

Jones, Bryan D., Derek A. Epp, and Frank R. Baumgartner. 2019a. Democracy, Authoritarianism, and Policy Punctuations. *International Review of Public Policy* 1 (1): 7–26.

Jones, Bryan D., Frank R. Baumgartner, and James L. True. 1996. *The Shape of Change: Punctuations and Stability in US Budgeting, 1947–96.* Chicago, IL: Paper presented at the Midwest Political Science Association.

Jones, Bryan D., Frank R. Baumgartner, Christian Breunig, Christopher Wlezien, Stuart Soroka, Martial Foucault, Abel Francois, Christoffer Green-Pedersen, Chris Koski, Peter John, Peter Mortensen, Frederic Varone, and Steffan Walgrave. 2009a. A General Empirical Law of Public Budgets: A Comparative Analysis. *American Journal of Political Science* 53:855–873.

Jones, Bryan D., Graeme Boushey, and Samuel Workman. 2006. Behavioral Rationality and the Policy Processes: Towards a New Model of Organizational Information Processing. In *Handbook of Public Policy*, ed. B. G. Peters and J. Pierre. Thousand Oakes, UK: Sage Publications.

Jones, Bryan D., Heather Larsen-Price, and John Wilkerson. 2009b. Representation and American governing institutions. *The Journal of Politics* 71 (1): 277–290.

Jones, Bryan D., Herschel F. Thomas III, and Michelle Wolfe. 2014. Policy Bubbles. *Policy Studies Journal* 42 (1): 146–171.

Jones, Bryan D., Sean M. Theriault, and Michelle Whyman. 2019b. *The great broadening: How the vast expansion of the policymaking agenda transformed American politics*. University of Chicago Press.

Jones, Bryan D., Tracy Sulkin, and Heather Larsen. 2003. Policy Punctuations in American Political Institutions. *American Political Science Review* 97:151–170.

Jones, Bryan. 1994. *Reconceiving Decision-Making in Democratic Politics: Attention, Choice and Public Policy*. Chicago: University of Chicago Press.

Jones, Bryan. 2001. *Politics and the Architecture of Choice*. Chicago: University of Chicago Press.

Kahneman, Daniel. 2011. *Thinking Fast and Slow*. New York: Farrar, Straus, and Giroux.

Karch, Andrew. 2009. Venue Shopping, Policy Feedback, and American Preschool Education. *Journal of Policy History* 21 (1): 38–60.

Kingdon, John. 1984. *Agendas, Alternatives, and Public Policies*. New York: Longman Classics.

Krehbiel, Keith. 1992. *Information and Legislative Organization*. Ann Arbor, MI: The University of Michigan Press.

Levere, Jane L. 2020. From Piano to Dreamer: The Inspiring Story of Tereza Lee: WQXR Editorial. *WQXR*. New York Public Radio. May 12. https://www.wqxr.org/story/piano-dreamer-tereza-lee/.

Lindblom, Charles. 1959. The Science of Muddling Through. *Public Administration Review* 19:79–88.

Lupia, Arthur and Mathew D. McCubbins.1998. *The Democratic Dilemma: Can Citizens Learn What They Need to Know?* Cambridge, UK: Cambridge University Press.

Patashnik, Eric M. 2023. *Countermobilization: Policy Feedback and Backlash in a Polarized Age*. Chigago, IL: University of Chicago Press.

Preston, Julia, and John H. Cushman. 2012. Obama to Permit Young Migrants to Remain in U.S. *The New York Times*. The New York Times. June 15. https://www.nytimes.com/2012/06/16/us/us-to-stop-deporting-some-illegal-immigrants.html.

Romo, Vanessa, Martina Stewart, and Brian Naylor. 2017. Trump Ends DACA, Calls on Congress to Act. *NPR*. NPR. September 5. https://www.npr.org/2017/09/05/546423550/trump-signals-end-to-daca-calls-on-congress-to-act.

Sabatier, Paul and Weible. 2007. The Advocacy Coalition Framework: Innovations and Clarifications. *Theories of the Policy Process, Second Edition*. Boulder, CO: Westview Press.

Schattschneider, Elmer E. 1960. *The Semisovereign People.* New York: Holt, Reinhart, and Winston.

Senator Hatch (UT). 2001. Introduction of the DREAM Act. Congressional Record 147:110 (August 1, 2001) p. S8581. Available from: ProQuest® Congressional; Accessed: 6/30/24.

Simon, Herbert A. 1957. *Models of Man, Social and Rational: Mathematical Essays on Rational Human Behavior in a Social Setting.* New York: John Wiley and Sons.

Simon, Herbert A. 1983. *Reason in Human Affairs.* Stanford, CA: Stanford University Press.

Simon, Herbert A., and Associates. 1986. Decision-Making and Problem-Solving. *Research Briefings: Report of the Research Briefing Panel on Decision-Making and Problem-Solving.* Washington DC: National Science Academy Press.

Snyder, James M., and Michael M. Ting. 2002. An Informational Rationale for Political Parties. *American Journal of Political Science* 46 (1): 90–110.

Stolberg, Sheryl Gay, and Thomas Kaplan. 2018. Government Shutdown Ends after 3 Days of Recriminations. *The New York Times.* The New York Times. January 23. https://www.nytimes.com/2018/01/22/us/politics/congress-votes-to-end-government-shutdown.html.

Wildavsky, Aaron. 1964. *The Politics of the Budgetary Process.* Boston: Little, Brown.

Workman, Samuel G., Bryan D. Jones, and Ashely Jochim. 2009. Information Processing and Policy Dynamics. 2009. *Policy Studies Journal* 37:75–92.

Behavioral Approaches: How Nudges Lead to More Intelligent Policy Design

Peter John

A quiet revolution has taken place in public agencies across the world. Experts and policy-makers have discovered how to use insights from the study of human behavior to design better policies. Often called nudge, behavioral public policy is no fad and has embedded itself into the working practices of public organizations worldwide. As Naru (2024) finds in his recent international survey, the number of behavioral public policy bodies increased from 201 to 631 between 2018 and 2024, a trend observed for all continents.

While the quest to understand behavior has always been an important aspect of the social sciences, with behavioral research regularly informing public decision-making, work in economics and psychology occurring since the 1970s has given much more powerful impetus behind the use of behavioral science. In due course, such work appealed to those wanting to solve public problems and improve the quality of public services. The

I thank Liz Richardson for her comments on an earlier draft of this chapter.

P. John (✉)
King's College London, London WC2B 4PH, England
e-mail: peter.john@kcl.ac.uk

B. G. Peters and P. Zittoun (eds.), *Contemporary Approaches to Public Policy*, International Series on Public Policy,
https://doi.org/10.1007/978-3-032-06026-6_7

energy that has come from recent strides in knowledge has helped create an integrated and cross-disciplinary research agenda. Academics, students, and media professionals as well as participants in the public policy process want to know more about what drives human behavior and how to change it for the common good. The result is a step-shift in the use of behavioral ideas to redesign policies. These innovations started from some relatively modest applications, such as the redesign of tax reminders; now behavioral science is applied to core topics in policy implementation, such as welfare and pensions. Behavioral public policy is a common currency of today's decision-makers with the word nudge being used to denote this interest.

Behavioral science appears at first sight at least to offer an uncontroversial and low-cost way of designing more efficient policies. It often appeals to political parties across the ideological divide; it can operate in contrasting institutional contexts and at different levels of governance. There is usually little dispute among policy-makers about whether such a technique should apply or not; rather, the debate is about which behavioral cue works, where it operates best, and what is the size of the expected effect. This lack of controversy is one reason for the success of behavioral public policy; another is the ease with which it can be understood. Behavioral science is a field where the insights from the academy can readily find their way into the policy agenda in a way that is immediate and comprehensible to policy-makers, overcoming the barriers to knowledge transfer that has dogged the utilization of policy-relevant scientific knowledge hitherto (John 2013a, 2018). The behavioral agenda has been supported by randomized controlled trials (RCTs) that evaluate different behavioral cues. An experiment is a particularly appropriate way to test for the efficacy of interventions in this field as it offers proof of the concept as well providing precise estimates of savings delivered and benefits achieved.

Regarded in this way, the development of the behavioral policy agenda is a useful innovation for today's policy-makers, mainly targeted toward the delivery of public services and concerned with ensuring greater efficiency in the use of the tools of government. It fits largely within existing understandings about the use of science to improve policies, which may be regarded as an aspect of paternalism as practiced in most mature democracies. Light-touch policies to encourage better behavior can be introduced with relatively little debate and controversy because usually their objectives are not thought to be controversial, and the means of implementation do not appear to affect citizen rights and freedoms.

Behavioral science need not only apply to already implemented policies simply to correct for poor delivery systems and to compensate for past failures to engage citizens. Behavioral approaches have much to offer the decision-making process itself: they can help guide more informed policies and make a better connection between citizens and governments. A more behavioral take on decision-making itself can ensure that policies are designed in more citizen-centered ways. Above all, behavioral policy is about responding to concerns on the public's agenda. The relevance of the science of human behavior is because the same human actors who are the target of human interventions can also be subject to the same nudge-based approach. Decision-makers, the politicians and the bureaucrats, respond to cues and behavioral incentives in the same way as citizens and are similarly subject to defaults and prompts. Like citizens they are limited in how they use information, which is just how the classic writers in public policy described them (e.g., Simon 1947; Lindblom and Braybrooke 1963). Subject and object in the behavioral agenda switch around: the citizen or interested public, usually the recipient of cues, is now the deliverer of them; the politicians and civil servant become the new recipients. In this way, the behavioral agenda, so often accused of being top-down and paternalist, can become a route to holding decision-makers accountable and improving decisions at the top as citizens and groups can use behavioral cues to encourage policy-makers to act in more sensible and publicly conscious ways. Even though the use of rational evidence is not abandoned in this account, the conveying of that evidence is much better achieved when the actors themselves are not regarded as rationally weighing alternatives as assumed in the traditional economic decision-making model. In this way, citizens can convey preferences that fit the grain of decision-making rather than buffet up against standard operating procedures that so often exclude them. How this works in practice can only be sketched out here, but it logically follows from the ideas on behavior change that governments have rolled out so effectively in recent years. What starts as minor tweaks to policy implementation can end up transforming the decision-making process as a whole and in ways that improve policies and their outcomes, perhaps in radical ways.

In this chapter, the elements to this argument are traced. The text below starts by recounting the beginnings of behavioral sciences as currently conceived and then setting out the expansion of interest that has ensued. The next step is to report on how such ideas have had a large impact on governments at all levels across the world, but also to note how decision-making itself has been influenced by more behaviorally informed ideas. The subsequent section discusses the paradox that the very decision-makers themselves are subject to the same biases as the objects of behavioral economics, which might imply limitations in the choices of such interventions. Here this chapter re-engages with the classics of decision-making theory in public policy. To set out the later part of the argument, the chapter notes how behavioral sciences need not depend on a top-down approach but can incorporate citizen voice. The following section goes one step further and reviews how citizens and other groups can use nudges to alter the behavior of policy-makers in socially beneficial ways. The final and concluding part discusses how behaviorally informed measures could be integrated within the policy-making process in ways that advance the effective use of evidence and nudge decision-makers to formulate better policies.

BEHAVIORAL ECONOMICS AND BEHAVIORAL SCIENCE

The study of behavior has been central to social science since its foundation, and academics have always sought to understand it. In political science, for example, models to understand behavior, such as voter decisions, are core to the discipline and appear in its early texts on the subject (e.g., Campbell et al. 1960) (see also Annex). A more concerted approach to studying behavior is a more recent phenomenon. Significantly, it emerged from the discipline of economics. Economics has long been a privileged discipline in social science and policy-makers have given economists precedence. As traditionally conceived, economic behavior has been widely assumed to be the consequence of cost–benefit assessments by individuals or firms so that an increase in the cost of an activity can be associated with a proportionate reduction in the incentive for carrying on with it and the other way round with respect to benefits. In public policy, a regulation that increases the costs of rule violation should lead to the reduction of the harmful activity (Becker 1968). The intelligent policy-maker needs to know how citizens or other actors trade costs and benefits in deciding how to act so they can adjust the tools of government—law/regulation and finance in particular—to achieve a desired policy outcome, for example, by increasing penalties to deter crime. Such ideas have been powerful as they provide micro-foundations that explain private action and offer a framework to assess governmental behavior designed to achieve collective purposes.

The economic or rational model has also influenced how governments approach policy-making, which can be seen as the choice between alternatives whose costs and benefits need to be evaluated. The model features prominently in introductions to public policy, such as in Allison's Model I in his *Essence of Decision* (1960). Despite generations of critics, not least students of public policy, pointing out the limitations the rational actor model, it has proved to be highly resilient, structuring the way in which governments seek advice. It has influenced the institutional framework of knowledge-searching within the bureaucracy and in other public institutions, whether it is options analysis by bureaucrats, the review of alternatives by commissions of inquiry, or the interrogation of experts by legislative committees. As Leach writes, the rational model satisfies a profound need among policy-makers to have the options set in front of them with their costs and benefits even if policy-makers want also to be free of following the conclusions that flow from such advice (Leach 1982). The review of alternatives based on rational responses to signals dominates most approaches in evaluation whether it be cost–benefit analysis or budget planning. It is possible to see how public and private actions are joined together in the same system with citizens and organizations appraising signals from different sources and decision-makers using rational models to choose the best action to influence how individuals and organizations respond to those signals.

The utility-maximizing rationally choosing individual is often believed to be something of an oversimplification based on a narrow conception of the drivers of human behavior. The approach is often believed to be worth the effort because it boils down human motivations to their essentials and then creates a simple framework that presents clear choices for policy-makers. It is a heuristic that tells them what to do in particular situations. It is also possible to complicate the framework by introducing cognitive limitations, such as search costs, to show how human actors might not be efficient at responding to signals. That the framework can survive an intense onslaught of criticism is tribute to its attraction and salience rather than obstinacy and stubbornness on the part of intellectuals and policy-makers. The economic or rational model remains core to understanding decision-making and can help improve policy, even taking account of behavioral science. One of the common mistakes commentators often make is to assume that the edifice of rationally linked actions understood in a framework of choice and efficiency crumbles because of innovations in behavioral economics. Many tweaks can be introduced.

The key innovation was the work of Kahneman and colleagues who started their investigations in the 1960s and became highly influential in the following years (Kahneman 1973; Kahneman and Tversky 1979; Kahneman et al. 1982). Both Kahneman and Tversky were psychologists who used insights from theories of judgment to understand how biases and cognitions affect the way in which human beings make choices. They carried out a series of striking experiments, which can be read more informally in Kahneman's *Thinking, Fast and Slow* (2011). These scholars showed the limitations individuals have in carrying out even very simple calculations of costs and benefits, even by those with very high levels of training in statistics. In social psychology, such ideas are not original, but they had been rarely applied outside the laboratory, especially for economic choices. In this way, decision-making can be seen as the result of biases—such as to avoid loss as in prospect theory, or where people prefer to remain with the default option or seek to confirm their point of view (confirmation bias) or express regret that may lead to preference reversal (Loomes and Sugden 1982). These biases become important when people must think or act without a large amount of reflection—that is, thinking fast—because of the necessity of speed and the attraction of conforming to habit. From this well of theory that Kahneman and others had outlined, other economists started to test the implications of such behavioral influences in a variety of substantive fields, such as over pension choice (Benartzi and Thaler 2004) or labor supply (Camerer et al. 1997). As a result, there are many studies showing applications of behavioral economics to practical problems in public policy where solutions can be offered to improve government interventions in a way that recognizes human biases and works with them to help both the individual and society at large (Benartzi et al. 2017, for a review see John 2018 and Banerjee and John 2025). Such is the number of studies that meta-reviews have been carried out that show the effect of nudges across a range of fields (Beshears and Kosowsky 2020, DellaVigna and Linos, 2022, Mertens et al. 2022), though with one review questioning these positive results when correcting for publication bias (Maier et al., 2022).

It is important to be precise about what was new about this kind of work as criticisms of standard economic/rational actor models have been staple fare throughout the twentieth and twenty-first centuries. After all, the theorist that public policy scholars most often cite with reference to decision-making, Herbert Simon, achieved fame by saying that heuristics inform decisions, which he developed in in the 1940s and 1950s (e.g., Simon 1957) and in which he was responding to formal models of decision-making just like modern behavioral economists do. It is possible to reach back to the start of economics for psychological insights, with one textbook stating that Adam Smith was the founder of behavioral economics (Cartwright 2011:5, see also, Oliver 2013b:6). What distinguishes the work of Kahneman and others is the greater integration of core ideas from psychology, empirical testing in the laboratory, and the use of the language and methods of economics, such as the formalization of theories and their testing in econometric models. These features of their work, particularly the last listed, have ensured their publication in the top journals in the field, such as *The American Economic Review* and *The Economic Journal*. Rather than operating on the fringes of economics, behavioral economics is in the mainstream because the approach does not attack the practice of economics in the centrality of formal theory and the presentation of econometric results (e.g., the countless robustness tests contained in appendices to papers). Indeed, applications of behavioral economics, such as to finance markets, are highly mathematical (e.g., Park and Sabourian 2011). Nor does behavioral economics challenge the implications of economic models for the nature of the state, the quest for efficiency, and the type of regulation of the market, at least not in a direct way. The basic relationships found in economic textbooks remain in place: behavioral economics merely offers a number of tweaks and additional considerations to deploy rather than a rethinking of the relationship between citizens, organizations, and the state. Moreover, Sugden (2004, 2018) uses the assumption of uncertain preferences to underpin the limited role of the state and the creation of efficient markets. The generation of efficiency by private individuals and organizations is not limited by their lack of clear preferences. The market economy is not uniquely micro-founded by full economic rationality. In Sugden's view, behavioral economics does not imply paternalism: it operates in a contractarian framework of mutual consent and publicity (Sugden 2013, 2018). Economists can sleep safe in their beds with such comforting conclusions: their world is not torn asunder by behavioral economics.

A more behavioral approach to understanding economic problems also fits neatly with dominant approaches to formulating public policy in western democracies whereby consensual decisions are formulated by technocrats and experts and approved by elected politicians. The norm of informed and intelligent decision-making is the goal of many leaders, such as politicians and civil servants. Even though political parties may wish to follow ideological objectives, few party leaders would argue the policy should not be informed by expert understanding about how citizens are going to react to government measures. The reason for having experts in government and well-run bureaucracies backed up by advice from peak bodies, such as professional associations and centers of research, is to make judgments about how to implement public policy in the best interests of the public and society at large. In fact, the insights of behavioral economics, when removed of their formal models and tests, can often be regarded as based on common sense and good practice, probably much more so than the simple version of economic model that has been so dominant for so long. It is this appeal of behavioral economics to the mainstream that is the source of its popularity and ensures its survival.

Key is *Nudge: Improving decisions about health, wealth and happiness* by Thaler and Sunstein (2008), which popularized this work using the eponymous term. This well-written and accessible volume brought to life examples of cognitive limitations from behavioral economics. It stated clearly that public policy-makers should not assume a huge amount of information-processing capacity on the part of individuals; rather, they should work with their biases and anchor points to create beneficial public policies. Rather than assuming that the provision of a large amount of information will lead to rational choices, more limited and clearly presented information, which ensures a default to the choice that is in favor of society, is much better. It does not matter that individuals do not think largely about these choices, because publicly interested bureaucrats, experts, and politicians are doing their thinking for them in their role as choice architects. An element of freedom is preserved because the individual could refuse the choice offered or even reject it out of prejudice. Few could argue against low-cost and sensible measures presented with colorful examples—such as painting a fly on men's urinals to help limit spillage when peeing, defaults to increase savings for retirement, and energy-saving devices. The book was regularly discussed in articles in respected newspapers and magazines. It could be bought from bookstands at airports; and its authors were often to be found on radio and television recounting homespun anecdotes. Never did economics appear so unthreatening.

Behavioral approaches had already caught the attention of policymakers long before the nudge book (e.g., Dawnay and Shah 2005) as they realized that they could use these insights to design policies. Behavioral economics has not been just the preserve of governments wanting a hands-off approach to regulation. It was the UK Labour government that produced the influential MINDSPACE (Dolan et al. 2010) decision-making tool that summarized the traits policy-makers could appeal to when redesigning policies. But it was the Conservative-led coalition government that set up the Behavioral Insights Team (BIT) directed by David Halpern, and who used behavioral insights more prominently. The team used RCTs to test out the various nudges (Haynes et al. 2012), which were codesigned by agencies and other actors in the public sector. An example was an initiative to test whether mobile text messaging would encourage those who owed a court fine to pay before further proceedings were taken against them, including visits by debt collection agencies or bailiffs. BIT and Her Majesty's Courts and Tribunals Service were able to find out that these mobile numbers were not yet used by the agency and then carried out two RCTs to test different kinds of messages that varied the personalization and detail on the message to show strong results (Haynes et al. 2013). Much of the early work of the team was about improving revenue collection, taking advantage of the large volumes of transactions and the ability of public agencies to vary the messages in a RCT and then choosing the most efficacious message in the subsequent rollouts.

BIT partnered with other parts of the government machine, such as Her Majesty's Revenues and Customs (HMRC), to produce a raft of powerful evidence (see Cabinet Office 2012). These trials allowed BIT to calculate nontrivial increases to government revenue and thus helped them show proof of the concepts they were applying. Alongside these trials, BIT sought to develop more behavioral approaches to public policy in fields such as energy, in terms of redesigning the regulated part of electricity bills; charitable giving, to encourage large institution's employees such as in banks to give to charity; health, to address key problems such as patients not turning up for general practitioners' appointments; and welfare, to motivate the unemployed to seek work and to improve the communication between employment centers and job seekers. In time, BIT spun out of government as a co-owned entity, hosted by the lottery funding body, Nesta.

This expansion of activities beyond the redesign of customer messages shows the power of the behavioral approach to address core features of the delivery of public policy. Partly because of the pedigree of nudge, there has been a tendency to associate behavioral interventions with the soft or informational tools of government, with the implication that the stronger and more authoritative tools are used less. This feature emerges in some critiques of nudge, such as an early House of Lords (2011) report, and in the work of health policy experts who believe that nudge throws away the essential tools of government (Marteau et al. 2011). But in practice even informational interventions have been closely linked to the use of other tools of government, so the court-fines nudge is just one step in a process that uses the law to very strong effect over the citizens. What is really going on is the use of behavioral insights to customize the operation of the tools of government so they work better, partly because even the authoritative tool of law and regulation involves compliance and depends on levels of trust on the part of the citizens and other actors. In this way, "all tools are informational now" (John 2013b) because each tool has to have an informational component to work effectively; now the behavioral revolution gives policy-makers a set of devices to improve the effectiveness of these tools. Nudges are just one part of the armory of behavioral economics: the approach might be better described as budge (Oliver 2013b) whereby policy-makers use the findings from behavioral economics in a variety of settings.

The behavioral revolution is profound in that it can reach all parts of the government or public organizational machine, across every kind of agency, activity, and functional field, using the same toolbox and approach, partly because most public activities can only operate with the cooperation of citizens or organizations. Even within a bureaucracy, lower-level actors need motivation and encouragement and the center needs to be skilful in harnessing collective knowledge. Decentralized bodies, such as community councils or local governments, have their own reference groups for whom behavioral insights apply.

As well as the wide application to the tools of government, there is an increasing realization that behavioral effects are strong and long-lived. Not only are policy-makers choosing a set of interventions that can apply across a range of settings, they can rely on bedding down behavior change. The conventional critique is that the effect sizes from behavioral interventions are small, but this is not the case and tends to be restricted to the information-provision interventions, whereas the use of more psychological mechanisms creates a much stronger effect. For example, with voter turnout, it is known that a range of campaign techniques can create behavioral change of between one and seven percentage points (see Green and Gerber 2008). However, if stronger behavioral cues are used, such as social pressure, it is possible to double these treatment effects (Gerber et al. 2008). The tendency for treatment effects to fade can be exaggerated too, largely because behavioral interventions can stimulate habit formation. Although interventions can stimulate reactance, that is, resistance against the intervention, it is possible that the change in behavior can be repeated after the occasion of the nudge; so, for example, with a voter-turnout intervention, it is possible for the respondent to carry on voting long afterward (Cutts et al. 2009). Private companies that use interventions know that they need to tweak interventions to ensure compliance and novelty is a big part of that. Public-sector users can use these techniques and change them from time to time, but they can also rely on the fact that the behaviors encouraged are perceived to be desirable and in the public interest, which can help entrench them as norms held by citizens. It is the openness of behavioral approaches to a variety of applications, without a dominant assumption that there is one behavioral cue that applies in all contexts, that has helped lead to the adoption of these ideas.

There is no worldview that needs to be accepted by every government agency. Only testing can find out how the context of a public decision can interact with the list of behavioral cues that may or may not apply. Theory is useful in coming up with a shortlist of likely interventions, but each needs evaluation in the field to deal with external validity. Usually, only one or two interventions may in the end prove efficacious, or there is a rank order of effect sizes from which the policy-maker may chose the one that is more consistent with other objectives such as legitimacy or equity. There has been no apparent limit to the application of behavioral ideas.

The UK has been prominent, but a larger influence has been felt in the USA, where one of the authors of Nudge, Cass Sunstein, became head of the Office of Information and Regulatory Affairs under President Obama. Subsequently in 2012, the White House set up its own behavioral policy unit, the Social and Behavioral Sciences Team (SBST), which operates in a similar way to BIT, and since 2017 was subsequently run out of the General Services Administration's Office of Evaluation Sciences. Behavioral science has influenced state governments in Australia, such as New South Wales with its Behavioral Insights unit, and Victoria, which has followed with a similar initiative. BIT example has influenced the design of public administration in Singapore, with interest being expressed by the European Commission and European governments, in particular, Germany, Holland, and Belgium. There is a large international interest in behavioral interventions, partly to address some of the weaknesses in international aid policy which require a change to ensure desired behaviors ensue after a financial allocation has been made by the donor country. Such themes are articulated in the World Development Report 2015: *Mind, Society, and Behavior*, which is a comprehensive review of behavioral science and its applications to less developed settings. Overall, there has been a diffusion pattern from US and UK outward to the rest of the world (John 2019; Naru 2024).

At the same time as the policy interest, the attention to behavioral policy in turn has stimulated a large amount of academic attention—often from outside economics and from disciplines that have always been interested in the application of behavioral ideas, such as in health policy research or other substantive fields such as transport and education. Academics in different disciplines speak a common language of policy intervention and management. Edited volumes show the interest across the academy, such as Oliver's *Behavioral Public Policy* (2013a), which has applications to the environment, health, work, finance, and transparency. Shafir's comprehensive *The Behavioral Foundations of Public Policy* (2013) contains chapters on employment, poverty, health, and savings among the many other topics covered. These have been followed up by Oliver's (2017, 2019, 2023) trilogy of books on behavioral public policy, looking at history, reciprocity, and political economy. The International Behavioural Public Policy Association is a home for these kinds of scholars and the journal *Behavioural Public Policy* is now the key place to publish these new works.

The Impact of the Behavioral Sciences on Decision-Making

The expansion of the behavioral sciences has not left public agencies unaffected. Of course, it is perfectly possible for bureaucrats and politicians to carry on with the same ways of working and simply to use behavioral insights to improve delivery and public managements as an add-on to standard routines and practices. However, this is not likely. The first reason for expecting an organizational impact is that using behavioral insights entails a pre-commitment to changing policies based on evidence and an admission that standard operating procedures need to change. It requires innovation to be adopted as a working assumption within the bureaucracy. This requires leadership from the center, powerful advocates at middle levels, and often a special unit in the bureaucracy with a reform-minded impetus. This is what has happened with the U.K. government (John 2014) where BIT was an officially sponsored change agent promoting innovation in the public sector. The second feature of behavioral public policy is that evidence and the use of experts become a more central feature of decision-making. Traditional evaluation, despite many attempts to integrate research, is done usually after the main policy-making decisions having taken place. With behavioral public policy, researchers, and by implication experts, who can be external to the organization, can set the agenda as to what kind of innovation to promote and then give instant feedback to policy-makers as to which one to choose. Research is integral to the exercise: the policy-maker needs the skills and mentality of the researcher to understand what is going on and the researcher has to adopt the pragmatism and sensitivity to context of the policy-maker. These research-policy teams can run behavioral public policy from start to finish.

The final feature that leads to innovation in bureaucracies is the orientation of the politicians, bureaucrats, and experts. It is often assumed that the use of behavioral insights is top-down, which implies technocratic assumptions about the role of the citizens that are revealed by the secrecy with which decisions are taken. But this need not be the case. The secret to the effective use of behavioral insights is the adaptation of existing means of delivering public policy to behavioral science, which involves a careful selection of the ideas that are likely to work in a particular context. Policy-makers have to rely on local knowledge because there needs to be a very precise customization of policy tools to ensure the effective delivery of the desired behavioral intervention. Even a letter designed to remind citizens to pay their taxes on time needs a very careful calibration so that the behavioral messages nest in the existing format of text and do not look awkward and out of place, while remaining prominent. That is, for behavioral interventions to work, it is not enough to copy insights from elsewhere or to implement what was designed in the laboratory: real-world field experiments need to be created, and these rely on a very practical assessments of what is possible. Local knowledge often comes from those personnel who have direct contact with the customer at the delivery end of the bureaucracy. In the end, behavioral policies need a thought experiment on the part of the intervener: the researcher needs to think what it is like to receive such an intervention—for example, the letter that hits the door mat and is opened in a hurry as recipient slugs back a coffee before heading out to work. In this way, the approach of the bureaucracy is more citizen-centered, having the mindset of a citizen rather than the state. The need to involve decentralized personnel can also appeal to those who are outside the agency and be suited for organizations that have close relationships to local publics, such as in locally elected government or voluntary and community groups. In this way, the nudge agenda is complementary with other tendencies within bureaucracies to become more citizen-friendly and responsive (see Fung 2006).

In one view, it is important that the bureaucrats do not consult too widely about the design of behavioral interventions, because if citizens find out about what is being done to them, they might not respond to the nudge: nudges need to work automatically and unconsciously. This might not be the case so much with publicly oriented policies. In fact, more inclusion of citizens in the design of policies and linking nudge policies that help citizens to think and reflect on policy outcomes (John et al. 2011, 2020) might be the way in which behavioral interventions become more embedded and accepted as legitimate by citizens. Hence the programme of nudge+ that enhances behavioral intervention with customized thinks (Banerjee and John 2021).

Behavioral Decision-Making

The paradox of behavioral public policy is that decisions that rely on limited cognitive capacity on the part of citizens are adopted and selected by politicians and civil servants who themselves have the same brains and emotions as the citizens they are targeting. One does need to be a believer in the enlightenment project of Saint-Simon to realize that politicians and bureaucrats have a different role than citizens: they are charged with making decisions for which they are held to account; the decision-making process is designed to allow for deliberation and stages that permit evidence and reflection to take place; and politicians have advisers, bureaucrats, and experts to help them make informed decisions to guard against implementing rash and unreflective policies. Just as the revolution in behavioral economics does not disrupt entirely notions of utility maximizing, most accounts of modern decision-making accept that an overload of information creates pressures on decision-makers to use heuristics and shortcuts that may in turn rely on human biases. Empirical accounts of decision-making going back to Simon (1947), then through to Allison (1971), Kingdon (1984), and Baumgartner and Jones (1993), stress the speed at which decision-makers must operate and their selective focus, where chance and positioning as well as the nature of the appeal can explain why policies are adopted. There is less surprise now that vast and meticulous collection of evidence and its evaluation, such as that presented in commissions of enquiry or official reports, are going to be trumped by on-the-hoof reactions to signals and to perceptions of crisis, such as the attempt to get out of a trap laid by a television interviewer and then the costs of retracting a policy commitment publicly stated in full view of the electorate. When policy is understood in this way, citizens and representatives cannot expect to get much from their representatives if they adopt what they think are the necessary procedures to get something addressed, that is, a calm reflection on the evidence and reasoned evaluation of the alternatives. Citizens and interest groups need to address the behavioral biases of decision-makers themselves. To get attention and hold representatives to account, citizens must become devotees of behavioral economics and administer the self-same signals that politicians are happy to dish out to the citizens.

It is here that the research arena of experiments on elites using behavioral cues offers insights into a more radical form of behavioral public policy. Such experiments have tended to be rare, but more have been carried out in recent years (see reviews in Grose 2014 and Kertzer and Renshon 2022). One experiment shows the necessity of such cues. Richardson and John (2012) randomly assigned local councilors to receive either a well-researched lobby letter or a less-well-researched on but found no difference in responses. A more behaviorally attuned experiment allocated legislators with poll results of something they were intending to vote on (Butler and Nickerson 2011), with positive effect. The polls made something salient to legislators that might otherwise have been lost in the vast amount of information they receive. In Chin (2005) and Chin et al. (2000), the treatment was the request for a personal meeting with the legislator to impact on responsiveness, which is another behavioral technique of seeking to personalize the message. Another method that has been used in these experiments is transparency, that is, making the actions of the policy-maker visible to others, especially electors. Grose (2010) conducted an experiment to show whether telling the representative that turning up to legislative sessions will be reported back to constituents and told to the media. All these techniques can work on policy-makers just as much as they work on citizens. We know from the experiments of Shafer, Loewen, and colleagues that decision-makers are just like citizens in responding to a cue with their biases (Sheffer et al. 2018), justifying interventions that go with the grain of those biases.

These are isolated research projects that are testing hypotheses about responsiveness to cues. But if such techniques become more readily used by the citizens in action groups to seek to hold policy-makers to account, there would be in effect a behavioral kind of public policy practiced by the citizens on policy-makers, creating an infinite regress of polices using behavioral insights being processed by citizens using behavioral insights to influence the very policy-makers using behavioral insights. In this way, the biases that are present in both decision-making and choices by citizens can be countered and addressed by signals that communicate desirable behaviors both for citizens and for those in public office too, who are encouraged by citizens to act more pro-socially, not by an appeal to reason but by using their biases and cognitions. This is not to assume that politicians and bureaucrats are not actively designing to act in the public interest but may fall from virtue just like citizens do. They need to be nudged to ensure they follow their own best conception of the interest. If citizens conveyed these nudges regularly, it might lead to an improved arena for making public decisions. Simply by extending nudge, however, it is impossible to rectify the inequality and paternalism that is inherent in current use of behavioral economics. For this to happen, it would need a lot of investment by groups to hold politicians to account-able; but there already is a mechanism through the internet and social media where politicians' actions can be critiqued by many observers and where feedback effects can rise quickly and convey norms and cues very efficiently (see Margetts et al. 2016).

The vision here is benevolent, both for the policy-makers nudging citizens and for citizens nudging policy-makers. But what is to stop policy-makers using nudges for personal advantage, such as re-election, by encouraging acceptability of policies that otherwise would be unpop-ular? What would prevent citizen groups using nudges for sectional gain, such as a powerful trades union representing groups of workers or a private company seeking a market advantage? Just as resources are unequal between groups for standard lobbying, so will be access to nudges, though nudges are not so expensive and can in principle be accessed by all. Cross-checking might also help to ensure that both sets of nudges prompt fairer decision-making.

CONCLUSION

Behavioral public policy is a new approach to decision-making that can be used by bureaucrats, politicians, and citizens. It applies the insights of the behavioral sciences to offer clear choices to decision-makers about what instrument or course of action is likely to lead to better societal outcomes. It deploys insights from psychology about the best motivator of a response to an incentive or message to act, relying on cognitions and judgments of the respondent that are activated or appealed to by the intervention. This is more effective than direct calls to comply or to act, which may not be believed or acted upon or which place far too much burden on individuals who already suffer from being overloaded by too much information. By being human-centered, sympathetic to how individuals approach decision-making, and appropriate to the social context in which individuals take their actions, policy-makers are more likely to get a desired response than by employing the many standard tools they have to choose from. The main task of the behavioral policy-maker is to identify the right cue in the appropriate context.

With such advantages it is no surprise that the behavioral agenda has been seized upon by today's policy-makers: it offers a common sense and practical way of dealing with public problems and of ensuring reasonable compliance with government commands and wishes. The benefits are demonstrable in terms of cost savings and greater number of pro-social behaviors achieved. There is potential for the transfer of the core ideas across functional areas, geographical locations, and levels of governance, making it a task of research to find out how a cue works in a particular context. There is every reason to expect that today's policy-makers are going to continue to practise behavioral public policy.

There is a wider and more ambitious application of behavioral ideas, which moves the focus away from the value-free context of the delivery of public policies to the process by which they are formulated, where the actors are the self-same decision-makers who authorize behavioral nudges. Here the task is more challenging, as it relies on citizens and groups using cues to nudge policy-makers so they realize their best conception of the public good. It is possible that nudges from citizens will help policy-makers produce better policies and in turn assist citizens in a self-reinforcing circle. In this way, behavioral public policy embraces both policy formulation and implementation, which is an extension of the vision that the founders of public policy intended when they started writing about decision-making in the mid-twentieth century.

AuthorContribution Contribution to the second edition of *Contemporary Approaches to Public Policy, Theories, Controversies and Perspectives (International Series on Public Policy)*, edited by B. Guy Peters and Philippe Zittoun, Palgrave Macmillan.

ANNEX: BEHAVIORAL APPROACHES IN PUBLIC POLICY

As the chapter indicates, the study of behavior is central to social science, and most empirical studies seek to investigate individual or collective behavior in some form, even if their focus is mainly on attitudes. There are whole branches of social science that focus on behavior, such as political behavior, which is about the study of elections and other participatory acts (while the study of attitudes and values is also core to this field). Within political science there was a field called behavioralism that assumed that social science was about observed behavior first and foremost, an approach that was popular in the 1950s and 1960s, and is still influential (Sanders 2010). More generally, it is possible to regard most of social science as often about or relating to behavior in some way. Even an institutional approach to political science or public policy has behavioral implications in people following rules and standard operating procedures. The standard rational choice approach is designed to predict how actors behave in response to incentives and the moves of the other players. To avoid such concept expansion and to ensure a behavioral approach helps understand problems in public policy, it is assumed that it incorporates insights from the study of psychology to understand how decision-makers behave, that is make decisions in public policy. The reference point is the standard rational actor model based on weighing up of alternatives, when cognitive science knows that actual decision-making is based on a more limited assessment of alternatives. This was the foundation for the incrementalist approach to public policy based on limited information processing (Lindblom 1959). This idea was picked up by Baumgartner and Jones (1993) in their agenda setting approach, but this fell short of a full-on behavioral approach, and these authors were more interested in the role of ideas as did much public policy scholarship in that period. Behavioral approaches also got squeezed out because of the prominence of the principal-agent model and varieties of institutionalism. This relative neglect paves the way for the starting point for this chapter, which is the revolution in understanding behavior which comes from outside public policy in the field of the psychological sciences and the emergent discipline of behavioral economics. At an earlier point in time in the study of public policy, Simon and colleagues were leading the behavioral approach; now public policy has fallen behind, with some exceptions such as in the study of policy failures and disasters (t Hart 1990). But the elite experiments discussed above provide the way in for a more developed behavioral approach to public policy directed to the classic problem of understanding decision-making in government but using recent findings in behavioral science to advance knowledge.

There is a temptation to think that large-scale quantitative analysis is the way to research individual or collective behavior, which perhaps comes from familiarity with mass surveys used in political behavior research. More common these days are field and other experiments that have been so popular with research on nudges (John 2017). But such a facility is not usually available to study public decision-making, even surveys of elites are rare. Records of what they do, such as voting for legislation, or changing their posts, only partly illuminates decision-making and is rarely a substitute for the case study and the historical approach, as was seen with Allison's (1971) work, and remains the core to the study of policy decisions. Experiments on elites have become possible and more frequent, as reviewed above, but are not a substitute for the use of good shoe-leather as done in classic qualitative work. Other techniques of qualitative work, such as comparative case studies, the long interview, coding of qualitative data, and the use of interpretation, are effective ways to study observed behavior, whereby its motivation is subtle and hard to elucidate so are rewarded by a mixed methods approach. With these various research methods to hand, there is no one dominant approach to the study of behavior. As with all social science, there should be openness and pluralism when selecting and using research methods to acknowledge the difficulty of understanding human behavior and its meaning, and an avoidance of using oversimplifying terms, such as positivism or realism, when applying methods (Dowding 2016).

REFERENCES

Allison, Graham T. 1971. *Essence of decision. Explaining the Cuban missile crisis.* New York: Harper Collins.

Banerjee, Sanchayan and John, Peter. 2021. Nudge plus: Incorporating reflection into behavioral public policy. *Behavioural Public Policy*, 1–16.

Banerjee, Sanchayan, and Peter John. 2025. Behavioral public policy: past, present, & future. *Policy and Society*, puaf012. https://doi.org/10.1093/pol soc/puaf012

Baumgartner, Frank R., and Bryan D. Jones. 1993. *Agendas and instabilities in American politics.* Chicago: University of Chicago Press.

Becker, Gary. 1968. Crime and punishment: An economic approach. *The Journal of Political Economy* 76: 169–217.

Benartzi, Shlomo, et al. 2017. Should governments invest more in nudging?. *Psychological Science* 28 (8): 1041–1055. https://doi.org/10.1177/095679 7617702501.

Benartzi, Shlomo, and Richard H. Thaler. 2004. Save more tomorrow: Using behavioral economics to increase employee saving. *Journal of Political Economy* 112 (1): 164–187.

Beshears, J., and H. Kosowsky. 2020. Nudging: Progress to date and future directions. *Organizational Behavior and Human Decision Processes* 161: 3–19.

Butler, Daniel M., and David W. Nickerson. 2011. Can learning constituency opinion affect how legislators vote? Results from a field experiment. *Quarterly Journal of Political Science* 6: 55–58.

Cabinet Office. 2012. Applying behavioural insights to reduce fraud, error and debt. London: Cabinet Office. https://www.gov.uk/government/uploads/system/uploads/attachment_data/file/60539/BIT_FraudErrorDebt_access ible.pdf.

Camerer, Colin, Linda Babcock, George Loewenstein, and Richard Thaler. 1997. Labor supply of New York City cabdrivers: One day at a time. *The Quarterly Journal of Economics* 407–441.

Campbell, Angus, Phillip E. Converse, William E. Miller, and Donald E. Stokes. 1960. *The American voter.* New York: Wiley.

Cartwright, Edward. 2011. *Behavorial economics.* Abingdon: Routledge.

Chin, Michelle L. 2005. Constituents versus fat cats: Testing assumptions about congressional access decisions. *American Politics Research* 33: 751–786.

Chin, Michele L., Jon R. Bond, and Nehemia Geva. 2000. A foot in the door: An experimental study of PAC and constituency effects on access. *Journal of Politics* 62: 534–549.

Cutts, David, Ed. Fieldhouse, and Peter John. 2009. Is voting habit forming? The longitudinal impact of a GOTV campaign in the UK. *Journal of Elections of Public Opinion and Parties* 19 (3): 251–263.

Dawnay, Emma, and Hetan Shah. 2005. *Behavioural economics: Seven principles for policy-makers*. London: New Economics Foundation.

DellaVigna, Srefano, and Elizabeth Linos. 2022. RCTs to scale: Comprehensive evidence from two nudge units. *Econometrica* 90 (1): 81–116.

Dolan, Paul, Michael Hallsworth, David Halpern, Dominic King, and Ivo Vlaev. 2010. *MINDSPACE: Influencing behaviour through public policy*. UK: Report for the Cabinet Office.

Dowding, Keith. 2016. *The Philosophy and Methods of Political Science*. Palgrave.

Naru, F. 2024. Behavioral public policy bodies: New developments & Lessons. *Behavioral Science & Policy*. https://doi.org/10.1177/237946072 41285614.

Fung, Archong. 2006. *Empowered participation: Reinventing urban democracy*. Princeton: Princeton University Press.

Gerber, Alan S., Donald P. Green, and Christopher W. Larimer. 2008. Social pressure and voter turnout: Evidence from a large-scale field experiment. *American Political Science Review* 102 (1): 33–48.

Lindblom, Charles E. 1959. The science of 'muddling through.' *Public Administration Review* 19 (2): 79–88.

Green, Donald P., and Alan S. Gerber. 2008. *Get out the vote: How to increase voter turnout*, 2nd ed. Washington, DC: Brookings Institution Press.

Grose, Christian. 2010. Priming rationality: A theory and field experiment of participation in legislatures. Presented at New York Univ–Coop. Congr. Elect. Study Exp. Polit. Sci. Conf., 5–6 February, New York.

Grose, Christian. 2014. Field experimental work on political institutions. *Annual Review of Political Science* 17: 355–370.

Haynes, Laura, Owain Service, Ben Goldacre, and David Torgerson, 2012 Haynes, Laura, Owain Service, Ben Goldacre, and David Torgerson. 2012. *Test, learn, adapt: Developing public policy with randomised controlled trials*. London: Cabinet Office.

Haynes, Laura, Donald P. Green, Rory Gallagher, Peter John, and David Torgerson. 2013. Collection of delinquent fines: A randomized trial to assess the effectiveness of alternative messages. *Journal of Public Management Research and Theory* 32 (4): 718–730.

House of Lords. 2011. *Science and technology sub-committee, 2nd report of session 2010–12, behaviour change*. London: The Stationery Office Limited.

John, Peter. 2013a. Political science, impact and evidence. *Political Studies Review* 11: 168–173.

John, Peter. 2013b. All tools are informational now: How information and persuasion define the tools of government. *Policy and Politics* 41 (4): 605–620.

John, Peter. 2014. Policy entrepreneurship in British government: The behavioural insights team and the use of RCTs. *Public Policy and Administration* 29 (3): 257–267.

John, Peter. 2017. *Field experiments in political science and public policy: practical lessons in design and delivery*, 1st ed. New York City: Routledge. https://doi.org/10.4324/9781315773025.

John, Peter. 2018. *How far to nudge: assessing behavioural public policy*. Cheltenham: Edward Elgar.

John, Peter. 2019. The international appeal of behavioural public policy: Is nudge an Anglo-American phenomenon? *Journal of Chinese Governance* 4 (2): 144–162.

John, Peter. *How far to nudge assessing behavioural public policy*. Cheltenham: Edward Elgar.

John, Peter, Sarah Cotterill, Alice Moseley, Liz Richardson, Graham Smith, Gerry Stoker, and Corinne Wales. 2011. *Nudge, nudge, think, think: Experimenting with ways to change civic behaviour*. Bloomsbury: Academic.

John, Peter, Sarah Cotterill, Alice Moseley, Liz Richardson, Graham Smith, Gerry Stoker, and Corinne Wales. 2020. *Nudge, nudge, think, think: Experimenting with ways to change citizen behaviour. In Nudge, nudge, think, think*, 2nd ed. Manchester: Manchester University Press.

Kahneman, Daniel. 1973. *Attention and effort*. Englewood Cliffs: Prentice-Hall; Kahneman, Daniel. 2011. *Thinking, fast and slow*. London: Penguin.

Kahneman, Daniel. 2011. *Thinking, fast and slow*. New York: Farrar, Straus and Giroux.

Kahneman, Daniel, and Amos Tversky. 1979. Prospect theory: An analysis of decision under risk. *Econometrica* 47 (2): 263–291.

Kahneman, Daniel, Paul Slovic, and Amos Tversky. 1982. *Judgment under uncertainty: Heuristics and biases*. Cambridge: Cambridge University Press.

Kertzer, Joshua, and Jonathan, Renshon. 2022. Experiments and surveys on political elites annual review of political science 24: 529–550

Kingdon, John W. 1984. *Agendas, alternatives, and public policies*. Boston: Little, Brown.

Leach, Steve. 1982. In defence of the rational model. In *Approaches in public policy*, ed. Steve Leach and John Stewart. London: Allen & Unwin.

Lindblom, Charles E., and David Braybrooke. 1963. *A strategy of decision: Policy evaluation as a social process*. New York: Free Press.

Loomes, Graham, and Robert Sugden. 1982. Regret theory: An alternative theory of rational choice under uncertainty. *Economic Journal* 92: 805–824.

Margetts, Helen, Peter John, Scott Hale, and Taha Yasseri. 2016. *Political turbulence – How social media shape collective action*. Princeton: Princeton University Press.

Maier, Maximillian, František Bartoš, T. D. Stanley, David R. Shanks, Adam J. Harris, and Eric-Jan. Wagenmakers. 2022. No evidence for nudging after adjusting for publication bias. *Proceedings of the National Academy of Sciences* 119 (31): e2200300119.

Marteau, Theresa M., David Ogilvie, Martin Roland, Marc Suhrcke, and Michael P. Kelly. 2011. Judging nudging: Can nudging improve population health? *British Medical Journal* 342: 263–265.

Mertens, Stephanie., Mario Herberz, Ulf J. J. Hahnel, and Tobias Brosch. 2022. The effectiveness of nudging: A meta-analysis of choice architecture interventions across behavioral domains. *Proceedings of the National Academy of Sciences* 119, e2107346118.

Oliver, Adam. 2013a. *Behavioural public policy*. Cambridge: Cambridge University Press.

Oliver, Adam. 2013b. From nudging to budging: Using behavioural economics to inform public sector policy. *Journal of Social Policy* 42 (4): 685–700.

Oliver, Adam. 2017. *The origins of behavioural public policy*. Cambridge, UK: Cambridge University Press.

Oliver, Adam. 2019. *Reciprocity and the art of behavioural public policy*. Cambridge, UK: Cambridge University Press.

Oliver, Adam. 2023. *A political economy of behavioural public policy*. Cambridge, UK: Cambridge University Press.

Park, Andreas, and Hamid Sabourian. 2011. Herding and contrarian behavior in efficient financial markets. *Econometrica* 79: 973–1026.

Richardson, Liz, and Peter John. 2012. Who listens to the grassroots? A field experiment on informational lobbying in the UK. *British Journal of Politics and International Relations* 14: 595–612.

Sheffer, Lior, Peter J. Loewen, Stuart Soroka, Stefan Walgrave, and Tamir Sheafer. 2018. Nonrepresentative representatives: An experimental study of the decision making of elected politicians. *American Political Science Review* 112 (2): 302–321.

Shafir, Eldar, ed. 2013. *The behavioral foundations of public policy*. Princeton: Princeton University Press.

Sanders. D. 2010. "Behavioural Analysis". In *Theory and methods in political science*, eds. David Marsh and Gerry Stoker, 3rd Ed. Palgrave Macmillan.

Simon, Herbert. 1947. Administrative behavior. New York: Free Press.

Simon, Herbert. 1957. *Models of man*. New York: Wiley.

Sugden, Robert. 2004. The opportunity criterion: Consumer sovereignty without the assumption of coherent preferences. *American Economic Review* 94 (4): 1014–1033.

Sugden, Robert. 2013. The behavioural economist and the social planner: To whom should behavioural welfare economics be addressed? *Inquiry: An Interdisciplinary Journal of Philosophy* 56 (5): 519–538.

Sugden, Robert. 2018. *The community of advantage: A behavioral economist's defence of the market*. Oxford: Oxford University Press.

Thaler, Richard H., and Cass R. Sunstein. 2008. *Nudge: Improving decisions about health, wealth and happiness*. New Haven

t Hart, Paul. 1990. *Groupthink in government: a study of small groups and policy failure*. Amsterdam: Swets & Zeitlinger.

Tools Approaches

Helen Z. Margetts and Christopher C. Hood

Various writers on public policy have used—and still use—a 'tools' or 'instruments' approach to make sense of the complexity of contemporary policy-making. There is something attractive about breaking down the complex, abstract concept of 'public policy' into a more prosaic metaphor, as a combination of tools. It holds the promise of making the study of public policy simpler and easier to understand. Perhaps another reason for its attraction is that it suggests a solubility to policy problems, just as most problems around the house can, actually, be fixed with a reasonably simple toolbox that may be purchased in a DIY store, or most dental

Christopher Hood died on 3rd January 2025, before this article could be finished. His passing is both a personal loss to Helen Margetts and a profound loss to public administration scholarship. This article reflects their collaborative thinking, but Helen Margetts completed the final version and takes responsibility for any shortcomings.

H. Z. Margetts (✉) · C. C. Hood
University of Oxford, Oxford, UK
e-mail: helen.margetts@oii.ox.ac.uk

problems be fixed by a dentist wielding a limited range of custom built instruments.

This chapter focuses on the various tools or instruments approaches to policy-making developed over recent decades. First it lays out the advantages of the approach and outlines the main variants. Second, it discusses the merits and drawbacks of the approach in general, and each perspective specifically. Third, the chapter discusses the challenges to the use of the approach, in terms of how each of the variants copies with change in the policy-making environment by focusing on one particularly fast-moving and important change—the availability and use of digital tools and data for policy-making, and the widespread use of such tools by society at large. Fourth, it shows how this particular challenge might be overcome, particularly by the tools approaches developed by the authors of this chapter and other chapters in this book.

Where Does It Come from and Why Is It Different?

What distinguishes the tools approach from other ways of looking at or analyzing public policy? As noted above, a key attraction of the tools approach is the idea of simplifying this complex concept, making more tangible the abstract idea of policy. For example, if we can break public policy down into distinct elements, it may aid the comparison of policy-making across sectors, across locations and over time, or assist the process of policy evaluation. It also implies agency or control, in contrast to (for example) institutional approaches, with their implicit path dependency. It encapsulates the idea that there are choices to be made, and that the selection of instruments can make policy-making better, or more efficient, or socially optimal in some way:

> public policy is fundamentally conceived as pragmatic—that is, as a political and technical approach to solving problems via instruments; that it views such instruments are "natural"; they are viewed as being "at our disposal," and the only questions they raise relate to whether they are the best possible ones for meeting the objectives set; and that the central set of issues is around the effectiveness of instruments. (Lascoumes and Le Gales 2007)

If we can think of the different choices available to policy-makers for any particular policy, and look back in time to see the results where certain choices were made, then we can start to think of what might be the *best* option—and therefore find out what works and what doesn't in particular contexts. And in analytical terms, it gives us a way to distinguish between different types of policy, providing us with a taxonomy for public policy-making.

These advantages vary according to the type of instruments or tools approach used, however. Not all instruments-based approaches do cut through complexity, particularly when they provide long lists of possible tools with little clear analytical distinction between them. Some approaches focus on the practical choices available to policy-makers, and lack analytical validity, while some focus purely on analyzing policies after the event, and do not provide the idea of choice. So first we provide a brief summary of the main approaches that have been used.

ALTERNATIVE TOOLS-BASED APPROACHES

Approaches to the tools of government vary according to how much they delve into the 'how' and 'who' of policy-making. There is a continuum from, on the one hand, authors who discuss the internal organization or institutional complexity of government, or differences between policy-makers themselves within the governmental context. At the other end of the spectrum, there are approaches which treat government like a 'black box', and consider the difference between tools only in so far as they touch upon the world outside, and how they change individual, collective or organizational behaviour in society at large.

At the 'inside government' or 'institution-led' end of this spectrum, there are approaches that focus on different specific forms of organization through which public policy is conducted, and indeed this is central to the traditional mission of public administration. One way of doing this is to consider variants based around whether the public sector, private firms or third-sector organizations or some combination (such as public–private partnerships) are providing a service or utility, or regulating an industry. These are hotly contested issues in many countries, so conceiving instruments in the sense of alternative organizational types clearly links to issues of enduring salience.

One example of this 'institution-led' approach is provided by Lester Salamon's (2002) *The Tools of Government* (a development of the earlier work, *Beyond Privatization*, Salamon and Lund 1989), which pays considerable attention to various forms of public–private partnerships. Salamon's general argument is framed by the new types of institutional form available for public policy that were central to a 'new governance' paradigm linked with the rise of 'New Public Management' during the 1980s–2000s. These new institutional arrangements were enthusiastically embraced in the US by Osborne and Gaebler in their 1992 book *Reinventing Government*, probably the first (of very few) books on public administration to become a bestseller which formed a key plank of Clinton and Gore Administration's National Performance Review of the 1990s. Osborne and Gaebler draw on Salaomon's earlier work to provide their own list of 'tools' or 'Alternative Service Delivery Options', laid out in an Appendix A at the end of the book (pages 332–346), but in their case they are precisely that—a (long) list of 36 options, and there is little analytic derivation or clarity on how they were derived.

Another tools approach at this end of the spectrum may be described as the politics-of-instrument-choice approach, which focuses on the politics that lies behind the selection of whatever tools governments use, whether conceived as generic instruments or as forms of organization and was developed by one of the authors of this book, Guy Peters, and his colleague Stephen Linder (1989, 1998). They distinguish four approaches to the understanding of public policy instruments, contrasting what they call 'instrumentalists' (those who concentrate on and often seek to champion some particular tool, such as those economists who see price mechanisms as the answer to every policy problem), 'proceduralists' (those who see tool selection as a product of political processes that are so complex and unique to every case that it is impossible to make any general assessment of 'appropriateness'), 'contingentists' (those who see the appropriateness of tool use as depending on types of task, for instance as between 'compliance cultures' and cultures of resistance to government policy) and 'constitutivists' (those who see the appropriateness of tool use as turning on subjective and contested meanings). They make the case for 'constitutivism' replacing instrumental or contingency as the dominant approach, arguing that there is 'a growing understanding that instrument selection is not a simple mechanical exercise of matching well-defined problems and equally well-defined solutions. Rather, it is fundamentally an intellectual process of constituting a reality and then attempting to work within it' (Linder and Peters 1998, p. 45).

It could be argued, however (as do Hood and Margetts 2007) that to compare the tools favoured or perceived by policy participants with others that could have been chosen or perceived by others with different ideological or cognitive baggage cannot be done without some overall categorization of the tools available in principle, to play against those actor perceptions. In that sense, this approach does not really provide options to prospective policy-makers for selecting policy tools, unless it is to think themselves into one of the types presented; it assumes the existence of such a categorization as a point of departure—whether in the form of institutional types or broader methods of intervention—for exploring why political actors choose the policy instruments they do. That is because such an understanding necessitates a comparison between the tools that a given set of decision-makers chose to tackle the problems they faced with those that they could have chosen, but either did not see or did not use.

Meeting this kind of challenge to the politics-of-instruments approach, Pierre Lascoumes and Patrick Le Gales (2007) in a special issue of *Governance* argue in favour of what they call a political sociology of public policy, arguing that 'By emphasizing the political sociology of policy instruments, we want to stress power relations associated to instruments and issues of legitimacy, politicization, or depoliticization dynamics associated with different policy instruments'. They argue that it is essential to move beyond functionalist approaches, to see public policy from the angle of the instruments that structure policies: '....public policy instruments are not tools with perfect axiological neutrality, equally available: on the contrary, they are bearers of values, fueled by one interpretation of the social and by precise notions of the mode of regulation envisaged'. In this way, they provide 'meta-tools' to understand the complexity of the policy-making environment.

At the other end of the continuum between 'inside government' and 'black box' perspectives are generic 'institution-free' approaches to cataloguing the toolkit. As with the other approaches, this general approach can be traced back to an age before modern policy analysis. In the late eighteenth and early nineteenth century, for instance, the utilitarian philosopher Jeremy Bentham was much preoccupied with cataloguing some of the different ways of controlling crime (for example, by incarcerating prisoners or transporting them to Australia) and of providing public services. And economists have long been concerned with identifying different generic instruments for the conduct of economic policy, for instance in distinguishing price mechanisms and rationing systems. Perhaps the most well-known, generic account of policy instruments is the distinction between 'carrots, sticks and sermons' as alternative methods of intervention and control, originating in a 1960s analysis of types of organizational control by the famous sociologist Amitai Etzioni (1961), developed and introduced into the public policy literature by Evert Vedung (Bertelmans-Videc et al. 1998).

While 'carrots, sticks and sermons' might be used in any organization, an institution-free tools approach developed specifically for government is that pioneered by Hood (1983) and later developed for the digital age by Hood and Margetts (2007). This approach argues that for any policy problem government has four basic tools at its disposal: nodality, the property of being at the centre of social and information networks; authority, the legitimate legal or official power to command or prohibit; treasure, the possession of money or fungible chattels which may be exchanged; and organizational capacity, the possession of a stock of people, skills, land, buildings and technology. The analysis is refined by breaking down each of the four NATO tools into 'effecting' and 'detecting' tools—that is, tools for gathering information as well as for modifying or shaping behaviour in other ways. In this approach, any policy solution will be composed of some combination of these tools, each of which has advantages and disadvantages in terms of being more or less expensive or renewable, for example. This approach has developed in other variants in the public policy literature. Elmore (1987) conceived government instruments as variants on a four-fold division of basic intervention strategies, comprising mandates, inducements, capacity-building and system-changing. Anne Schneider and Helen Ingram (1990) elaborated and modified this approach with a closely similar but fivefold categorization, comprising authority tools, incentive tools, capacity tools, symbolic or hortatory tools and learning tools.

In the middle of the continuum between 'institutions-as-tools' and generic approaches, there are tools-based perspectives on public policy which use a mixture of institutions and generic tools to make up their toolkit. Again, there are antecedants here; even in the early 1950s, the famous American public policy scholars, Robert Dahl and Charles Lindblom (1953) attempted to catalogue a range of socio-economic instruments available to government as a mixture of institutions-as-tools and the generic institution-free approach. Perhaps the most extensive mixed approach comes from the Canadian public administration scholar Michael Howlett (1991, 1993, 2000, 2005, 2007, 2009a, b). Building on his earlier work in a chapter in his edited book (2007), he provides a 'taxonomy of taxonomy' of policy instruments, within the basic NATO categories of Hood's Tools of Government (which he terms substantive instruments) and a raft of procedural instruments such as education, training, institutions, formal evaluations, institutional reform. For each of these categories, he produces a spectrum of policy instruments across a continuum of the level of state provision, ranging from voluntary to compulsory. He goes on to identify a range of factors or variables that influence instrument choices in specific directions, using here the organization specific categories of market, direct provision, regulation and voluntary, community instruments. These various categorizations and sub-divisions mean that he amasses quite a heavy toolbox; in Howlett (2005), for example, he builds on his previous work to delineate a spectrum of both 'substantive' and 'procedural' instruments, breaking them down into ten and twelve sub-categories respectively.

More recently, Peter John in *Making Policy Work* (2011) typifies this mixed approach, with his 'six broad levers, which express themselves as resources that governments have available to manipulate, in varying degrees, so as to influence public policy outcomes'. Of these, two are 'institution-free' tools—public spending and taxation; and law and regulation, while three tools are based on the internal workings of government: institutions and institutional reform; bureaucracy; and public management. Another two are defined by the author as 'non-standard'; information, persuasion and deliberation; and networks and governance. Of these 'non-standard' tools, the former might be seen as analogous to 'Nodality' in Hood and Margetts' terms, and the latter 'soft levers of networks' is more about the system of governance, but is separated out as being almost beyond the capacity of the state or other public actors. In this sense, the approach does not treat government as a 'black box', because the author sees no clear boundary line between state and society, so argues for the 'softness' and indirectness and blurred boundaries of contemporary governance—but at the same time, might be accused of rendering the concept of 'tool' so soft as being almost impossible to wield usefully.

CHALLENGES TO THE TOOLS APPROACH

A key challenge to any tools-based approach is 'what can we use it for'? How does it aid our understanding of policy-making, for example by comparing policies over time or exploring differences between jurisdictions? And to what extent might it be used to improve policy-making, in terms of making it more efficient, effective, equitable or ethical, or at least to evaluate policies that have already been carried out, in order to learn lessons and make better policy in the future? The various approaches outlined above pick up these gauntlets in different ways.

With regard to understanding public policy, and allowing us to make comparisons across policies, all approaches face the trade off between simplicity and comprehensiveness. The different approaches provide different taxonomies of policy, which range from the most basic and simple—the 'carrots, sticks and sermons' approach—to the most complex mixed approaches, which endeavour to incorporate all possible dimensions of policy-making. The 'carrots, sticks and sermons' classification is the most parsimonious, achieving the greatest simplicity. But there are some instruments that are not easily classified under this parsimonious variety of headings. One such example is the case where environments are physically or digitally structured so as to shape behaviour, for example by making violation impossible, or very costly, such as fencing to shape crowd behaviour, for instance at sporting events or near pedestrian crossings on the roads. This set of activities—sometimes called 'architecture', as in the literature on digital codes (Lessig 1999) or 'choice architecture' in the language of behavioural 'nudge' experiments (Thaler and Sunstein 2008)—cannot really be forced into the 'CSS' trichotomy. But it has historically been one of the most important ways by which governments have gathered information and shaped behaviour, has been taken as a central aspect of government activity by philosophers from Bentham to Foucault and is likely to remain so, particularly with digital technology.

Hood's (1983) and the later Hood and Margetts (2007) Tools of Government approach is also parsimonious, and perhaps the most conceptually based, resting on theoretical and conceptual foundations rooted in the theory of cybernetics, the foundational science of control, and in the basic and distinctive properties of government rather than of organizations in general. It does not purport to be comprehensive in terms of incorporating all possible organizational instruments or forms, but it does make a claim to be exhaustive in terms of being able to discuss any public policy in terms of its tools make-up. In this way, the four NATO tools can be used for comparative analysis in at least two ways; to assess policy change over time, and to compare the way that the tools are used across different governments, levels of government or government agencies (Hood and Margetts 2007: 126–143). For example, countries vary enormously in the way they use treasure, from a tax base of around 17 percent of the GDP in China or India, to 45 percent or so in Sweden, reflecting enormous differences in the extent to which government uses treasure for purposes such as welfare state payments to citizens and protection of the environment. Likewise, although in practice all government departments or agencies will use a mixture of tools, they may be categorized in terms of the dominant tool they employ; a foreign office or department of state, for example, tends to be characterized by nodality as the dominant tool, because their operations depend upon being at the centre of informational networks, while they tend to lack large-scale organizational capacity, financial resources or legal authority, except in so far as they link to other departments.

The institution-based approaches are less well placed to undertake this comparative analysis. They clearly perform a valuable function in terms of cataloguing the different organizational forms available to government, and delving into the politics and cognitive processes that lie behind the choice of different policy tools provides important insight into the policy process. But these accounts tend to be based on heuristic lists of strategies for control or managerial intervention, the foundations of which are left largely implicit in most cases. For instance, Salamon's (2002) Tools of Government takes a broad, eclectic view and argues that 'tools' can be understood in many different dimensions (singling out for particular attention the aspects of 'directness', visibility, coerciveness and automaticity), but what foundational set of categories underpins the four dimensions of instrumentality or 14-point schema that Salamon picks out is far from clear. Osborne and Gaebler's 36 point schema is even more dislocated from any foundational conceptual framework, with both the alternative service delivery options and their table indicated which sector is suited to which instrument springing as if from nowhere in their 14 page appendix. So these approaches can only really aid understanding when the analyst has the book in front of them, rather than providing an analytic framework which is easily remembered and brought into play at any point.

Other mixed approaches such as the John and even more so the Howlett approach are comprehensive, and this sense offer a 'whole of public policy' approach to readers, but in so doing lose out on simplicity and analytic derivation, and the idea of explicit policy choices in any particular public policy between the different tools. Howlett offers a range of categorizations so complex that it is very difficult to work out what a policy-maker might be choosing between. Everything is covered, but the bewildering array of instrument classifications does not entirely make up in terms of comprehensiveness what is lost in simplicity. In general, this is the challenge of the mixed approach.

So how do the various approaches tackle the ask of policy evaluation, for example by providing a way of working out if the selected tool is more economic, efficient, effective or equitable or ethical than any of the available alternatives? Here the 'institutions-as-tools' or 'politics-of-instrument' approaches may seem at first glance to have the upper hand. They are geared at understanding the internal workings of the state—and what effect that has on the policy that emerges. Salamon's approach, for example, is likely to lead to a focus on how different institutional forms perform in terms of efficiency and effectiveness, making it easier to evaluate the cost of policy or services (although proponents of this approach have tended to rest on a normative belief that private sector solutions, where possible, are more efficient, rather than actually embarking on the evaluation). Furthermore, this approach might be used to assess tools in terms of how citizens can be involved in policy-making, allowing the analyst to understand the extent to which they may be regarded as transparent or democratic. For example, if a policy is implemented by a private organization rather than a public one, governed by the terms and conditions of the contract, it is less likely that citizens will be able to provide input to policy-making or service delivery.

In contrast, at the other end of the spectrum, a generic tools approach will take the discussion away for such questions, because there is no mechanism for observing how different policies lead to more or less efficient administrative or institutional forms. However, it is possible to think about the question of what makes a good choice of tools, and lead to an 'intelligent' policy design (Hood and Margetts 2007: 144), for example through the consideration of which mix of tools would work for which policy 'job', and which tool works in which circumstances, and also the moral acceptability of choices in terms of satisfying ethical criteria, such as justice and fairness. With perhaps most claim for an evaluative technique attributable to this tools approach, the tool mix may be considered under the heading of economy, although not one of monetary expense. They argue that the desired policy effect must be achieved as economically as possible from the perspective of both government and citizens, in terms of the 'spending' of governmental resources, and the minimum burden, in terms of form-filling, obligations and highly visible signs of governmental presence, on the general public. Saving in this latter sense would mean visiting on the public at large more 'trouble, vexation and oppression' (Smith 1910: 309) than is absolutely necessary. These two possible ways of being economical with the use of tools do not necessarily lead in the same direction, leading to a sophisticated analysis of how the use of tools might satisfy both of these aims. Not only do these two dimensions conflict, but the 'economy' requirement may conflict with any moral dimension for policy-making; for example, custodial treatment for offenders might seem to be the most economic way of treating alcoholics, in terms of minimizing bureaucratic effort and impact on the population at large, but it would definitely arouse some ethical hackles.

Such an analysis is not really possible with the instruments as tools approach. For instance, categorizing different organizational forms available to government only makes sense as an account of policy intervention if it can be supplemented by an analysis of the intervention instruments that those organizations can use or are likely to use. It is often said that organizations at the core of government tend to be used when it comes to the most authority-intensive instruments of policy, while the use of nodality and treasure is often entrusted to a range of other organizational forms, such as special-purpose authorities or contract organizations. But there are some important exceptions to that rule; a Treasury department or Ministry of Finance at the centre of government being the most obvious example. Most of the generic approaches—and some of the mixed ones—use 'organization' in the generic sense—'organizational capacity' (Hood 1983) or 'bureaucracy' (John 2011). The direct use of people and equipment for physical processing of one kind or another does not obviously match with any single administrative form. It is used both by bodies at the 'core' of government, such as armies and the police, and by bodies nominally independent from government, such as private firms operating under contract to government, or intelligence agencies. Indeed, the advantage of keeping generic accounts of government tools and categories of forms of government institution analytically separate is precisely that institutional type and method of intervention may not always be tightly connected.

Coping with a Changing (Digital) World

The real test of a tools based approach to understanding public policy—or indeed any approach discussed in this book—is if they can cope with the changing world, for example by providing a way to understand how public policy changes over time in response to exogenous events. After all, public policy is the business of understanding, dealing with and even changing the world outside government, so part of governing is to keep up with societal or environmental change.

One of the key changes to the context in which policy-making takes place in the last decades is the widespread use of digital technology by both society and government, particularly since use of the internet and social media became widespread. These are the first digital technologies that have become widely domesticated into everyday life, bringing societal innovation, and transforming the way that ordinary citizens work, shop, socialize, organize, entertain, inform and educate themselves and communicate with each other. Such technologies and applications are also heavily implicated in the rise in societal mobilization, demonstration and protest which brought some authoritarian regimes to collapse in the Arab Spring of 2011 and have challenged democratic states across the world, particularly since the financial crash of 2008 (Margetts et al. 2016). As a result, the ways in which government can—or cannot—influence the outside world through policy-making are in a period of flux. Governments have long used such technologies; they led the development of large-scale information systems for administrative operations from the 1960s onwards, and since that time complex information systems have become integral to organizations of all kinds, including government, offering new possibilities for policy innovation, alternative organizational forms and ways of interacting with citizens (Margetts 1999; Dunleavy et al. 2006, 2023). But with the advent of the internet, governments tended to lag behind citizens in capitalizing upon these possibilities, so these are the first digital technologies which citizens have used earlier and to a greater extent than governments. Most recently, we have seen the advent of data-driven technologies, particularly Artificial Intelligence (AI). At first, AI technologies were developed principally by and for private sector firms, but during the 2010s, there was huge interest in AI from governments also (Margetts and Dorobantu 2019, 2023). Governments were interested in these technologies for the improvement of services and policy-making, but also the extent to which the use of technologies by malicious actors could become a threat to governments (Bengio et al. 2025). At the end of 2022, with the launch of Chat GPT and a whole host of other Large Language Models (LLMs), the possibilities of AI were opened up to citizens. We are only at the beginning of being able to understand the effect of these developments on policy-making.

Theoretically, any of the 'tools' approaches discussed above could help to explore what difference this widespread use of digital and data-driven technology makes to the array of policy instruments, and hence to policy-making. They tend not to be used to do that, mainly because people who research public policy and administration—the 'tools' scholars—and the 'internet' or 'technology' scholars, looking at how digital technologies shape societal change, have tended to live in different worlds (Hood and Margetts 2007). But any approach aimed at making sense of contemporary policy-making and aiding policy-makers in a rapidly changing world needs to take account of shifts brought about by technological change, both in terms of the challenges to governance posed by a digitally enabled society, and the new opportunities for government to use digital technologies, to increase efficiency for example, or to interact with citizens in innovative ways. This sense-making is even more important in the wake of the 2020-2 global Covid-19 pandemic, which necessitated huge shifts in the way these technologies were used.

For any of the institutions-as-tools approaches, the emphasis will be on the changing set of institutional and organizational arrangements available to government in the era of 'digital era governance' (Dunleavy et al. 2006; Margetts and Dunleavy 2013; Dunleavy and Margetts 2023). Digital technology has long paved the way for forms of privatization and outsourcing to global corporations that were not available in the pre-digital age (Margetts 1999; Dunleavy et al. 2006, Margetts and Dunleavy 2024). Much has been written about the way such developments reshape organizations in a geographical sense, for instance in having 'back office' functions once co-located with strategy units or front-line delivery conducted in different regions, countries or even continents, and by workers in their own homes. And digital technology makes new forms of organization possible by dramatic reduction of transaction costs for certain kinds of activity, facilitating the rise of digital labour and micro-labour markets (Lehdonvirta 2014), and the opening up of new markets for public services and utilities. For instance, electric power is a good that cannot readily be stored once it has been generated, meaning that a spot market was not really practicable (and indeed would have been unimaginable) in the early twentieth century when electric power generation developed, and in effect the only organizational alternatives were direct state organization or regulated private monopoly. But by the late twentieth century, a virtual spot market in electric power became possible through digital technology, creating the possibility of a different (commercial market) kind of provider structure (see Foster 1992: 73) as did new possibilities for users of utilities such as gas and telephones to choose among alternative providers in a way that would have been either impossible or very costly in the pre-digital age (Hood and Margetts 2007).

Since then, virtual organizations with no physical presence visible to customers have proliferated all over the world, and although they have mostly originated outside government, they do offer new types of contract arrangements and ways of interacting with citizens that would have been unimaginable 20 years earlier. And during the pandemic, governments themselves were required to embark on virtualization on a major scale, as lockdowns and social distancing measures made many organizational processes impossible. Use of technologies that allowed 'working from home' and online interactions in every possible context was essential to continuing administrative operations, including paying benefits, conveying information, wielding authority and a whole raft of bureaucratic processes. After the pandemic, working from home practices are being re-evaluated, with requirements for staff to be in the office a minimum number of days per week. But there is no doubt that the pandemic period and the massive acceleration of platforms like MS Teams and Zoom have widened our ideas about what organizational forms are viable, and accelerated innovation in digital interaction.

Digital technology also raises important questions for the politics-of-instruments approach to the tools of government, although Linders and Peters (1998) did not discuss it. We would expect that this approach would concentrate on the use of digital technology by government, rather than by citizens—as it is here that policy-makers are presented with choices. On the face of it, technology seems to be a dramatic case of what they call 'instrumentalism'. Digital technology tends to be treated by, or presented to, governments as a panacea for many of the problems associated with traditional bureaucratic functioning—such as high cost, inflexibility, overload, difficulties in tracking down elusive lawbreakers—and thus to figure large in upbeat trade-off-free political visions of new ways to deliver public services and to 'do more for less', at least since the 1993 US National Performance Review presented information-age technology as a pathway to several kinds of bureaucratic salvation and even more since the rise in internet use and the advent of data-driven technologies such as machine learning and artificial intelligence.

However, interests may be equally important in driving this policy 'instrumentalism', and research has shown how the outsourcing of government's own information systems and digital technology has spawned large markets of global computer services providers (Systems Integrators) to government, in some countries (such as the UK) highly concentrated and oligopolistic (Margetts 1999; Dunleavy et al. 2006). Through the 2010s, these markets reshaped around the role played by the huge technology corporations of Silicon Valley (SV) through the provision of cloud services and the development of AI. So even while the influence of the Systems Integrators lingers on:

> ......with the current generation of data-driven technologies, governments will be directly exposed to buffeting winds of change driven by SV firms. Increasingly, policy, administrative, financial, and regulatory decisions—indeed, governments' capacity to govern—will depend in part on the capacity of administrative elites to understand and deploy these technologies and manage their political economy relationships with the technology industry. (Margetts and Dunleavy 2024)

The obvious historical parallel is with the way that nineteenth-century Europe saw many kinds of arms manufacture move from a domain dominated by state arsenals to one dominated by private arms companies, albeit closely linked with governments. If the nineteenth and early twentieth centuries saw the rise of the military–industrial complex, the late twentieth century saw the rise of an information–industrial complex with large corporate interests in treating digital-age technology as a universal solution looking for problems. Of course, the solution has often turned into the problem, as the endless roll call of government IT fiascos, troubled contract relationships and disappointed expectations shows (Margetts 1999; Hood and Margetts 2007; Dunleavy et al. 2006; Margetts and Dunleavy 2024). Such problems were epitomized in the Horizon IT scandal at the UK Post Office during the 1990s, caused in part by the Post Office's failure to manage its relationship with its contract provider, Fujitsu. In general, however, the politics-of-instruments cannot do much to distinguish different effects of digital era change on policy because it is so often presented in a politics-free way, making it attractive to all the possible variants of policy-makers.

Furthermore, any approach which conceptualizes tools as being internal to government, will be challenged when it comes to changes taking place in society at large, such as the widespread use of digital platforms, particularly social media. The rise of so-called general purpose AI in the form of Large Language Models (LLMs) poses an even greater challenge to a view of tools as internal. LLMs can be used to perform a wide variety of tasks, responding to simple queries or 'prompts' with realistic text or images, that can appear as if it was generated by humans. Although the first of these models (GPT3) was only released into society at the end of 2022, there was already evidence by the start of 2024 that large tranches of public sector personnel are using these models at work, in healthcare, education, social care and emergency services (Bright et al. 2024). With this trend will come a whole range of external influences on the information sources used by public sector workers, as well as for ordinary citizens in their interactions with government.

At the other end of the spectrum, generic 'institution-free' approaches to analyzing the tools of government—the classification of generic forms of action for the purpose of exploring alternatives and combinations—are the most well-suited to understanding digital era change in society, and the challenges it presents to government. For these approaches, the question posed by the digital age is how far and in what ways the new technology has changed each of the tools in the box. For this generic approach, at some level, the basic resources available to government do not change with changes in technology, so the repertoire of tools is unchanged. Carrots, sermons and sticks or nodality–authority–treasure–organization remain the fundamentals in a digital age as in any other. In that sense, digital technology doesn't bring fundamentally new instruments to government of the same order as nodality, authority, treasure and organization, any more than the railway age of the nineteenth century brought fundamentally new principles to the law (see Holmes 1920: 196).

However, digital technologies do make a difference to how policymakers can wield these tools. That is, such technologies may 'sharpen' the tools, making them easier to use or more effective when they are used, or blunt them, by making them more difficult to wield in a technologically savvy society. Indeed, the tools of government have really come of age as 'digital tools', rather than tools which make use of digital technologies. It is hard to imagine what 'non-digital' nodality would mean. Technologies are completely intertwined with every act of authority, every challenge to authority. In an increasingly 'cashless' society, most treasure exists only digitally and although that does not change its nature as a conditional or unconditional incentive, it does open new possibilities for how it may be used as a policy tool. And organizational capacity is moving ever nearer to being 'digital by default', particularly after the accelerated shift online necessitated by the 2020 pandemic. There are some generalized effects on all tools; Hood and Margetts (2007) observed a general 'narrowcasting' effect, whereby all four tools could be more easily targeted at groups of people, whereas blanket coverage or individualized interactions do not necessarily become easier. Targeted social media advertising is one such example, as used by many political parties and governments since the mid-2010s to gear their political messages at people with certain demographics, interests or affiliations. In the most advanced form, targeting narrows down to a personalization or individualization of treatment, as in moves towards personalized healthcare based on people's genetic identifiers (Dudley et al., 2014), or other personal characteristics. This personalization trend has speeded up with the advent of general purpose AI in the form of LLMs, which offer the possibility of LLM-based personalized virtual assistants or chatbots for a range of public sector tasks. Most governments are working on LLM-based chatbots offering personalized advice for interacting with government and within sectors, personalized chatbots are being offered for a whole range of support functions, from mental health counselling to personal educational tutors.

The most interesting implications, however, may come from examinations of the individual tools. For organizational capacity for example, it might be argued that there is in general a move away from the use of government's stock of people, buildings and equipment and towards a more informational (or nodal) approach, where web-based platforms can harness citizens in a form of isocratic administration (Margetts and Dunleavy 2013; Dunleavy and Margetts 2023), where they manage their own affairs in the same way that internet banking has allowed people to take over some responsibilities (and some of the administrative effort) from their bank, reducing the need for organizational capacity. The advent of mobile healthcare, whereby patients monitor chronic conditions in their own homes using wearable technologies such as smart watches, and communicate back to health professionals, may also reduce the need for organizational capacity (in terms of nurses measuring blood pressure and heart rate, for example). The pandemic period illustrated the possibilities for remote consultations in primary care using digital platforms such as Zoom and MS Teams, although public pressure for in-person contact with doctors seems to have inhibited continuing growth of the practice after the pandemic.

Conversely, the tool of authority can become more difficult to wield in a society where the internet, social media, mobile communications and LLMs are ubiquitous, allowing citizens to generate and share information and misinformation at scale. Governments can struggle to keep up with a tech savvy citizenry, particularly when citizenries rise up, riot, rebel or revolt, as in mass protests against the financial crisis and austerity from 2008 and the uprisings of the Arab Spring from 2011, and indeed in almost every country since then. And authoritarian states need to wield an increasingly sophisticated technological apparatus to censor, block or otherwise restrict citizens' use of the internet to maintain control or repressive regimes, as in China, Russia or Iran. In China, massive digital platforms like WeChat and Baidu offering social media and payment services are used also for surveillance of citizens, while western social media platforms like WhatsApp, X and Facebook are blocked. Research has shown that censoring efforts are focused on any conversation that might engender, reflect or lead to collective action, rather than discussion of controversial issues per se (King et al., 2013; Wright 2014). Similarly, in Iran, the regime have used internet shutdowns and blocking of communications platforms like WhatsApp (in 2024) to repress anti-government protests, especially since 2022, when the death of 22-year-old Mahsa Amini at the hands of the 'morality police' for violation of the country's hijab rules sparked a series of protests against the regime. The shutdowns pushed protestors to use state-run local networks (intranets), much more vulnerable to surveillance, just as the Chinese state uses WeChat and Baidu. As in China, the regime also uses facial recognition technology, initially in the pandemic to photograph and then find people who were not wearing masks properly, and later to do the same for women not wearing the hijab (Bushwick 2022).

It is nodality as a tool where government has most to gain—or lose— from the digital age. Widespread use of the internet, social media and AI-powered platforms such as ChatGPT across society and the economy can challenge government nodality. In the original articulation of the Hood's 1983 Tools approach, nodality was defined as something that government possesses 'by virtue of being government' (Hood 1983), but in the twenty-first century, nodality—being embedded in social and information networks—is bestowed on any user of the internet as a 'peer-to-peer' network, providing ordinary citizens with unprecedented capacity to receive, share and disseminate information across their own large-scale networks. This universalization of nodality is one of the most exciting characteristics of the domestication of the internet into everyday life, but governments can be slow to capitalize on the possibilities, and experience a net loss of nodality. To lose nodality is for government to cede power and even the very idea of what it means to be a state. Nowhere has the importance of nodality been demonstrated as well as in the crisis-hit years of 2020-2. One of the things that distinguish governments' ability to take their countries out of the public health crisis and forward to economic recovery was their nodal capacity to provide their citizens, firms and public agencies with timely information about the spread of the virus, about risk, danger and health services, and about constantly shifting guidance and legal constraints regarding social distancing, masks, opening and closing of businesses and so on (Margetts et al. 2021). And during the pandemic, competition for nodality became particularly acute. Social media platforms were used to generate and spread what the World Health Organization called an 'Infodemic' of misinformation and a 'tsunami' of hate speech during the crisis. Tackling these nebulous but sustained and serious threats, particularly now that the generation and dissemination of misinformation can be turbocharged and targeted with AI through so-called 'deepfake' images, video and audio, will require an 'army' of researchers with technological tools of the kind that government has not proved itself successful in building in the past.

The nodality of non-state actors can be a direct challenge to government. In the summer of 2024, the incoming Labour government in the UK faced anti-immigration protests riots across the country after false claims circulated regarding the perpetrator of a knife attack in which three children were killed. Far-right groups and social media personalities, using group chats on the messaging platform Telegram and more mainstream platforms such as X, played a major role in spreading misinformation (using slogans like 'save our kids') and inciting the violence, particularly the far-right activist Stephen Yaxley-Lennon ('Tommy Robinson'), even though he himself was in a Cyprus hotel, escaping a contempt of court order for similar crimes committed earlier. Government nodality is also challenged by the companies that operate social media platforms and thereby have huge nodality themselves in terms of shaping global social and informational networks. This challenge was illustrated well in 2024 by the owner of X (formerly Twitter) Elon Musk, who from the US unleashed an onslaught of verbal attacks on the new UK prime minister Sir Keir Starmer, hugely amplified across his own platform. He also gave a huge boost to Yaxley-Lennon's nodality when he reinstated his formerly banned Twitter account in 2023, as well as temporarily pinning the message 'Free Tommy Robinson' to the top of his own X-feed, with 211 million followers in January 2025.

The way that digital technologies, or rather society's relationship with these technologies, impact on each of the tools varies greatly according to context, so investigating the relationship between digital technologies and the tools is also useful at sectoral level. For example, as noted above organizational capacity may be reduced in healthcare, but may have to increase in other contexts, such as in the 'army' of cybersecurity experts required to deal with modern-day criminal activity and terrorist threats, especially in the age of AI. Some Silicon Valley figures, such as the former Google CEO Eric Schmidt, argue that national governments face huge security threats from non-state actors repurposing general purpose AI such as LLMs for their own ends, through biological warfare, for example (Morgan, 2024). Unlike other threats, such as nuclear warfare, these tools are easily accessible and cheap and their application is in no way limited to large states as is the case for nuclear weapons, for example, due to the scarcity of uranium. Likewise, nodality is easier to secure in some contexts—such as indeed, healthcare, where people are strongly incentivized to communicate directly and co-operate with healthcare organizations or to a benefits agency. In others, such as taxation or security, where keeping hold of nodality is vitally important, it can be more difficult. And both governments and citizens face threats to nodality from other quarters, for example where so-called 'phishing' sites trick citizens into paying for services that government are offering for free, such as a health insurance card, or an application for citizenship. Public figures with high nodality on social media don't necessarily threaten government nodality, but they can when they enter political life, as Yaxley Lennon and Musk have shown. Both these figures have also threatened the tools of authority, with disregard for legal institutions, and organizational capacity, through their capacity to incite physical action, mob violence and armies of trolls on digital platforms, all of which must then be tackled by government. They can be confronted—in 2024, for example, the Brazilian court banned the use of X in Brazil until Musk blocked accounts spreading misinformation. Musk eventually backed down, paying a fine of $5 million and banning profiles and re-opening X offices in Brazil that he had closed. But Brazil's 22 million users, making it one of the largest markets for the platform, probably had something to do with that.

So how useful are 'mixed' tools approaches at incorporating the effects of digital change? In the most complex and differentiated (Salamon 2002; Howlett 2011), it is less viable to consider changing patterns within the schema in any meaningful way although Howlett (2009b) does discuss 'e-communications' in his discussion of government communication as a policy tool, loosely based on the nodality concept. But John's (2011) schema has been developed to tackle the question directly, arguing that 'All tools are Informational now' (2013) and that the key to all interventions is the provision of information to change behaviour. John (2013) argues that 'there is a distinction between the provision of a tool of government, such as a new law or new tax, and how the citizen or organization receives information about it', and suggests that behavioural interventions based on experimental 'nudge' approaches made popular by the book of the same name (Thaler and Sunstein 2008) and developed in particular by the Behavioural Insights Team in the UK government are the best way to introduce and develop policies, taking some of the load from 'expenditure' of the other tools. In a way, this could be construed as a recognition of the importance of nodality (in Hood's terms) and an appreciation of choice architecture (missing from generic approaches, as noted above) as a tool, but in another sense it misses the concept of centrality and capability embodied in the term. After all, without nodality, and the capacity to disseminate information across populations, it is not possible to nudge. However, in the end, this mixed approach and the generic approach are not so very far apart. In the NATO schema, most policies are in practice a mix of the available tools, and the questions are of the emphasis placed on nodality within that mix, rather than completely replacing it with (say) authority, which is rarely viable. So the idea that all tools rely on government's ability to communicate them to citizens— and persuade them to comply—is commensurate with the argument that 'all tools are informational now', while explicit recognition of nodality's importance might enhance the potential for 'recalibrating the instruments of state' (John 2013).

Methodology: Researching the Tools of Government

How should we research the tools of government, and what methodologies might we use to measure their use? The work on instruments discussed above tends to be qualitative. Both the 'institution-led' and 'politics-of-instrument-of-choice' approaches are proposed largely through frameworks and typologies and evidenced descriptively. They do not lend themselves to meaningful measurement or comparison. Likewise, it is difficult to see how to measure a 'political sociology of policy instruments' approach, or the issues of legitimacy, politicization or depoliticization dynamics associated with different policy instruments.

For 'black-box' tools approaches, it is easier to ask methodological questions, as there is the possibility to measure the difference between tools in so far as they touch upon the world outside, in terms of policy inputs or outputs for example. For the Hood 'Tools' approach, the relative analytical simplicity of the NATO schema can be explored empirically and even quantitatively. The development of a methodology for doing so was not an endeavour upon which Christopher Hood himself was keen to embark, saying that he was 'reluctant to pack a suitcase for a journey he was not going to travel'. However, Hood and Margetts (2007) did consider what the suitcase might look like, in a chapter on 'Comparing the Tools of Government', which discussed how we might compare government's use of the tools with other organizations; how we might look at the use of the tools across different governments or different levels of government or agencies; and how we might examine the changing use of the tools over time. The chapter includes a discussion of measurability and how the 'huge, apparently exponential increase in quantitative data on government performance and activity' of the 2000s might be turned into 'effective measures of government's toolkit' (Hood and Margetts 2007: 139). After a number of Christopher's careful caveats, the chapter suggests that Treasure is probably the tool that is most easily turned into numbers, 'and has indeed been used as a way of comparing what government does over time or across countries or policy sectors', particularly for military spending (Pryor 1968). Authority and organization present greater challenges, because of less reported data but also the 'conceptual difficulties of measuring authority are severe', with the counting of number and length of laws as a highly questionable index of legislative use of authority. De Soto's and Diaz (2002) experimental method of comparing governmental use of authority across countries in which subjects do comparable things (such as set up a high street shop, replace a lost driving license and enter the country) probably remains the best hope of measuring authority. But even after a decade of data-driven methods for surveying and experimenting with the public, it remains the case, as Hood and Margetts (2007) observed, that 'the cost, effort and bureaucratic resistance involved in measuring authority that way are anything but trivial'. Likewise for organization, figures for government employment tend to be even more problematic than government spending data, with a huge range of variations in methodologies for calculating even seemingly simple metrics, such as number of police.

For one tool, nodality, the prospects for a methodology of measurement have improved significantly since the 2007 book. Even then, the 'comparison' chapter already pointed to two methodologies that might be used to measure nodality. First, an experimental method analogous to that of de Soto and Diaz (2002), where subjects were asked to 'search' for government information on the open web, allowed researchers to assess how well governments provided it (Escher et al. 2006). Second, the field of 'webmetrics' allowed the calculation of metrics for the network of linkages between websites, which was used to compare the relative nodality of audit offices in four countries (Petricek et al. 2006; Escher et al. 2006). Since that time, other scholars have packed a more complex suitcase for measuring nodality and travelled further down the road. Margetts and John (2024) make a case for 'rediscovering' nodality, and lay out a research agenda for measuring this tool qualitatively and quantitatively, at individual and system level. Hood (1983) suggested that nodality was something government possessed almost by virtue of being government, as a watchtower or watermill in societal information networks. In contrast, Margetts and John (2024) argue that in a digital world, many actors (including ordinary citizens themselves) have far greater possibility to accumulate nodality, challenging government's monopoly position, and in thinking about nodality, we need to focus on the whole constellation of actors and intermediaries in a policy system. Journalists play a crucial intermediary role by highlighting key policy issues and taking them out of narrow policy conversations and into the wider information ecosystem (including social networks). Political representatives act as a conduit to bring constituents' or electors' concerns to the attention of other policy actors such as governmental organizations, as well as feed policy developments back to their supporters. NGOs and other civil society organizations are important in highlighting the concerns of citizens and feeding them into policy conversations. There will also be actors out to mislead citizens or pollute the information environment with misinformation. A system-level analysis of nodality requires understanding how these intermediary actors shape the nodal relationships between governments and citizens in terms of detecting and effecting. Some of these ideas are explored quantitively in Castro-Gonzalez et al. (2024)

which breaks nodality down into two dimensions, active nodality of elite actors in policy conversation in social networks, and inherent nodality relating to an actor's institutional position (such as being a minister). They explore the relative nodality of elite actors (political representatives and journalists) in policy conversations on social media. These (highly quantitative) techniques might be developed in the future to compare the relative nodality of individual and institutional actors across governments and levels of government, and across the information ecosystem more generally.

CONCLUSIONS

The tools approach is an attractive way to understand policy-making, due to the way it seems to offer the potential of breaking down the complex concept of policy into constituent components and thereby provide a taxonomy for public policies. The attraction of the approach has long appealed to writers on public policy, and has received particular attention in the last three decades, with a number of variants on the basic tools concept. We have considered the various approaches here under two dimensions. First, we consider the extent to which they delve inside government and consider institutions as tools, or treat government as a black box and consider the various resources that government can use to act upon society at large. The second dimension is the extent to which they provide a parsimonious selection of tools or types of tool, with the attraction of simplicity, or whether they provide a 'thick' array of types and sub-types with the advantage of comprehensiveness.

Along the first dimension, Linder and Peters (1989) and Salamon (2002) consider respectively the different political choices made in terms of policy instruments and the alternative administrative possibilities for government as tools; while at the other end Elmore (1987), Hood (1983) and Hood and Margetts (2007) identify generic tools which may be implemented by any organizational form. A number of mixed approaches employ both generic tools and institutional forms (John 2011), or produce a 'taxonomy of taxonomies' that endeavour to capture the advantages of either end of the spectrum (Howlett 2005). The parsimonious approach is embodied in the Elmore approach and to some extent captured by Hood's Tools of Government, while by offering a much more extensive and subdivided taxonomy, the mixed approaches endeavour to make up for in terms of comprehensiveness what they lose in simplicity.

All tools-based approaches, along with other approaches that provide a taxonomy, face the challenge of what they may be used *for*. The approaches covered here are definitely well used. The generic tools approach conceived of by Hood (1983) and developed by Hood and Margetts (2007) has 1,254 citations in total, while Howlett's work on instruments probably reaches the same total when all the articles and books with the word instrument in the title are added together (Howlett 1991, 1993, 2000, 2004, 2005, 2009a, b, 2010). Salamon (2002) has over 1,700 citations, while Peters and Lindner's work on instruments probably reaches around 1,150 and John's (2011, 2013) more recent approach which has 220. So they are definitely being used by scholars of public policy, but to what extent may they be used for the task of policy evaluation, or at least for comparison over time, across countries, levels of government or at department or agency level, is less clear. In the end, to be able to really make these comparisons or evaluations with any kind of clarity, it is essential to have a clear way to lay out the tools in the box, in categories (such as screwdrivers, hammers, pliers and so on, where there is some rough difference between functionality and mechanism, albeit with some overlaps). It has been argued that by treating government as a 'black box' and focusing on how it interacts with society, a generic tools approach can provide this simple and elegant way to think about public policy. It does so, however, through a radical simplification of core concepts of public policy, ignoring the internal organization of government and by implication the entire field of public administration. But it does lend itself to an understanding of what works where, to comparison across countries and over time and in particular, to an understanding how policy-making is changing in the rapidly changing technological—and social—context of the digital era.

BIBLIOGRAPHY

Bengio, Y., Mindermann, S., Privitera, D., Besiroglu, T., Bommasani, R., Casper, S., Choi, Y., Fox, P., Garfinkel, B., Goldfarb, D., and Heidari, H. 2025. *International ai safety report*. arXiv preprint arXiv:2501.17805.

Bertelmans-Videc, M., R. Rist, and E. Vedung. 1998. *Carrots, sticks and sermons: policy instruments and their evaluation*. New Brunswick, NJ: Transaction.

Bright, J., F. Enock, S. Esnaashari, J. Francis, Y. Hashem, and D. Morgan. 2024. Generative AI is already widespread in the public sector: Evidence from a survey of UK public sector professionals. *Digital Government: Research and Practice.* https://dl.acm.org/doi/pdf/10.1145/3700140.

Bushwick, S. 2022. How Iran is using the protests to block more open internet access. *Scientific American,* October 13. https://www.scientificamerican.com/article/how-iran-is-using-the-protests-to-block-more-open-internet-access/.

Castro-Gonzalez, L., S. Chakraborty, H. Margetts, H. Rajpal, D. Guariso, and J. Bright. 2024. Who is driving the conversation? Analysing the nodality of British MPs and journalists on Twitter. arXiv preprint arXiv:2402.08765.

Dahl, R. A., and Lindblom, C. E. 1953. *Politics, economics, and Welfare.* New York: Harper.

De Soto, H., and H. P. Diaz. 2002. The mystery of capital. Why capitalism triumphs in the west and fails everywhere else. *Canadian Journal of Latin American & Caribbean Studies* 27 (53): 172.

Dudley, T., J. Listgarten, O. Stegle, S. E. Brenner, and L. Parts. 2014. Personalized medicine: From genotypes, molecular phenotypes and the quantified self, towards improved medicine. In *Pacific symposium on biocomputing*, vol. 20, 342–346.

Dunleavy, P., H. Margetts, S. Bastow, and J. Tinkler. 2006. *Digital era governance: IT corporations, the state, and e-government.* Oxford University Press.

Dunleavy, P., and H. Margetts. 2023. Data science, artificial intelligence and the third wave of digital era governance. *Public Policy and Administration.* https://journals.sagepub.com/doi/pdf/10.1177/09520767231198737.

Elmore, R. F. 1987. Instruments and strategy in public policy. *Review of Policy Research* 7 (1): 174–186.

Escher, T., H. Margetts, V. Petricek, and I. Cox. 2006. Governing from the centre? Comparing the nodality of digital governments. In *Annual meeting of the American political science association*, vol. 31.

Etzioni, A. 1961. A comparative analysis of complex organizations: On Power. *Involvement and their correlates.*

Foster, C. D. 1992. *Privatization, public ownership and the regulation of natural monopoly.* Oxford: Blackwell.

Holmes, O. W. 1920. The path in law. *Collected Papers*, pp. 167–202. London: Constable.

Hood, C. 1983. *The tools of government.* London: Macmillan.

Hood, C., and H. Margetts. 2007. *The tools of government in the digital age.* London: Palgrave Macmillan.

Howlett, M. 1991. Policy instruments, policy styles, and policy implementation. *Policy Studies Journal* 19 (2): 1–21.

Howlett, M. 2000. Managing the "hollow state": Procedural policy instruments and modern governance. *Canadian Public Administration* 43 (4): 412–431.

Howlett, M. 2004. Beyond good and evil in policy implementation: Instrument mixes, implementation styles, and second generation theories of policy instrument choice. *Policy and Society* 23 (2): 1–17.

Howlett, M. 2005. What is a policy instrument? Policy tools, policy mixes and policy implementation styles. In *Designing government: From instruments to governance*, ed. F. Eliadis, M. Hill, M. Howlett. Montreal: McGill Queens University Press.

Howlett, Michael. 2009a. Governance modes, policy regimes and operational plans: A multi-level nested model of policy instrument choice and policy design. *Policy Sciences* 42 (1): 73–89.

Howlett, M. 2009b. Government communication as a policy tool: A framework for analysis. *Canadian Political Science Review* 3 (2).

Howlett, M. 2011. *Designing public policies: Principles and instruments*. Abingdon: Routledge.

John, P. 2011. *Making policy work*. Taylor & Francis.

John, P. 2013. All tools are informational now: How information and persuasion define the tools of government. *Policy & Politics* 41 (4): 605–620.

King, G., J. Pan, and M. E. Roberts. 2013. How censorship in China allows government criticism but silences collective expression. *American Political Science Review* 107 (02): 326–343.

Lascoumes, P., and P. Le Gales. 2007. Introduction: Understanding public policy through its instruments—From the nature of instruments to the sociology of public policy instrumentation. *Governance* 20 (1): 1–21.

Lehdonvirta, Vili, and Edward Castronova. 2014. *Virtual economies: Design and analysis*. MIT Press.

Linder, S. H., and B. G. Peters. 1989. Instruments of government: Perceptions and contexts. *Journal of Public Policy* 9 (01): 35–58.

Linder, S. H., and B. G. Peters. 1998. The study of policy instruments: Four schools of thought. In *Public policy instruments. Evaluating the tools of public administration*, ed. B. G. Peters and F. K. M. Nispen. Cheltenham: Edward Elgar.

Margetts, H. 1999. *Information technology in government: Britain and America*. Routledge.

Margetts, H., and P. Dunleavy. 2013. The second wave of digital-era governance: A quasi-paradigm for government on the Web. *Philosophical Transactions of the Royal Society of London a: Mathematical, Physical and Engineering Sciences* 371 (1987): 20120382.

Margetts, H., and Dorobantu, C. 2019. Rethink government with AI. *Nature* 568 (7751), pp. 163–165.

Margetts, H., and Dorobantu, C. 2023. Computational social science for public policy. In *Handbook of computational social science for policy*, pp. 3–18. Cham: Springer International Publishing.

Margetts, H., and P. Dunleavy. 2024. The political economy of digital government: How Silicon Valley firms drove conversion to data science and artificial intelligence in public management. *Public Money & Management*: 1–11. https://www.tandfonline.com/doi/pdf/10.1080/09540962.2024.2389915.

Margetts, H., and P. John. 2024. How rediscovering nodality can improve democratic governance in a digital world. *Public Administration* 102 (3): 969–983. https://onlinelibrary.wiley.com/doi/pdfdirect/10.1111/padm.12960.

Margetts, H., John, P., Hale, S., and Yasseri, T. 2016. *Political turbulence: How social media shape collective action*. Princeton University Press.

Morgan, S. 2024. The double-edged sword: Opportunities and risks of AI in biosecurity, georgetown security studies review.

Osborne, D., and T. Gaebler. 1992. *Reinventing government: How the entrepreneurial spirit is transforming the public sector*. Reading, MA: Addison-Wesley.

Petricek, V., T. Escher, I. J. Cox, and H. Margetts. 2006. The web structure of e-government-developing a methodology for quantitative evaluation. *Proceedings of the 15th International Conference on World Wide Web*, 669–678.

Salamon, L. M., ed. 2002. *The tools of government: A guide to the new governance*. Oxford University Press.

Salamon, L. M., and M. S. Lund, eds. 1989. *Beyond privatization: The tools of government action*. The Urban Institute.

Schneider, A., and Ingram, H. 1990. Behavioral assumptions of policy tools. *The Journal of Politics* 52 (2): 510–529.

Smith, Adam. 1910. *The wealth of nations*, 2 vols. London: Dent (first pub.1776).

Thaler, M. and Sunstein, C. 2008. *Nudge*, pp. 1–304. Yale University Press.

Wright, Joss. 2014. Regional variation in Chinese internet filtering. *Information, Communication & Society* 17 (1): 121–141.

Bounded Rationality and Garbage Can/ Multiple Streams Models of Policy-Making

Nikolaos Zahariadis

> I have said almost all I think interests you. You should now choose what
> is most beneficial to the city and all of you.
> Demosthenes, *Third Olynthiac*, 36

Demosthenes' oration contains the main elements of the policy-making
process: deliberation, interests, framing, political conflict, and collective
goals. He anticipates by 2350 years the emergence of the policy sciences
and encapsulates many of the difficulties encountered in policy-making
when goals are not widely shared, attention is fleeting, choice is biased
by framing effects, and collective benefits differ from individual interests.
Under these conditions, the utility of synoptic rationality is limited.

In this chapter, I analyze the relationship between two alternatives
to synoptic rationality: bounded rationality and garbage can/multiple
streams models of policy-making. The term framework is used as identification of "a general list of variables that should be used to analyze
different types of phenomena of interest" (Ostrom et al. 2014, 270).

N. Zahariadis (✉)
Rhodes College, Memphis, TN, USA
e-mail: zahariadisn@rhodes.edu

Models make precise assumptions under certain conditions and observe a limited set of variables to specify relations between variables outlined in a framework. Therefore, a framework is understood here as a generalized family of models. Bounded rationality is an argument, not really a model, first articulated by Herbert Simon in his classic *Administrative Behavior* (1976). The garbage can model of organizational choice was first proposed by Cohen et al. (1972), Kingdon (1995) adapted it as a framework to policy-making. My aim is to briefly discuss the structure and functions of each separately, stress commonalities and differences, assess strengths and weaknesses, and highlight the contribution of these related frameworks to the study of public policy.

THE ARGUMENT IN BRIEF

Limitations on rational, optimizing behavior significantly complicate the aims of public policy. In his "policy orientation" Lasswell (1951, 8) articulates the main goal: to produce knowledge for a purpose, i.e., solve "the fundamental problems of man in society." Bounded rationality and garbage cans enrich this aim and add new twists.

- Bounded rationality stresses cognitive, computational, and organizational limitations in

    a. rational problem-solving and
    b. political quasi-resolution of conflict.

- Multiple streams/garbage cans offer additional aims:

    a. meaning and identity-creation and
    b. legitimation through participant and problem activation.

How do bounded rationality and multiple streams affect the policy orientation? They make three contributions. First, process affects content. How the process unfolds influences the policy outputs a system produces. If useful knowledge (intelligence) is the fundamental task, the gathering of intelligence clearly biases the intelligence of gathering. Second, there are practical limitations to human rationality which depend on individual capacities and organizational environments. Optimal solutions to "man's problems" are likely to prove utopian expectations. Third, greater ambiguity, political contestation, and time constraints in the policy process likely lead to more politicized, disjointed, truncated, and non-rational policy-making.

It is important to note, both frameworks of policy-making do not reject rational models of policy-making, but they seek to:

- Develop models that more closely match empirical observations of how policy is actually made.
- Explain decisions in situations that rational or other frameworks leave unexplained or simply assume away.
- Build on many similarities while simultaneously containing differences.

As originally formulated, the frameworks describe decision-making processes within organizations. The constructs have since been adapted to policy-making. While both bounded rationality and garbage cans/ multiple streams will be discussed, emphasis in this chapter will be placed on multiple streams to capture the differences of the approach from traditional models of policy-making.

BOUNDED RATIONALITY AND THE BIAS OF CHOICE

Two foundational works elaborate on the concept of bounded rationality: Simon's (1976) *Administrative Behavior* and March and Simon's (1958) *Organizations*. The fundamental premise is: human rationality is goal-intending and bounded or limited. Simon follows the methodological individualist tradition and makes three profound observations.

- Individuals have computational and cognitive limitations. Therefore, attention and search processes are neither costless nor complete.
- Individuals use satisficing rules of selection (i.e., good enough solutions relative to an aspiration level).
- Environmental cues, roles, and perceptions affect decision processes.

March and Simon add an organizational dimension to decision-making: parallel v. serial processing capabilities. Stressing the impact of the environment, they postulate bounded rationality within organizations.

- Organizations are social institutions which manage conflict.

- Action programs are developed to serve (sometimes) contested goals by semi-autonomous units.
- Organizations solve problems by factoring them into smaller pieces which are then distributed to different units.
- The level of conflict and the degree of hierarchy determine decision styles (analytical *v.* bargaining).

The logic of this argument has been adapted to policy-making, but it has also been subsumed by other policy frameworks. Bounded rationality currently does not exist as a distinct model as Simon originally formulated it, but as the fundamental logic or series of assumptions within other frameworks. For example, Allison's (1971) organizational and bureaucratic (to an extent) models, what he terms models II and III respectively, derive inspiration from March and Simon's work. The former model discusses the impact of an organization's standard operating procedures and the latter the role bureaucracy plays in perceiving threats and formulating preferences. Lindblom's (1959, 1963) disjointed incrementalism is stimulated by bounded rationality although it is more overtly political through the process of partisan mutual adjustment. Most rational choice, especially rational institutionalist, theorists today subscribe to the notion of bounded rationality: e.g., Williamson's (1985) and Epstein and O'Halloran's (1999) transaction cost theory, Scharpf's (1997) actor-centered institutionalism, and Ostrom et al. (2014) institutional analysis and development framework.

In sum, bounded rationality makes assumptions about individuals and the environment (Simon 1957) and essentially views policy-making as a problem of individual decisions and institutional aggregation. Computational and cognitive limitations substantially bias the search and selection processes while organizational cues and slack (excess supply of resources relative to demand) favor some solutions over others.

AMBIGUITY, GARBAGE CANS, AND MULTIPLE STREAMS

This framework derives inspiration from Cyert and March's (1963) *A Behavioral Theory of the Firm* and Cohen et al. (1972) garbage can model. The organizational variant follows the garbage can model while the policy variant fleshes out Kingdon's (1995) multiple streams approach (MSA). At the center is ambiguity; it "refers to a lack of clarity or consistency in reality, causality, or intentionality" (March 1994, 178). It clearly implies multiple and often irreconcilable ways of thinking, which often create confusion, ambivalence, and contradictions. Ambiguity complicates rationality even more than Simon did, but it also more closely approximates conditions in many public sector or educational organizations. Taking March and Simon's ideas as a starting point, it claims that not all organizational decisions will be made via boundedly rational processes; rather under certain conditions decision processes call for a fundamentally different interpretation. The garbage can/multiple streams approach is a systemic (not individual) level framework.

The main aspects of the organizational variation of the approach are:

- Four streams of variables flow in an organization: problems, solutions, participants, and choice opportunities.
- Decisions are made mainly by allocating attention through activating or overcoming temporal constraints and biases. Most decisions in garbage cans are not made by problem resolution but by flight (when problems leave the choice arena) or oversight (by action before the activation of problems) (Cohen et al. 1972). The process is generally sensitive to energy load (the resources needed to make a decision) and problem load (rise in the number of problems). In this way, the content of problems or solutions is as significant as—or even less than (March 1994, 218)—the process and timing of decisions.
- Loosely coupled parts of the organization develop separate tools and contain different repertories of action. Such repertories in the form of slack enable organizations to make decisions under stress without engaging in lengthy search and evaluation of alternatives (Cyert and March 1963).
- Organizations are viewed as political coalitions that engage in problemistic search and seek to avoid uncertainty (Cyert and March 1963). Information is used as both a signal of competence and a symbol of reaffirming social values (Feldman and March 1981, 177). In this way, information gathering is not only costly in the economic sense, but it also acquires powerful symbolic significance in the political sense.
- Organizational learning takes place in an environment of short attention spans with loose connections between actions and consequences (March and Olsen 1976b).

- Decision processes are organized, implemented, and legitimated through variable problem and participant activation (what Cohen, March, and Olsen call access and decision structures).

Adapting these ideas to the realm of policy-making, Kingdon (1995) argues agenda-setting and alternative specification are the result of the coupling or interplay of three factors—relatively independent streams of problems, policies, and politics—during open policy windows in either the problem or the politics streams. Zahariadis (2003, 2008b) later expands the argument to the entire policy-making process. Each stream has its own dynamic and constraints. The flow of problems is influenced by sudden changes in indicators, focusing events, feedback, and problem load (number and difficulty). Solutions bubble to the top of the policy stream depending on value acceptability, technical feasibility, and the degree of integration in sub-systemic policy networks. The receptivity of policy-makers in the political stream is a function of party ideology (Zahariadis 2003), the national mood, and political turnover. Figure 1 provides a schematic representation of the main elements of the multiple streams approach. The original garbage can simulation is curiously divorced from human agency, conceiving decision rules as a function of energy expended relative to total effective energy available to the organization (Bendor et al. 2001). In contrast, Kingdon emphasizes the role of policy entrepreneurs who use various strategies to couple the three streams in the policy-making process.

The approach explains all decisions in part—part of the time. Scope conditions (assumptions) are specified to more clearly circumscribe explanatory power: problematic preferences, unclear technology, and fluid participation. They are properties that measure ambiguity and apply to "organized anarchies," such as educational institutions (March and Olsen 1976a; Weick 1976), national governments (Kingdon 1995), international organizations (Zahariadis 2008a; Herweg 2017), bureaucracies and governance (Peters 2002; Olsen 2008), or situations (Rommetveit 1974). The approach specifies first- and second-order conditions:

- first-order scope conditions apply to the institutional environment, i.e., particular organizations and inter-organizational environments (Clarke 1989) tend to approximate these conditions;

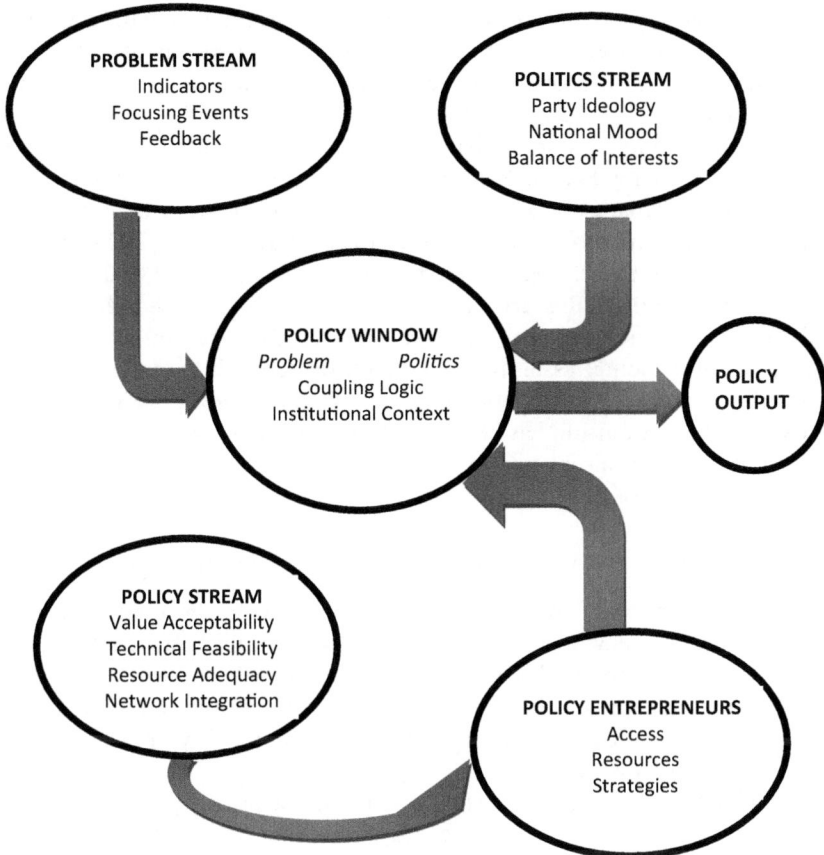

Fig. 1   Diagram of the multiple streams framework

- second-order scope conditions apply to situational environments, i.e., the issue itself approximates a garbage can—e.g., policy reform or administrative reorganization (Natali 2004; Olsen 1976, 1988).

There is overlap between the two sets of conditions in the sense that not all policies made by national governments approximate the stated conditions, but many decisions will likely not be easily explained by rational or even boundedly rational processes. Conversely, there will be some decision processes in more rational environments where greater clarity and consistency abound, such as local governments (Henstra 2010), business firms, or non-governmental organizations, that will tend to become garbage cans. Finally, there may be tightly coupled parts of a loosely coupled system that also produce or result in garbage can processes (Crecine 1986). Figure 2 presents the argument about scope conditions schematically. The empirical/theoretical literature (as opposed to computer simulations) is vast. One study, DeLeo et al. (2024, 2), has found that a simple Google Scholar search yields over 30,000 citations of Kingdon's book. Research has overwhelmingly explored the former (national governments) without paying systematic attention to carefully relaxing fundamental assumptions or shifting scope boundaries in order to build a more robust theory (but see Padgett 1980; Weiner 1976). Relatively little attention has been paid to the two latter scope possibilities.

Additional specifications are made to fully investigate the flow and linkages in the policy process.

1. The fundamental logic follows temporal sorting through:

   a. Emphasis on policy windows. They provide the context within which policy takes place. These are analytical constructs that help define a temporal beginning and end, a policy rhythm, and some sense of organizational boundaries. Time horizon and temporal rhythm affect conflict intensity and accountability in public policy (Zahariadis 2015a).

   b. Sequential selection processes. Unlike a priori specification and ordering of preferences, garbage can theorists emphasize preferences revealed through action.

   The implications of temporal sorting include:

   c. The order of alternative presentation biases selection.

   d. Attention focus is critical in specifying agendas and selecting among alternatives.

   e. Search strategies are mostly guided by heuristics and time pressure.

2. Decision rules are defined mainly by political processes [bargaining, persuasion, coercion via institutionalized hierarchy (Cyert and March 1963), or manipulation of frames, symbols, salami tactics, and emotion (Herweg et al. 2023)].

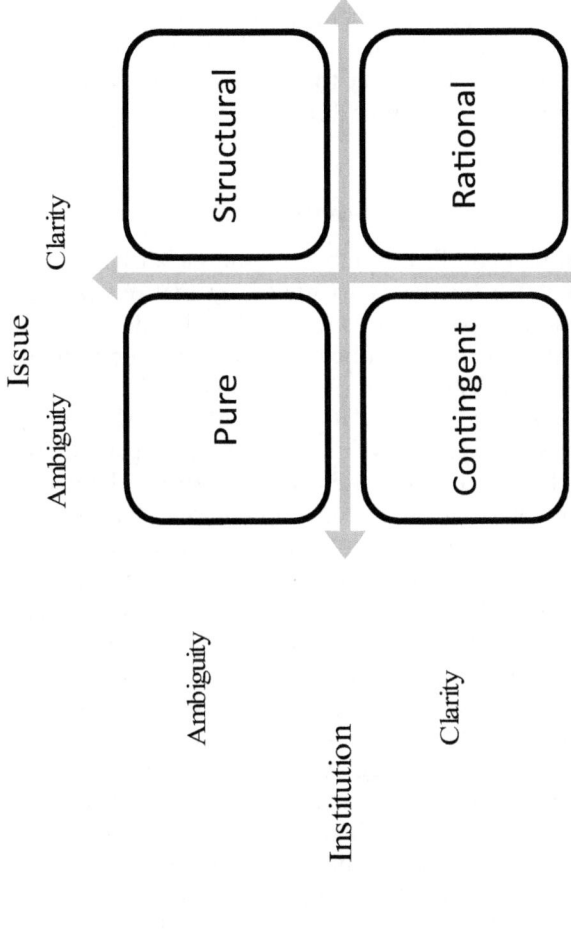

Fig. 2 Types of garbage cans by issue and institution

3. Participant activation affects search and selection. The fact that participants move in and out of choice arenas due to expertise, position, and alternative demands on their time results in shifting attention and temporally biased outcomes (March and Romelaer 1976).

4. Policy entrepreneurs use a repertory of specific strategies to couple the streams. Indeed, entrepreneurs have spawned a literature in their own right (e.g., Petridou and Mintrom 2021) and have added an important dimension of agency to the framework. Policy-makers and policy entrepreneurs are often different actors (Kingdon 1995).

Methodology

The MSA is methodologically adaptable to multiple analytical techniques. Although most scholarship tends to utilize qualitative case studies for empirical verification purposes, there is literature that derives implications through computer simulations (Cohen et al. 1972; Fioretti 2024; March and Weissinger-Baylon 1986; Lomi and Harrison 2012; Zahariadis 2003) and statistical analysis (Travis and Zahariadis 2003; Fowler 2019).

Since Kingdon's seminal study in 1984, the emergent literature has followed mainly the qualitative case study approach. Utilizing mostly interviews, documentary analysis, and ethnographic narratives, analysts have sought to explain shift in the policy agenda or policy change although a few have also examined implementation (Herweg et al. 2023). The results have yielded mixed success because some studies are not as rigorous or theoretically informed as they should be in order to build on the framework and move the literature forward (Zohlnhöfer et al. 2022). For example, concepts such as policy windows, as not well measured in the literature because they appear simply as events that policy-makers somehow know are important triggers for change. Yet, Kingdon reminds us that perceptions matter. Herweg et al. (2015) similarly argue that conditions that put a policy-maker's re-election at risk are more likely to gain attention. To capture this condition empirically as a policy window, researchers must make a plausible argument that policy-makers believed their re-election chances were threatened by nonaction. Such a determination requires probing interview questions. For example, Dolan (2021, 177) demonstrates that the serious threat of being ousted triggered

Prime Minister Howard to believe that lack of response to the Australian Millennium Draught would endanger his re-election.

Choosing an appropriate analytical technique depends mainly on the nature of the research question and, of course, the availability of data. Small-N studies are better served qualitatively while large-N research may need to employ statistical methods. Some scholars using the MSA employ multi-methods (e.g., Fowler 2019), but most use qualitative studies while some veer toward quantitative analysis. Those using case study designs and qualitative methods rely mainly on interviews and document analysis but on occasion fail to incorporate variance in the dependent variable (for a discussion, see Töller 2023) or neglect to interview enough or the "right" interviewees (for a discussion, see DeLeo et al. 2024, Chapter 4).

On the quantitative side of methodology, the MSA raises concerns with information demands and the number of terms in the guiding equation. For example, coupling necessitates the use of inclusion of both additive and multiplicative terms. With five core elements, a complete MSA test becomes somewhat unwieldy with results that are difficult to interpret. Engler and Herweg (2019) suggest overcoming this drawback by either condensing the streams' readiness for coupling into one variable or by testing partial couplings only. For example, DeLeo and Duarte (2022) use regression analysis to explore the dynamics of the problem stream and conduct a qualitative case study of the other streams and coupling activities. Others use qualitative comparative analysis (e.g., Sager et al. 2019) to explore combinations of determinants which make it particularly likely that Swiss cantons opt for complementary healthcare policy activity.

Benefits of the Framework

The MSA provides many benefits as a framework to analyze the policy process. First, it decouples and often reverses the rational problem–solution sequence, explaining the possibility and specifying the conditions under which policies are in search of a rationale. As Wildavsky (1987, 3) explains, "the solution is part of defining the problem...In policy analysis, the most creative calculations concern finding problems for which solutions might be attempted."

Second, it synthesizes agency and structure but avoids biases of aggregation in collective action. Assumptions are made about organizational or collective choices and processes, not individual decisions. In so doing, the approach subscribes to the proposition advanced by Simon (1981,

221) that in nearly decomposable systems detailed explanations or theories of lower level units are not needed to explain higher level phenomena (Bromiley 1986, 121–122).

Third, ambiguity is an enabler of policy-making. It explains both policy change (through successful coupling) and policy inertia (through unsuccessful coupling).

Fourth, the framework travels well to local (e.g., Henstra 2010; Liu et al. 2010), national—such as US, Germany, France, UK, Norway, Greece, Sweden, and Burkina Faso (e.g., Zahariadis 2003; Pierre and Peters 2005; Ridde 2009; Guldbrandsson and Fossum 2009; March and Olsen 1976a)—and supranational (e.g., Ackrill and Kay 2011; Richardson 2006; Lipson 2007) levels.

Fifth, the framework also travels well across policy sectors—defense policy (e.g., March and Weissinger-Baylon 1986); foreign policy (e.g., Travis and Zahariadis 2002; Durant and Diehl 1989; Zahariadis 2005; Mazzar 2007); global policy (e.g., McCann 2012); transport policy (e.g., Chen 2011; Khayesi and Amekudzi 2011); environmental policy (e.g., Brunner 2008); education policy (e.g., McLendon 2003; Protopsaltis 2008; Corbett 2005); health policy (e.g., Blankenau 2001; Guldbrandsson and Fossum 2009; Oborn et al. 2011); trade and welfare policies (e.g., Ackrill and Kay 2011; Natali 2004); security and crisis management (e.g., Birkland 1997, 2004).

Sixth, it pays close attention to meaning-making, rituals, myths, interpretation, and symbolism (March 1994). Choices don't only have instrumental dimensions in the sense of attempts to address actual or perceived problems but also symbolic dimensions in the meaning-making or identity-creation sense. March (1991, 110) boldly makes this point: "it is hard to imagine a society with modern ideology that would not exhibit a well-elaborated and reinforced myth of choice, both to sustain social orderliness and meaning and to facilitate change." Policy entrepreneurs use symbols and other coupling strategies to create meaning and bias selection toward pet projects (Zahariadis 2003). In this way, meaning-making becomes a symbolic endeavor of policy-maker competence and outcome legitimacy. Such governmental cues are then transmitted to elites and mass publics to create, reinforce, support, oppose, or change shared meanings and beliefs about political efficacy and effectiveness (Edelman 1971).

Issues and Prospects

Nevertheless, there are still unanswered questions that need further treatment. In this section, I discuss some of these issues and sketch a brief research agenda.

First, are the streams really independent? While Robinson and Eller (2010), Mucciaroni (1992), and Bendor et al. (2001) claim that's an empirical misspecification because problems and solutions tend to track each other, their contention is off the mark. Stream independence is an analytical assumption that is not subject to empirical verification. Solutions or problems have the potential to attach themselves to a wide range of different choices. "The liberating effect of this assumption is to provide a place in the theory for frequently observed phenomena such as 'accidents of timing.' It also includes the apparently erroneous process in which a solution is chosen that seems not to solve the original problem" (Cohen 1986, 63). One may think of streams existing *as if* they are independent.

Second, how is the dependent variable specified? Is the approach better at explaining major policy changes, as some authors contend (e.g., Hayes 2006), or can it explain small incremental steps with equal precision? If the latter, what role do policy windows play in bringing about small or no changes?

Third, while much is made of policy entrepreneurship, the approach lacks an integrated theory of entrepreneurship and more specifically a repertoire of successful and unsuccessful strategies of coupling. Petridou and Mintrom (2021), Mintrom and Norman (2009), and Brouwer and Biermann (2011) offer some possible avenues, but their suggestions have yet to be integrated into the approach. Does the approach change if one strategy is involved rather than another? If so, in what ways does it change?

Fourth, can policy windows be modeled in ways that elevate their impact beyond that of *deus ex machina*? Multiple streams argues policy change occurs during open windows. But recognition of open windows is often little more than post hoc rationalization. Kingdon (1995, 166) defines windows as "opportunities for action on given initiatives," arguing they exist as much in the minds of participants as they do in objective reality, i.e., change in administration (177). Because their existence is contested—some analysts may think a window is open and others will not—can policy change occur in the absence of a window, and if so, how will we know? For example, Howlett (1998) finds evidence of predictable or routine windows in media mentions and parliamentary debates and committees, but he finds no evidence of random or unpredictable windows. If some of these windows are a function of perceptions, could evidence simply be a matter of articulating perceptions (or not) rather than a signal of objective features? Greater specification is clearly needed to make this concept far more analytically tractable and easier to measure.

Moreover, what happens when windows are endogenized, i.e., when they are opened by entrepreneurs? Crecine (1986, 116) offers the intriguing possibility of bureaucrats creating opportunities, such as dramatizing deficiencies of weapons systems in order to create demand for specific technologies or establishing task forces or commissions, as a way of linking particular problems to specific solutions. Leaders of government in many countries are given the constitutional mandate to dissolve parliament at will, i.e., open (or close) policy windows. Some have used this mandate with great skill and expediency, e.g., Margaret Thatcher in 1983, and others have not, e.g., Jacques Chirac in 1997. Do coupling strategies change in these situations? Furthermore, how does the process change when more than one window open at the same time? Is there a hierarchy of windows, and if so, what are the implications for coupling? To complicate matters even more, do policy windows affect partial couplings, as Dolan (2021) claims? And if so, how?

Fifth, what is the role of institutions? Some analysts contend the processes are essentially random without much structure or without being placed within familiar institutional terrain (Mucciaroni 1992; Schlager 2007). Kingdon (1995, 229–230) contends institutional constraints exist but in unconventional form. More to the point he claims fluidity should not be confused with randomness: "[the model] is structured in the same way that a river is fluid, but its banks usually restrict its movement. The process cannot flow just anywhere" (Kingdon 1995, 223). This criticism is highly unusual because the original garbage can model explicitly specifies hierarchical and specialized access and decision forms as examples of structure (Cohen et al. 1972). Can the original insights of institutional structure be more clearly integrated into multiple streams?

Sixth, what role does feedback play in biasing attention or search? While Kingdon (1995) discusses feedback as part of problem definition, the process surely affects the policy and politics streams as well. Feedback from past failures helps spark the search for new solutions that might overcome previous shortcomings. Moreover, feedback lag clearly affects the receptivity of policy-makers and the broader public to new ideas. The original garbage can model envisioned a process of organizational learning through feedback channels. Multiple streams has yet to systematically integrate this idea to the policy process.

Seventh, what role do emotion and cognition play in enabling coupling? Zahariadis (2003, 2005, 2015b) specifies some hypotheses using from prospect and affect priming theories. Because people hate losing more than they like winning, prospect theory predicts they will make riskier decisions to recoup losses. In terms of multiple streams, the implication is that if solutions espoused by entrepreneurs are large deviations from the status quo, successful coupling is more likely when problems are framed as losses. Affect congruence theory suggests people process mostly information that agrees with their mood. By implication concessions in policy arguments are more likely under a positive national mood. Zahariadis empirically tests these hypotheses in the cases of Greek and U.S. foreign policies, but much more work needs to be done to replicate verification.

Eighth, the MSA involves more than just agenda-setting or policy formulation. It also calls for the study of implementation under ambiguity (Ridde 2009; Baier et al. 1986; Taylor et al. 2021). Zahariadis (2008b) develops such a research program linking implementation to Europeanization. Fowler (2023) elaborates on how such an implementation framework applies to and affects a democratic setting. Such theoretical and more importantly empirical work has barely started.

Finally, although the MSA paints an unusual, almost capricious picture of policy-making, it barely mentions problems of political power. Some analysts (Peters 2002; Zahariadis 2008a) contend political power actually plays a major role in favoring some policy entrepreneurs and policy-makers over others. As Peters (2002, 14) boldly claims: "The most fundamental paradox is that a system of governance that is assumed to be ... open, inclusive, and indeterminate may be more determined by power than are more structured systems." What role do democratic legitimation and participation play in such a system? Cohen et al. (1972) discuss some implications of what they call an open decision structure (where all participants get to deliberate during all choice opportunities in the can). Can these implications be adapted to the policy-making process through accountability or representation loops? If so, do they enhance or inhibit democratic processes?

One possible way to address the issue of democracy is to differentiate between symbols and content. Decisions in garbage cans, particularly those which involve administrative reorganization, contain both instrumental elements and symbolic value. Democratic legitimacy is gained through rhetoric, such as improving efficiency or effectiveness, even though there are few attempts to empirically assess the effects of reorganization. Quite often major changes, as March and Olsen (1983, 290) boldly assert, symbolize "the possibility of effective leadership; confessions of impotence are not acceptable." In other words, decisions in garbage cans affirm legitimate values and institutions regardless of the actual content or (re)distribution of political or economic power. Democracy is exercised by celebrating intent and the efficacy of collection action.

Another way to address complications with accountability is to apply the MSA to non-democratic states. For example, Herweg et al. (2022) adapt the MSA to non-democratic regimes and derive testable hypotheses. Van den Dool (2023) further probes the applicability and the need for adaptation in the Chinese context. Once there is a sizable literature, then comparisons can be made between the two types of systems and lessons drawn.

Conclusion

Policy-making is often a complicated process involving hundreds of actors and/or institutions, each bringing its own competences, values, resources, and understanding of the process. To make it comprehensible, scholars and policy-makers analytically simplify the process in order to gain greater tractability comprehending the outcome. Such simplifications come at a cost because they reflect the resources and biases of the simplifiers. Simon (1976) began his extensive work on bounded rationality driven by a desire to explain why decision-making did not always follow rational conventional wisdom. Rationality has a normative privileged position because "we want to be rational" (Elster 1989, 28). Following the rational model at the policy level ensures procedural fairness and optimizes outcome effectiveness. All options are considered, thereby ensuring dissenting voices will be heard, and policies are selected on the basis of yielding the most benefits. The model is tempting, but Simon observed it is also unrealistic. His main contribution is to supplement (not supplant) rational decision-making in organizations (he initially had public sector organizations in mind) by bringing them closer to what analysts and participants actually observe. Doing so enhances the empirical validity of models of policy-making but also complicates them substantially by increasing the amount of information needed to explain or predict phenomena.

The person who "gave birth" to both organizational bounded rationality and garbage cans is not Simon but March. Strongly influenced by Simon, March shifted foundational assumptions and amended theories of organizational choice to areas that are still considered to be pathological deviations. Organizational (and policy) goals are frequently opaque and contentious yet policies are still made, utilizing processes that are not well understood by transient participants. He questioned the pre-existence of purpose, the primacy of rationality, and the necessity of consistency, and instead introduced the goal of developing the organizational technology of foolishness (March 1976). Under ambiguity, a choice process, he contended, does more than provide a basis for action. "It provides an occasion for defining virtue and truth, for discovering or interpreting what is happening...for distributing glory and blame for what has happened... It is an occasion for socialization" (March 1994, 218). These ideas have found their way into the broader endeavor of the policy sciences (to be sure in bits and pieces), enriching models and enhancing the aims of the policy process.

To return to Lasswell's policy orientation, bounded rationality and garbage cans/multiple streams question synoptic rationality but do not reject rational behavior. They simply specify alternative models under specific conditions that more closely approximate what analysts observe in the policy process. They remain fundamentally embedded within a broader information processing and interpreting view, indicating limitations and explaining deviations and pathologies. En route, they point *a* (not *the*) way toward solving "the fundamental problems of man in society" but caution the road involves many detours and dead-end alleys toward multiple destinations some of which we may never reach.

REFERENCES

Ackrill, R., and A. Kay. 2011. Multiple streams in EU policy-making: The case of the 2005 sugar reform. *Journal of European Public Policy* 18 (1): 72–89.

Allison, G.K. 1971. *Essence of decision*. Boston: Little, Brown & Company.

Baier, V.E., J.G. March, and H. Saetren. 1986. Implementation and ambiguity. *Scandinavian Journal of Management Studies* 2 (3–4): 197–212.

Bendor, J., T.M. Moe, and K.W. Shotts. 2001. Recycling the garbage can: An assessment of the research program. *American Political Science Review* 95 (1): 169–190.

Birkland, T.A. 1997. *After disaster: Agenda setting, public policy and focusing events*. Washington, D.C.: Georgetown University Press.

Birkland, T.A. 2004. The world changed today: Agenda-setting and policy change in the wake of the September 11 terrorist attacks. *Review of Policy Research* 21: 179–200.

Blankenau, J. 2001. The fate of national health insurance in Canada and the United States: A multiple streams explanation. *Policy Studies Journal* 29 (1): 38–55.

Bromiley, P. 1986. Planning systems in large organizations: A garbage can approach with application to defense PPBS. In *Ambiguity and command*, ed. J.G. March and R. Weissinger-Baylon. Marshfield, MA: Pitman.

Brouwer, S., and F. Biermann. 2011. Towards adaptive management: Examining the strategies of policy entrepreneurs in Dutch water management. *Ecology and Society* 16 (4): 5. https://doi.org/10.5751/ES-04315-160405.

Brunner, S. 2008. Understanding policy change: Multiple streams and emissions trading in Germany. *Global Environmental Change* 18: 501–507.

Chen, Z. 2011. Is the policy window open for high-speed rail in the United States? A perspective from the multiple streams model of policymaking. *Transportation Law Journal* 38 (2): 115–144.

Clarke, L. 1989. *Acceptable risk? Making decisions in a toxic environment*. Berkeley and Los Angeles: University of California Press.

Cohen, M.D. 1986. Artificial intelligence and the dynamic performance of organizational designs. In *Ambiguity and command*, ed. J.G. March and R. Weissinger-Baylon. Marshfield, MA: Pitman.

Cohen, M.D., J.G. March, and J.P. Olsen. 1972. A garbage can model of organizational choice. *Administrative Science Quarterly* 17: 1–25.

Corbett, A. 2005. *Universities and the Europe of Knowledge: Ideas, institutions and policy entrepreneurship in European Union higher education policy, 1955–2005*. New York: Palgrave Macmillan.

Crecine, J.P. 1986. Defense resource allocation: Garbage can analysis of C3 procurement. In *Ambiguity and command*, ed. J.G. March and R. Weissinger-Baylon. Marshfield, MA: Pitman.

Cyert, R.M., and J.G. March. 1963. *A behavioral theory of the firm*. Englewood Cliffs, NJ: Prentice Hall.

DeLeo, R., and A. Duarte. 2022. Does data drive policymaking? A Multiple Streams perspective on the relationship between indicators and agenda setting. *Policy Studies Journal* 50 (3): 701–724.

DeLeo, R., R. Zohlnhöffer, and N. Zahariadis. 2024. *Multiple streams and policy ambiguity*. Cambridge University Press.

Dolan, D.A. 2021. Multiple partial couplings in the multiple streams framework: The case of extreme weather and climate change adaptation. *Policy Studies Journal* 49 (1): 164–189.

Durant, R.F., and P.F. Diehl. 1989. Agendas, alternatives, and public policy: Lessons from the US policy arena. *Journal of Public Policy* 9 (2): 179–205.

Edelman, M. 1971. *Politics as symbolic action.* Chicago: Markham.

Elster, J. 1989. *Solomonic judgements.* Cambridge: Cambridge University Press.

Engler, F., and N. Herweg. 2019. Of barriers to entry for medium- and large-n multiple streams applications: Methodologic and conceptual considerations. *Policy Studies Journal* 47 (4): 905–926.

Epstein, D., and S. O'Halloran. 1999. *Delegating powers: A transaction cost politics approach to policy making under separate powers.* New York: Cambridge University Press.

Feldman, M., and J.G. March. 1981. Information in organizations as signal and symbol. *Administrative Science Quarterly* 26 (2): 171–186.

Fioretti, G. 2024. Emergence and evolution of organizations out of garbage can dynamics: A few insights for the theory of the firm, entrepreneurship, and industrial economics. *Industrial and Corporate Change* 33 (4): 808–830.

Fowler, L. 2019. Problems, politics, and policy streams in policy implementation. *Governance* 32 (3): 403–420.

Fowler, L. 2023. *Democratic policy implementation in an ambiguous world.* Albany, NY: State University of New York Press.

Guldbrandsson, K., and B. Fossum. 2009. An exploration of the theoretical concepts policy windows and policy entrepreneurs at the Swedish public health arena. *Health Promotion International* 24 (4): 434–444.

Hayes, M.T. 2006. *Incrementalism and public policy.* Lanham, MD: University Press of America.

Henstra, D. 2010. Explaining local policy choices: A multiple streams analysis of municipal emergency management. *Canadian Public Administration* 53 (2): 241–258.

Herweg, N. 2017. *European Union policy-making: The regulatory shift in natural gas market policy.* New York: Palgrave.

Herweg, N., C. Huß, and R. Zohlnhöfer. 2015. Straightening the three streams: Theorizing extensions of the Multiple Streams Framework. *European Journal of Political Research* 54 (3): 435–449.

Herweg, N., N. Zahariadis, and R. Zohlnhöfer. 2022. Travelling far and wide? Applying the multiple streams framework to policy-making in autocracies. *German Political Science Quarterly* 63: 203–223.

Herweg, N., N. Zahariadis, and R. Zohlnhöfer. 2023. The Multiple Streams Framework: Foundations, refinements, and empirical applications. In *Theories of the policy process*, ed. C.M. Weible, 5th ed. New York: Routledge.

Howlett, M. 1998. Predictable and unpredictable policy windows: Institutional and exogenous correlates of Canadian federal agenda-setting. *Canadian Journal of Political Science* 31 (3): 495–524.

Kingdon, J. 1995. *Agendas, alternatives, and public policies*, 2nd ed. New York: Harper Collins.

Khayesi, M., and A.A. Amekudzi. 2011. Kingdon's multiple streams model and automobile dependence reversal path: The case of Curitiba, Brazil. *Journal of Transport Geography* 19 (6): 1547–1552.

Lasswell, H.D. 1951. The policy orientation. In *The policy sciences*, ed. D. Lerner and H. Lasswell. Stanford: Stanford University Press.

Lindblom, C.E. 1959. The science of muddling through. *Public Administration Review* 19: 79–88.

Lindblom, C.E. 1963. *The intelligence of democracy: Decision making through mutual adjustment*. New York: Free Press.

Lipson, M. 2007. A garbage can model of UN peacekeeping. *Global Governance* 1: 79–97.

Liu, X., E. Lindquist, A. Vedlitz, and K. Vincent. 2010. Understanding local policy making: Policy elites' perceptions of local agenda setting and alternative policy selection. *Policy Studies Journal* 38 (1): 69–91.

Lomi, A. and J.R. Harrison, eds. 2012. *The garbage can model of organizational choice: Looking forward at forty*. Bingley, UK: Emerald Group.

March, J.G. 1976. The technology of foolishness. In *Ambiguity and choice in Organizations*, ed. J.G. March and J.P. Olsen. Oslo: Universitetsforlaget.

March, J.G. 1991. How decisions happen in organizations. *Human-Computer Interaction* 6: 95–117.

March, J.G. 1994. *A primer on decision making*. New York: Free Press.

March, J.G., and H.A. Simon. 1958. *Organizations*. New York: John Wiley & Sons.

March, J.G., and J.P. Olsen. 1976a. *Ambiguity and choice in organizations*. Oslo: Universitetsforlaget.

March, J.G., and J.P. Olsen. 1976b. Organizational learning and the ambiguity of the past. In *Ambiguity and choice in organizations*, ed. J.G. March and J.P. Olsen. Oslo: Universitetsforlaget.

March, J.G. and P.J. Romelaer. 1976. Position and presence in the drift of decisions. In *Ambiguity and choice in organizations*, ed. J.G. March and J.P. Olsen. Oslo: Universitetsforlaget.

March, J.G., and J.P. Olsen. 1983. Organizing political life: What administrative reorganization tells us about government. *American Political Science Review* 77 (2): 281–296.

March, J.G., and R. Weissinger-Baylon, eds. 1986. *Ambiguity and command*. Marshfield, MA: Pitman.

Mazzar, M.J. 2007. The Iraq war and agenda setting. *Foreign Policy Analysis* 3 (1): 1–24.

McCann, L.M. 2012. Peacebuilding as global policy: Multiple streams and global policy discourse in the creation of the United Nations Peacebuilding Commission. Doctoral Dissertation, University of Colorado at Denver.

McLendon, M.K. 2003. Setting the governmental agenda for state decentralization of higher education. *The Journal of Higher Education* 74 (5): 479–515.

Mintrom, M., and P. Norman. 2009. Policy entrepreneurship and policy change. *Policy Studies Journal* 37 (4): 649–667.

Mucciaroni, G. 1992. The garbage can model and the study of policy making: A critique. *Polity* 24: 459–482.

Natali, D. 2004. Europeanization, policy arenas, and creative opportunism: The politics of welfare state reforms in Italy. *Journal of European Public Policy* 11 (6): 1077–1095.

Oborn, E., M. Barrett, and M. Exworthy. 2011. Policy entrepreneurship in the development of public sector strategy: The case of London health reform. *Public Administration* 89 (2): 325–344.

Olsen, J.P. 1976. Reorganization as a garbage can. In *Ambiguity and choice in organizations*, ed. J.G. March and J.P. Olsen. Oslo: Universitetsforlaget.

Olsen, J.P. 1988. Administrative reform and theories of organization. In *Organizing governance, governing organizations*, ed. C. Campbell and B.G. Peters. Pittsburgh: University of Pittsburgh Press.

Olsen, J.P. 2008. The ups and downs of bureaucratic organization. *Annual Review of Political Science* 11: 13–37.

Ostrom, E., M. Cox, and E. Schlager. 2014. An assessment of the institutional analysis and development framework and introduction of the social-ecological systems framework. In *Theories of the policy process*, ed. P.A. Sabatier and C.M. Weible, 3rd ed. Boulder, CO: Westview.

Padgett, J.F. 1980. Managing garbage can hierarchies. *Administrative Science Quarterly* 25: 583–604.

Peters, B.G. 2002. *Governance: A garbage can perspective*. Political Science Series #84. Vienna: Institute for Advanced Studies.

Petridou, E., and M. Mintrom. 2021. A research agenda for the study of policy entrepreneurs. *Policy Studies Journal* 49 (4): 943–967.

Pierre, Jon, and B. Guy Peters. 2005. *Governing complex societies*. New York: Palgrave Macmillan.

Protopsaltis, S. 2008. Theories of the policy process and higher education reform in Colorado: The shaping of the first state postsecondary education voucher system. Doctoral Dissertation, University of Colorado at Denver.

Richardson, J. 2006. Policy-making in the EU: Interests, ideas and garbage cans of primeval soup. In *European Union: Power and policy-making*, ed. Jeremy Richardson, 3rd ed. New York: Routledge.

Ridde, V. 2009. Policy implementation in an African state: An extension of Kingdon's multiple streams approach. *Public Administration* 87 (4): 938–954.

Robinson, S.E., and W.S. Eller. 2010. Participation in policy streams: Testing the separation of problems and solutions in subnational policy systems. *Policy Studies Journal* 38 (2): 199–216.

Rommetveit, K. 1974. Decision-making under a changing normative structure— The case of the location of Norway's third medical school. *Acta Sociologica* 17 (3): 256–272.

Sager, F., C. Rüefli, and E. Thomann. 2019. Fixing federal faults: Complementary member state policies in Swiss health care policy. *International Review of Public Policy* 1 (2): 147–172.

Scharpf, F.W. 1997. *Games real actors play: Actor-centered institutionalism in policy research*. Boulder, CO: Westview.

Schlager, E. 2007. A comparison of frameworks, theories, and models of policy processes. In *Theories of the policy process*, ed. Paul A. Sabatier, 2nd ed. Boulder, CO: Westview.

Simon, H.A. 1957. *Models of man*. New York: John Wiley & Sons.

Simon, H.A. 1976. *Administrative behavior*, 3rd ed. New York: Free Press.

Simon, H.A. 1981. *The sciences of the artificial*, 2nd ed. Cambridge, MA: The MIT Press.

Taylor, K., S. Zarb, and N. Jeschke. 2021. Ambiguity, uncertainty, and implementation. *International Review of Public Policy* 3 (1). https://doi.org/10.4000/irpp.1638.

Töller, A.E. 2023. The challenge of applying the Multiple Streams Framework to non-decisions and negative decisions. In *A modern guide to the multiple streams framework*, ed. N. Zahariadis, N. Herweg, R. Zohlnhöfer and E. Petridou. Cheltenham: Edward Elgar.

Travis, R., and N. Zahariadis. 2002. A multiple streams model of US foreign aid policy. *Policy Studies Journal* 30 (4): 495–514.

Van den Dool, A. 2023. The multiple streams framework in a nondemocracy: The infeasibility of a national ban on live poultry sales in China. *Policy Studies Journal* 51 (2): 327–349.

Weick, K.E. 1976. Educational organizations as loosely coupled systems. *Administrative Science Quarterly* 21 (1): 1–19.

Weiner, S.S. (1976). Participation, deadlines, and choice. In *Ambiguity and choice in organizations*, ed. J.G. March and J.P. Olsen. Oslo: Universitetsforlaget.

Wildavsky, A. 1987. *Speaking truth to power*, 2nd ed. New Brunswick, NJ: Transaction Publishers.

Williamson, O.E. 1985. *The economic institutions of capitalism.* New York: Free Press.

Zahariadis, N. 2003. *Ambiguity and choice in public policy: Political decision-making in modern democracies.* Washington, DC: Georgetown University Press.

Zahariadis, N. 2005. *Essence of political manipulation: Emotion, institutions, and Greek foreign policy.* New York: Peter Lang.

Zahariadis, N. 2008a. Ambiguity and choice in European public policy. *Journal of European Public Policy* 15 (4): 514–530.

Zahariadis, N. 2008b. Europeanization as program implementation: Effective and democratic? *Journal of Comparative Policy Analysis* 10 (3): 221–238.

Zahariadis, N. 2015a. Plato's receptacle: Deadlines, ambiguity, and temporal sorting in public policy. *Leviathan* 30: 113–131.

Zahariadis, N. 2015b. The shield of Herakles: Multiple streams and the emotional endowment effect. *European Journal of Political Research* 54 (3): 466–481.

Zohlnhöfer, R., N. Herweg, and N. Zahariadis. 2022. How to conduct a multiple streams study. In *Methods of the policy process*, ed. C.M. Weible and S. Workman. New York and London: Routledge.

The Narrative Policy Framework: A Storied Understanding of Public Policy

Rachel McGovern and Michael D. Jones

INTRODUCTION

Narratives are a fundamental driving force of politics and public policy. In the contemporary political landscape, the stories told shape, construct, and manipulate public perceptions. They are powerful enough to high-light previously overlooked social issues, mobilize stakeholders to support or oppose policies, and persuade individuals to adopt new positions. Narratives achieve this because they are the primary means through which we communicate and understand the social and political world. Effective narratives help us make sense of complex information by identifying villains who cause harm, victims who suffer from it, and heroes who seek to resolve it. Narratives provide meaning by connecting facts to values, emotions to actions, and coherence to time and events. Therefore, to truly understand public policy, we must understand narratives. This is the mission of the Narrative Policy Framework (NPF).

R. McGovern (✉) · M. D. Jones
Department of Political Science, Clemson University, Clemson, USA
e-mail: rnmcgov@clemson.edu

M. D. Jones
e-mail: mjone239@utk.edu

B. G. Peters and P. Zittoun (eds.), *Contemporary Approaches to Public Policy*, International Series on Public Policy,
https://doi.org/10.1007/978-3-032-06026-6_10

217

The NPF is a well-established empirical, scientific, and theoretical framework designed to understand the role of narratives within the public policy process. Within the NPF, narratives are defined as any statement or text that references a policy or policy stance and includes at least one character (Shanahan et al. 2013). This conceptualization of narratives differs notably from adjacent work on narratives in disciplines such as literary studies, narratology, and other academic fields, which often adopt broader, more comprehensive, definitions of narrative. For example, in narratology, one might find narrative broadly defined as a structured representation of a sequence of events, whether real or imagined (e.g., Herman 2009), a means of organizing temporal or causal relations (e.g., Genette 1983), or as a system of structuring human experience and meaning (e.g., Bruner 1991), among many other contending definitions. The NPF's definition of narrative does not require all the possible definitional permutations of narrative found in various disciplines to be present; it recognizes, however, the importance of these elements within various aspects of the broader framework, which we elaborate later in the chapter. What is particular to the NPF is that its primary focus is on *policy narratives*, which are narratives constructed around specific policy problems or issues (*see* Jones et al. 2023, p. 163). This focus distinguishes NPF policy narratives from other narrative studies, as well as from related concepts in policy literature, such as frames or discourse, by emphasizing the recognition and requirement of characters in relation to the policy issue (Jones et al. 2022).[1]

The study of narratives within public policy did not begin with the NPF. Initial explorations of narrative applications to public policy emerged in the late 1980s and early 1990s as a response to the dominant "decisionism" paradigm within policy analysis (Majone 1989). At that time, much of the policy literature was grounded in objective and positivistic orientations, focusing on studying and understanding policymaking through logical, sequential steps aimed at identifying optimal solutions based on objective criteria. Majone, along with other scholars (*see, for example,* Bacchi 2009; Stone 1997, 2012; Hindess 1977), critiqued this rational approach and reductionist perspective. They argued

---

[1] It is beyond the scope of this chapter to provide a high-resolution exploration of the nuanced differences between discourse, frames, and the NPF. For discourses and the NPF, we steer readers to Crespy and Nessel (2022); in respect to frames, we recommend Shanahan et al. (2018a, b, c) and Jones (2018).

that it reduced policymaking to overly simplistic processes that failed to capture the complexities and political contexts in which policies operate. Along the same lines, Deborah Stone (1997, 2012) famously rejected what she termed the "rationality project", contending that the idea of objective scientists using the scientific method to produce a single correct answer is inherently misguided. While scientific evidence can reduce uncertainty, she convincingly argued that it cannot eliminate ambiguity. Stone concluded that it is therefore inappropriate to rely solely on rational approaches to understand an inherently irrational political system. These critiques of rational approaches to policy sciences sparked a new wave of scholarship, with policy scholars arguing that policymaking does not operate within market models but rather within political models characterized by ongoing struggles over values, ideas, and morals. This shift in the literature at that time led to the incorporation of alternative methods and perspectives as a means to better understand how narratives shape, influence, and impact public policy.

This narrative movement within the policy scholarship laid the foundation for what would eventually become the NPF. As it exists today, the NPF is overtly derivative of the early work and debates on narratives and their relationship to policy sciences. The NPF distinguishes itself theoretically from other narrative approaches to public policy by adopting a relative understanding of human meaning-making in the world (post-positivist ontology) with a scientific approach to the generation of knowledge (objective epistemology) (Jones and Radaelli 2015). Within the framework, there is an acknowledgment of an objective reality; however, the NPF also recognizes that our understanding of it is inherently imperfect and driven by perception. Narratives can represent aspects of reality, yet they are constructed through the lens of individual and collective perceptions, values, biases, and norms. Consequently, narratives are not mere reflections of objective reality but are the reflections of narrators and audiences, and their interactions. Despite the socially constructed nature of narratives, the NPF allows for empirical observation and logical reasoning to scientifically study what these narratives are, how they present, and the meaningful patterns within them. Thus, the value of the NPF to the study of public policy lies in its ability to provide an objective approach to the study of subjective phenomena (Shanahan et al. 2018a, b, c).

In this chapter, we trace the evolution of narratives in public policy, starting with post-structuralist approaches to policy narratives, addressing the critiques of these perspectives, and examining the emergence of structuralist approaches. We conclude by exploring how these developments influenced the creation of the NPF as an empirical and scientific response to ongoing theoretical debates. The chapter then proceeds with an overview of the NPF, outlining its core theoretical assumptions, examining the policy contexts in which narratives have been studied, and presenting a discussion of the structure of narrative form and content. We then follow with a discussion about how the NPF has been applied to address key questions within various subfields of public policy research, as well as the methods used to investigate these questions. The chapter concludes with a general statement on the future directions and potential of the NPF.

Narrative Origins in Policy Sciences

Narrative scholarship has long been shaped by theoretical divides in narratology, particularly the division between structuralism and post-structuralism. Structuralism posits that narratives possess a fixed, underlying structure with identifiable and generalizable patterns and meanings (Propp 1968; Saussure 2005). Emerging from the early works of scholars such as Saussure (1916), Lévi-Strauss (1958), and Noam Chomsky (1957), structuralism emphasizes the importance of systems and structures that underpin human culture and thought. For structuralist approaches to narrative, this involves analyzing the semantic and syntactic structures, patterns, and binary oppositions that shape narratives (Genette 1983; Saussure 2005; Herman 2009). Structuralists often view text as a primary manifestation of discourse and language, making it the focal point of narrative analysis (Huisman 2005, p. 39). In contrast, post-structuralism challenges these assumptions, arguing that narratives are fluid, shaped by context, and subjected to multiple interpretations. Consequently, post-structuralism has tended toward the deconstruction of narratives to uncover inherent contradictions, ambiguities, and power dynamics, rejecting the notion of fixed or singular meanings (Huisman 2005; Derrida et al. 1981). These differing perspectives have fundamentally influenced how policy scholars approach and understand the role of narratives in public policy, laying the theoretical foundation for the development of the NPF (Jones and McBeth 2010).

Post-structuralism and Policy Narratives

The earliest applications of narrative analysis in policy studies were grounded in post-structuralist orientations to narratives. As stated earlier, these approaches emerged in response to the rejection of the rationality project and the traditionally objective, positivistic frameworks for understanding policymaking. Both post-structuralism and early narrative analysis emphasize the inherently subjective nature of both narrative and public policy, asserting that neither can ever be truly and entirely objective. Instead, both are shaped by the contexts in which they emerge. Early narrative analysis in policy studies aligned with these post-structural arguments that asserted meaning is context-dependent and shaped by power dynamics, values, and belief systems. This argument coincided with ongoing shifts in policy scholarship that recognized that language serves as a tool for evoking "favorable interpretations" of the political world (Edelman 1990, p. 103). This perspective aligns closely with the post-structuralist rejection of fixed meanings and patterns in language and narrative, as well as the critique of positivistic assumptions of rationality prevalent in the policy sciences.

Deborah Stone (1997, 2012) and Frank Fischer (2003) are widely credited for laying the foundational arguments of the theoretical importance of narrative analysis in policy scholarship. Before their contributions, policy studies largely focused on language and symbolism rather than storytelling itself. For instance, and before Fischer's work would come to fully embrace narrative, Fischer and Forester (1993) broadly argued that language shapes reality by defining policy problems—determining who gets what, when, and how—and framing acceptable solutions. Similarly, Edelman (1964, 1990) described language as a symbolic tool for justifying and rationalizing political actions and outcomes through powerful imagery (Smith and Larimer 2017). Together, these scholars emphasized how language and symbols shape public perceptions and influence policy outcomes.

Recognizing the central role of language in policymaking, scholars such as Stone (1997) shifted the focus toward storytelling and causal stories—which are narratives designed to define policy problems persuasively. These stories explain why and how problems occur, assign blame or responsibility for those problems, and highlight intended or unintended consequences of the problems (Stone 1989, p. 285). This emphasis on causal storytelling highlights the inherently political and subjective nature of problem definition, as competing narratives advocate preferred solutions and shape public perceptions around a given policy problem, a clear perspective also advocated in Fischer's later work (2003). Frank Fischer further argued for multi-method approaches to uncover how policy problems are framed, positing that diverse methodologies can reveal dimensions of meaning-making often overlooked by traditional policy analysis (Smith and Larimer 2017). Following the lead of these foundational arguments, early narrative analysis scholarship most often embraced interpretivist epistemologies, emphasizing how policy actors construct and interpret meaning through stories.

While Deborah Stone's work on causal stories provided a compelling illustration of how narratives shape policy problems and solutions, there remained a significant gap in developing a robust theoretical framework for systematically studying narratives in policy analysis. Addressing this gap, Emery Roe introduced one of the first comprehensive frameworks in his book *Narrative Policy Analysis* (1994). Roe's work offered an empirical alternative to the traditional, positivist, economics-focused approaches to policy analysis. Similarly to Stone and Fischer, he argued that studying and understanding narratives could help build political consensus and address complex policy problems. However, Roe extended the case for incorporating narrative approaches into policymaking by proposing a structured methodology that could replace or complement traditional policy analysis methods. Writing with Hukkinen and Rochlin (1990), Roe emphasized that narratives told by policy actors should not be treated as isolated units of analysis. Instead, these narratives could be connected to reveal broader narrative arcs, which together create the socially constructed reality of a given policy issue. This approach views narratives as interrelated stories that collectively shape an overarching policy reality.

Roe outlined *Narrative Policy Analysis* (NPA) in four distinct phases:

1. *Narrative Identification*: In contexts of high uncertainty, complexity, and polarization, researchers should identify policy narratives and the arguments supporting policy assumptions (Roe 1994, p. 155).
2. *Alternative Narratives*: Researchers should then identify alternative narratives that challenge the primary ones identified in the first step (Roe 1994, p. 155).

3. *Comparison and Synthesis*: Compare and contrast the dominant and alternative narratives to develop a comprehensive policy metanarrative (Roe 1994, p. 155).
4. *Recasting Problems*: Determine how this metanarrative can reshape the policy problem to make it more suitable for conventional analytical tools used in traditional policy analysis, such as microeconomics, legal analysis, statistics, organizational theory, and public management (Roe 1994, p. 155).

At the time of publication, the unique contribution of NPA was its ability to compare dominant and counter-narratives, providing researchers with means for analyzing narratives while offering practitioners a framework for facilitating deliberation without requiring consensus (Roe 1994; Hampton 2004). Unlike earlier approaches, NPA introduced a systematic framework that allowed narratives to be utilized similarly to traditional policy tools, such as statistics, economics, and conventional policy analysis. This represented a significant advancement by integrating narrative analysis into the methodological repertoire of policy studies. Building on Deborah Stone's argument that narratives are especially critical in contexts of high uncertainty or ambiguity, NPA demonstrated how narratives could be used to address policy issues where traditional methods often fail to deliver adequate answers. While Stone and Fischer emphasized the interpretive and symbolic dimensions of narratives, NPA moved beyond individual narratives to focus on the broader aggregation of these interpretations. By connecting individual narratives into larger arcs, NPA allowed for the narrative construction of overarching policy realities, emphasizing the interconnectedness of individual stories in shaping the collective understanding of policy domains. So, rather than rejecting the post-structuralist foundations of earlier narrative approaches, NPA adapted and refined them to meet the practical and methodological demands of policy analysis.

Around the same time as the development of NPA, Maarten Hajer (1993, 2005) introduced the concept of discourse coalitions. Hajer argued that narratives are not isolated units but serve as connectors within political networks, uniting groups of actors—referred to as discourse coalitions—around shared storylines. Hajer defined discourse as "an ensemble of ideas, concepts, and categories through which meaning is given to phenomena" (1993, p. 45). Discourse coalitions emerge when actors adopt storylines that resonate with their identities and align with their strategic goals. These coalitions leverage shared storylines to validate and institutionalize their discourses, persuading others and embedding their perspectives into policy frameworks. The success of a discourse coalition depends on the plausibility of its storyline, the credibility of its proponents, and the extent to which the storyline aligns with the social and political context of its audience (Hajer 2005, p. 47). Similar to Roe, Hajer's discourse coalitions emphasized the aggregation of narratives and illustrated the interconnectedness of individual narratives within larger discursive structures. By situating narratives within broader networks of meaning, Hajer demonstrated how storylines function as tools for shaping collective perceptions, framing policy problems, and driving political change.

Although NPA and discourse coalitions have advanced narrative analysis by moving beyond critiques of rationalist approaches to establish a more theoretically grounded and methodologically rigorous framework for policy analysis, their post-structuralist foundations and departure from rationalist and positivist traditions have often faced resistance within conventional policy studies. Most notably, Paul Sabatier (1999) criticized narrative analysis for lacking the empirical rigor required for scientific inquiry, dismissing it as overly interpretive and insufficiently robust for systematic policy research. This critique epitomized a growing tension in the field, as traditional policy scholars questioned whether post-structuralist narrative approaches met the methodological standards of falsifiability and hypothesis testing. These challenges inevitably shaped subsequent debates about narrative policy analysis and paved the way for the development of the NPF.

The Emergence of a Structuralist Approach to Policy Narratives

When examining the early post-structuralist narrative applications to public policy, the central argument running through each approach is the connection between narratives and meaning-making. This work demonstrates that through the dissemination of narratives, society assigns meaning and importance to policy problems. As such, narratives become the tools or lenses through which we begin to make sense of and understand how we socially construct and prioritize certain policy issues or interpretations over others, and why these meanings lead to specific policy effects at various stages in the policy process. However, a key critique of narrative analysis is that its foundation in post-structuralist approaches risks falling into relativism. Post-structuralism posits that all interpretations of policy outcomes can be seen as equally valid, making it challenging—if not impossible—to establish authoritative, external, or "objective" criteria for evaluating narratives (e.g., see Fischer 2003, p. 10). As a result, this relativism can render narratives *sui generis*, as their value and meaning are confined only to the specific context in which they are situated. Consequently, this raises important questions: If narratives are merely tools for constructing one version of reality, is it possible to identify generalizable narrative structures that transcend their context? Additionally, can narratives be integrated with positivist and empirical applications to provide more robust and objective policy analysis bridging the two opposing schools of thought? As a direct response to these concerns, and to the lack of a unifying and robust structuralist approach to policy narrative studies, the NPF was born.

Directly addressing critiques and broader concerns that narrative frameworks, such as NPA, were primarily a descriptive methodology rather than a theoretically robust approach capable of scientifically testing hypotheses or being clearly falsifiable, the 2005 article titled "The Science of Storytelling" by McBeth and colleagues marked a pivotal step forward in narrative studies in public policy. It responded to Sabatier's critique that narrative analysis was largely a constructivist activity with "very little concern with being sufficiently clear to be proven wrong" (1999, p. 138). The article proposed that if narratives were merely "political spin and meaningless", there should be no significant differences between opposing narratives from different interest groups (p. 421). However, findings demonstrated that narratives could indeed be scientifically studied, revealing statistically meaningful differences between competing narratives. This finding suggested that narratives are not random; rather, they play an important and measurable role in shaping public policy. These insights were the beginnings of what would later become the NPF. At the time of writing the 2005 article, there were only a handful of applications (*see* Golding et al. 1992; Ricketts 2007; Finucane and Satterfield 2005; McComas and Shanahan 1999; Morill et al. 2000) that applied narrative analysis in a positivist and empirical way. Building on these initial findings, the authors began to develop the framework for a structuralist approach to studying policy narratives (*see* Shanahan et al. 2008; McBeth et al. 2007; Jones 2010). In 2010, Jones and McBeth published the seminal article "A Narrative Policy Framework: Clear Enough to be Wrong?" which addressed the classic structuralism versus post-structuralism debate and introduced the NPF as an empirically testable framework that had the potential to be clear enough to be wrong, thereby countering Sabatier's critiques.

Jones and McBeth stated, "We see our framework not as a threat to post-positivist approaches to narrative but rather as an acknowledgment that narratives matter and that by studying them in a systematic empirical manner, positivists and post-positivists can engage in more productive debates over how stories influence public policy" (2010, p. 339). The authors further argued that post-structural scholarship has been predominantly inductive, qualitative, and based in interpretive methodologies. Consequently, it cannot engage in clear hypothesis testing, nor is it amenable to replication and falsification. To address this, the NPF identifies key narrative elements that are both generalizable and consistent across narratives and policy domains, enabling scholars to establish foundational structures of narratives. This structured approach facilitates the development of testable, empirical theories and models, allowing researchers to identify patterns and generate generalizable insights through systematic empirical analysis.

THE NARRATIVE POLICY FRAMEWORK

Like many other policy theories and frameworks, the NPF is grounded in a set of theoretical assumptions that underpin theory about how narratives operate within the policy world. While theoretical assumptions often remain implicit, the NPF explicitly outlines its five core assumptions. These assumptions address how the framework interprets and understands the nature of reality, how reality is created, and how to study and analyze that reality. For those applying the NPF, violating these assumptions may render the framework an inappropriate theoretical approach for their study. The five core assumptions are:

> *Assumption I—Social Construction:* The NPF assumes that the policy world is socially constructed. People both collectively and individually assign meaning and significance to various objects and processes associated with public policy. Therefore, to understand the meaning of something, we must understand how humans perceive it and how those perceptions can vary based on different subjective conditions and contexts.

Assumption II—Bounded Relativity: Because reality is inherently subjective, perceptions and interpretations vary greatly among different individuals and across different contexts, making reality relative to those variations. However, the relativity of these social constructions is bounded by "possible interpretations" constraining policy reality, such as belief systems, cultural norms, institutional rules, and ideologies. Therefore, reality is not random; rather, it is relative within these bounds.

Assumption III—Generalizable Structure: The NPF adopts a structuralist approach to narratives, positing that all narratives possess a specific and generalizable structure that is identifiable across different types of narratives and contexts. Thus, while reality is socially constructed and relatively bounded, there exists an identifiable structure that transcends these variations.

Assumption IV—Three Levels of Analysis: The NPF operates at three levels of analysis. The first level is the micro level, focusing on individuals. The second is the meso level, which examines groups and coalitions. The third level is the macro level, which addresses cultural and institutional narratives. All three levels operate simultaneously and interact with each other. The demarcation between these levels stems both from the need to operationalize varied units of analysis and from the theoretical understanding that narratives exist and function differently at each level, producing variable effects.

Assumption V—Homo Narrans Model of the Individual: The Homo Narrans model posits that storytelling is the primary way humans communicate, understand, and reason. This theoretical assumption emphasizes that storytelling is inherent and natural to the human experience, suggesting that it is a fundamental characteristic of all human language and communication.

The Structure of a Narrative: Form and Content

As previously stated, the NPF takes a classic structuralist approach to understanding narratives (Jones et al. 2022a, b). This means that the NPF, embracing some of the narratology approaches to stories (*see* Herman 2009, pp. 23–26), views and analyzes narratives through their underlying structures and components. From a theoretical standpoint, this means that narratives are composed of and connected through the relationships and functions of various narrative elements within a broader story. In the context of the NPF, this involves examining narrative elements such as characters, setting, and plot, and analyzing how these elements interact and connect to the shape of the narrative and convey a message or meaning.

By taking this structuralist approach, the NPF systematically identifies and analyzes common patterns and structures within policy stories. To do this, the NPF breaks down narrative into two components—form and content—and further breaks down these components into narrative elements. Narrative form includes the traditional structural elements we think of when we think of a story: characters, setting, plot, and the moral of the story. Characters are the entities, whether animate or inanimate, who give action and direction to a story. This action unfolds through a plot, where time and interaction shape a sequence of events into a cohesive storyline. These actions occur within a broader policy setting, and the outcome of this narrative is some kind of moral to the policy story. These four narrative form elements act as the structural core of a policy narrative and can be generalized across all policy contexts. They can be further understood as follows:

> *Characters:* Characters are the most well-established and studied narrative element within the framework. Given that the minimum definition of a narrative includes a character, they are central to most NPF policy narrative operationalizations. Traditionally, villains, victims, and heroes have been the three primary character archetypes within the framework. Victims are those harmed by a policy problem, heroes intervene to mitigate the policy problem or mobilize action to address it, and villains perpetuate or cause the policy problem. As the framework has evolved, additional characters have been incorporated into the NPF. For instance, research on coalition conflict introduced allies and opponents (Merry 2016), while beneficiaries—those who gain from policy solutions—were also identified (Weible et al. 2016). However, these are not the only possible character archetypes, as future research will likely reveal others.
>
> *Setting:* Setting refers to the broader policy environment or context within which a narrative is situated. This could include the physical, political, or institutional conditions that frame the story, as well as geographical locations, historical background, and cultural factors that impact the contextual framing of the policy issue. The setting

helps the audience situate and orientate the story within space and time (Shanahan et al. 2018a, b, c).

Plot: The plot in a narrative connects characters and settings, forming a story arc through a sequence of policy events over time. While many NPF studies have relied on Deborah Stone's (2012) story-lines—stories of change (transformation or progress) and stories of power (control and influence)—recent work has expanded and reconceptualized this approach. Kuhlmann and Blum (2020) applied Lowi's policy typology (regulatory, distributive, and redistributive), while others have framed plot through action verbs depicting character interactions (Crow et al. 2017a, b), universal themes (Kuhlmann and Blum 2021), problem definitions (Kear and Wells 2014), or time-based narrative analogies (Boscarino 2019). Ruff et al. (2022) most recently integrated Stone's storylines, redefining them as past and future policy impacts driven by the interplay between heroes and villains over time.

Moral of the story: The moral of the story within a policy narrative is the broader lesson or message that the narrative aims to convey to the audience. In many policy narratives, this is traditionally the policy solution; however, it could also be a call to action or some kind of moral lesson. The moral can be explicit, with a hero clearly stating what the policy solution should be, or implicit, with the narrative having a general thematic undertone that expresses a certain ideology or value.

In addition to narrative form, the NPF identifies narrative content as a core component. Unlike form, narrative content is more context-dependent, focusing on the substantive elements that convey the story's message. Thus, NPF researchers often focus on what is *actually* being communicated within these structures and what messages that conveys. Narrative content allows narrative structure to be amenable to the meaning-making process.

Operationalizing and generalizing narrative content can be challenging, but NPF scholars have identified various narrative content elements that are generalizable across different narrative contexts: narrative strategies and belief systems. However, while these elements may appear across contexts, their impact and effects may substantially vary. The three most widely recognized and operationalized narrative strategies are the Devil-Angel-Solidarity (DAS) shift, causal mechanisms/strategies, and the scope of conflict. Additionally, other scholars have identified policy beliefs as a core narrative content element, often focusing on cultural theory (Thompson et al. 1990), or political ideology (e.g., Barker and Tinnick 2006).

Devil-Angel-Solidarity Shift: Originally stemming from the work on advocacy coalitions (Weible et al. 2009), the DAS shift has become a widely applied narrative strategy to measure how coalitions portray themselves and their opposition (Merry 2019). The devil shift occurs when policy actors emphasize the villain character to focus blame on their opponents. Conversely, the angel shift involves emphasizing heroes, resulting in a self-portrayal as saviors addressing policy problems. Recently, the solidarity shift has been introduced, which emphasizes victims and the undue harm being caused to them (Smith-Walter et al. 2022). The DAS shift is a way of measuring the role and effect of character portrayal within policy conflict.

Causal Mechanism/Strategies: Causal strategies in narratives function as mechanisms that assign blame and responsibility for policy problems, often providing justification for proposed solutions and linking characters to both problems and solutions. Most NPF studies draw on Stone's (2012) four causal theories: intentional, inadvertent, accidental, and mechanical causality. These theories are distinguished by whether actions are purposeful or unguided and whether consequences are intended or unintended. Mechanical and accidental causes are unguided, with the former producing intended consequences and the latter unintended ones. In contrast, intentional causality involves purposeful actions with intended outcomes, while inadvertent causality arises from purposeful actions leading to unintended results.

Scope of Conflict: Building on Schattschneider's (1975) classic work, the NPF posits that policy narratives strategically expand or contain policy conflict. Narrators may portray their coalitions as winning—emphasizing policy benefits, advocating solutions, or framing issues as isolated—or losing, by highlighting the costs of the status quo, using dramatic language, and linking issues to broader controversies (Stephan 2020; Jones 2018). Melissa Merry (2016, 2018) further explores how persuasive narratives achieve this through proximity: expanding conflict by making problems feel personally relevant and featuring relatable characters, or containing conflict by minimizing proximity. Coalitions also leverage allies and opponents to define conflict boundaries and engage external actors beyond the subsystem.

Policy Beliefs: To operationalize and capture the social construction of narrative meaning, policy beliefs are viewed as the contextual, symbolic, or metaphorical lenses through which individuals interpret policy (Jones et al. 2022a, b). While scholars (Shanahan et al. 2011a, b, 2013) have utilized characters as a proxy and measurement of policy beliefs, other operationalizations have been theoretically grounded in political ideology (Lakoff 2016) and Cultural Theory (Williams and Kuzma 2022; McMorris et al. 2018; Jones 2014a, b). For example, utilizing Cultural Theory allows researchers to systematically understand how different cultural worldviews such as that of an egalitarian or an individualist differentially work to imbue content within a narrative (such as an American Flag) with meaning inherent to that worldview, which in turn communicates that worldview's shared beliefs and values to those able to recognize it as such.

Most NPF research has approached each element independently, operationalizing, coding, and analyzing the element's presence and effects separately from one another. From an applied and scientific perspective, this has been necessary to develop the NPF into a robust framework that is clear enough to be falsifiable. Thus, this disaggregation and isolation of each element has been driven by empirical necessity rather than theoretical rationale. As an unintended consequence, the framework has not effectively connected the elements and examined them holistically to determine their integrated and aggregated effects. The framework has now advanced to the point where we can reliably capture characters, plots, settings, and morals. Therefore, as the framework progresses, the next steps will likely involve reliably and empirically reintegrating these elements to further theoretical development. This will likely involve understanding what these elements do together, how they connect to one another, and how their presence or absence shape narrative effects.

What is and Where are Policy Narratives?

As previously stated, within the NPF, the traditional operational definition of a narrative includes a reference to a policy or policy stance and at least one character (Shanahan et al. 2013). However, it is also understood that not all narratives are the same. Some narratives are more complete, rich, and complex, while others are more austere. What is unique to the NPF, though, is that it provides clear definitional parameters for what constitutes a narrative, making it possible for narratives to be not only identifiable but also measurable. The completeness of a narrative is determined by the number and extent of narrative elements present. Many NPF studies have established a narrativity index, allowing researchers to assess how complete or incomplete a narrative is based on the presence and extent of narrative elements within a given narrative (Brewer 2019; Boscarino 2019; Shanahan et al. 2018a, b, c; Huda 2019; Crow and Lawlor 2016; McBeth et al. 2012).

Policy narratives exist all around us, in any medium or context within the political and policy worlds where communication occurs. The most widely studied policy narratives within the NPF tend to come from public consumption documents. These have largely been newspaper articles (Wolton et al. 2022; O'Donovan 2018; Blair and McCormack 2016), public statements or press releases by government officials (Huda 2019; O'Leary et al. 2017), and government and nonprofit reports (Gray and Jones 2016; Olofsson et al. 2018). Scholars have also examined speeches, such as the State of the Union address and legislative sessions (Peterson 2023). Additionally, there has been growth in NPF analysis on social media platforms like X, formerly known as Twitter (Merry 2016, 2018, 2019; Gupta et al. 2018). Visual content, such as YouTube videos, has also been used in NPF studies (McBeth et al. 2012). Given that the NPF assumes narrative is the central way individuals process information, communicate, and reason, any and all mediums of communication can, and should, be utilized as a source of policy narratives.

THE CORE QUESTIONS OF PUBLIC POLICY AND THE ROLE OF THE NPF IN ADDRESSING THEM

The field of public policy, though relatively young compared to its counterparts in Public Administration and Political Science, has generated multiple intellectual tracks. Each track addresses a distinct set of inquiries that guide the study, analysis, and practice within the field. It is thus beneficial to explore how the NPF has been, and could be, applied to develop and pursue answers to the core questions of each policy subfield. While the NPF emerged from policy process scholarship and remains closely associated with it, this should not limit its recognition as a versatile and valuable tool across all areas of policy scholarship. Indeed, the NPF is one of the most adaptable policy process frameworks, capable of being coupled with a wide range of theories and methodologies. Therefore, a primary concern of applying NPF to policy research should be whether and why the analysis of a narrative matters in the given context (Schlaufer et al. 2022a, 2022b).

NPF and The Policy Process

The literature on the policy process is primarily concerned with understanding how policy change and development interact with various policy actors, events, institutions, and settings (Weible et al. 2018). Smith and Larimer (2009, p. 18) note that while the literature aims to establish a unifying theory of the policy process, it has instead developed multiple theories that explain the political dynamics of policymaking and how different key elements affect the overarching process. The common thread across these disparate approaches is a broad, yet fundamental question (*see* Smith and Larimer 2009): How and why do public policies emerge, evolve, and change over time? It is through this common question that permeates the literature that we assess the NPF and the policy process more generally.

Unlike other applications of narrative analysis, the NPF emerged primarily from the literature on the policy process and is closely connected to other theories within this scholarship. Thus, the core guiding question of the NPF has traditionally been: *What role do narratives play* in explaining how and why public policies emerge, evolve, and change over time? To that end, NPF studies have explored the role of narratives within coalition conflict, finding that political coalitions will strategically use a variety of narrative strategies to either expand or contract the scope of conflict (Merry 2016; Smith-Walter et al. 2016). Other research has found that narratives can drive and shift political attention (Peterson 2018, 2023). As a result, narratives can have substantial influence on shaping and influencing public opinion (Shanahan et al. 2013), as well as influencing the policy agenda (Peterson and Jones 2016). Narratives can also be powerful enough to create a focusing event and open windows of policy opportunity (McBeth and Lybecker 2018).

It should be noted that while NPF research has primarily focused on understanding the role of narratives in agenda setting and the formulation stages of the policy process (Schlaufer et al. 2022a), there has also been work addressing narratives at a more holistic policy process level. Most notably, Crow and Jones (2018) argue that narratives can be observed as "central to the policy process—constituting public policy instruments, persuading decision makers and the public, and shaping all stages of the policy process" (p. 217). The reason for this is that narratives have various effects—they can persuade, mobilize, and manipulate (Jones et al. 2022). Consequently, narratives can serve as political tools at different intervention points within the policy process (Crow and Jones 2018).

For example, at the micro level, narratives have been shown to be highly effective in persuading individuals by providing cognitive shortcuts or heuristic imagery. For instance, several studies have demonstrated that respondents are more likely to support policy positions or adopt behaviors suggested in a policy narrative when exposed to hero characters, as compared to other character archetypes (Raile et al. 2022; Shanahan et al. 2019; Jones 2014a, b). Conversely, at the meso level, research has highlighted the influence of narrative strategies such as framing coalitions as winners or losers and manipulating the scope of conflict. These strategies can significantly shape the narrative landscape and sway public perception, often leading to narrative manipulation within policy debates (Shanahan et al. 2013). However, among these influences, the role of narratives in directing attention has been increasingly examined, though it remains an emerging area of study.

Holly Peterson (2018), for instance, argues that narrative mechanisms extend beyond persuasion and manipulation to influence the policy process and drive policy change through attention. Unlike persuasion, which aims to alter opinions, attention operates by mobilizing existing biases to prioritize a policy narrative's message and prompt action. Peterson explains that narratives with compelling characters and relatable conflicts are particularly effective at capturing and activating attention. Furthermore, narratives that incorporate emotional appeals are successful at maintaining engagement and driving sustained focus. Narratives, therefore, play a crucial role in drawing policy attention and shaping the policy agenda. By highlighting specific problems, solutions, and actors, narratives mobilize biases within public opinion, influence policymaker and institutional priorities, and ultimately affect policy outcomes. Thus, narratives are fundamental tools in shaping a policy image (Peterson 2023).

These theoretical insights have been applied across a wide range of policy domains, demonstrating the versatility of the NPF. Substantively, the NPF has also been applied across a variety of policy domains. Most applications have been in the environmental and energy policy field, with a few examples examining fracking (Stephan 2020; Gottlieb et al. 2018; Blair and McCormack 2016; Zanocoo et al. 2018; Galloway et al. 2024), Yellowstone buffalo regulation (McBeth et al. 2012; McBeth et al. 2010, 2005), climate change (Peterson 2023; Wolters et al. 2021; McBeth et al. 2022), and wildfire policy (Crow et al. 2017a, 2017b; Alamsyah 2022). Other applications have studied narratives in education and children's policy issues such as critical race theory in schools (Bertrand et al. 2024) and child welfare protection (Kuenzler and Stauffer 2023). While other scholars have examined social issues such as gun control (Merry 2016; 2018; 2019; 2020; Smith-Walter et al. 2016; Schwartz 2023) and transgender rights (Flores et al. 2023).

In addition to diverse policy applications, NPF scholarship has examined the critical role and relationship of media and narratives in shaping the policy process. The NPF has yielded significant insights into the relationship between the policy process, narratives, and both traditional and social media (e.g., Crow and Lawlor 2016; Gupta et al. 2018). Research shows that stories are often the primary means through which political information is communicated, presented, and understood. To explore media's role in the policy process, NPF scholars have examined how narratives are presented (Shanahan et al. 2011a, b), framed (Crow and Lawlor 2016), debated across media outlets (Gupta et al. 2018; Merry et al. 2016), and how they influence policy outcomes (McMorris et al. 2018).

NPF and Policy Analysis

The core questions guiding policy analysis are those that revolve around selecting, implementing, and evaluating solutions for specific policy problems. For example, policy analysis addresses questions such as (*see* Clemons and McBeth 2020): What is the problem, and why is it significant? Who is affected by the problem? What are the possible policy alternatives? How should policymakers balance conflicting values and interests?

As previously mentioned, early narrative theoretical contributions positioned narrative analysis as an alternative to traditional policy analysis methods to address core questions. These efforts were justified by the recognition that all human knowledge, including science, is shaped by the normative assumptions and societal meanings of the world it seeks to understand (deLeon 1992). Consequently, policy analysis must account for the social constructs through which policy targets define societal problems to identify politically feasible solutions (Fischer 2003). This necessitates an understanding of the often varied and conflicting interpretations of a policy problem's objective conditions and facts, an area where the NPF excels.

Clemons and McBeth (2020) emphasize that narratives play a critical role in raising societal awareness of policy problems. While data, studies, and statistics can draw attention to issues, they argue that "good stories" are essential—though not always sufficient—to capture public attention (p. 13). A compelling story identifies and defines the policy problem, names the villain responsible, highlights the victim harmed, and presents a hero who can resolve the issue through a specific policy solution. More robust narratives may also attribute blame, establish causality, or provide supporting evidence for the problem and proposed solution (Stone 2012). Additionally, they can outline stakeholders' perceptions of costs and benefits by identifying winners and losers (Crow and Berggren 2014). Most importantly, these narratives often reflect deeper policy beliefs and values embedded within their structure (McBeth et al. 2010).

Incorporating narratives into stakeholder assessments enhances policy analysis by revealing how individual stakeholders socially construct policy issues and where their perceptions diverge. For example, McBeth et al. (2016) demonstrated this through their analysis of a local river restoration project, where stakeholders focused on the characters presented in narratives and their influence on the overall message. They found that portraying villains could be divisive and increase stakeholder resistance, while highlighting victims drew attention to the policy problem and its solution, fostering consensus. Additionally, they observed that narrative strategies, such as the use of scientific evidence, can be effective but must be applied selectively based on the stakeholder audience.

The NPF offers a valuable policy analysis lens for understanding the social constructs, values, and beliefs that shape policy problems and solutions. By emphasizing the strategic role of narratives in capturing attention and fostering consensus, the NPF complements traditional policy analysis methods and addresses core questions about how and why policies emerge, evolve, and change. Whether through identifying key characters, assigning blame, or reflecting stakeholder perceptions, narratives provide policy analysts with tools to navigate the often-conflicting interpretations of policy issues, potentially leading to more politically feasible and informed solutions.

NPF and Policy Implementation

Policy implementation involves translating policy decisions into practice and ensuring they achieve the desired outcomes. For implementation scholars then, the primary focus is on studying to what extent a policy was effective in achieving its intended outcomes. Thus, rather than exploring which solutions are feasible, as in policy analysis, the key questions revolve around whether there was success or failure in implementation processes. Core questions in this area often include (*see* Sager et al. 2017): How are policies put into action? What factors influence the success or failure of policy implementation? What effects does a policy have, and who benefits from those effects?

NPF research has largely overlooked the policy implementation stage, but scholars have recently begun addressing this gap. Stauffer et al. (2024) offer early theorizing on how NPF can illuminate the dynamics of policy implementation, particularly the discretionary power of street-level bureaucrats and resulting outcome variations. They propose that NPF can uncover which narrative strategies most influence support or resistance to policies and whether these narratives seek to legitimize or delegitimize them. Such analyses can highlight key narrative elements driving successful or failed implementations and their significance.

Effective implementation, however, is also almost always largely dependent on the institutions enacting the new policy. The NPF could also be useful in understanding how a new policy may alter prevailing institutional arrangements and rules, as well as the dominant macro narrative within that institution. For example, recent work suggests that narratives likely define the roles of policy actors within an institutional arrangement through their character portrayals. Additionally, institutional narratives guide behavior and decision-making within an institution, influencing actor interactions and shaping the outcomes of implementation (McGovern and Jones 2024). By analyzing these narratives, the NPF could provide insights into how institutional dynamics affect the implementation process and identify potential areas for improving policy outcomes.

Methods for Answering these Questions

The growing adoption of the NPF in the policy literature has resulted in the increasingly robust methods developed by scholars to address core research questions. Grounded in structuralist approaches to narratives and science, much of the extant NPF scholarship has leaned into quantitative methodologies (Jones et al. 2022a, b). However, the framework is also quite compatible with diverse epistemological positions and methodological approaches (*see* Gray and Jones 2016). As such, there has been notable growth in qualitative and mixed-methodogical applications of the NPF, reflecting its versatility and adaptability across different research agendas (*see, for example,* McMorris et al. 2018; Weiss 2020; Huda 2019).

The first step in addressing narrative questions is understanding what constitutes narrative data and identifying its sources. In most applications of the NPF, content analysis has been the primary method for capturing and coding narrative data (Shanahan et al. 2018a, b, c). This typically involves the development of an NPF codebook, which applies deductive narrative elements to code data. While coding is often performed at the paragraph level, it can also be employed at the sentence or document levels of analysis (Jones et al. 2022a, b). Traditionally, NPF scholars have focused on publicly available documents consumed by the public (Shanahan et al. 2018a, b, c). Examples include news articles (Gottleib et al. 2018), tweets (Merry 2016), political speeches (Peterson 2023), policy-related documents (O'Donovan 2018), and multimedia sources like YouTube videos (Lybecker 2015, 2018). Beyond content analysis, other methods such as experiments (McMorris et al. 2018; Liu and Yen 2024; Flores et al. 2023), surveys (Shanahan et al. 2011a, b), interviews (Gray and Jones 2016), and focus groups (Smith-Walter et al. 2020) have also been employed to capture and code narrative data, particularly in studies examining narratives at different levels of analysis. Micro-level narrative studies often rely on these data acquisition methods to investigate individual-level narrative phenomena. In contrast, meso-level studies have predominantly used content analysis to explore group-level narratives, particularly those disseminated through media or organizational communication. Macro-level studies, while also relying on content analysis, are more limited in their applications and scope, reflecting the challenges of capturing broad, system-level narratives.

Once narrative data is captured, the next step is analyzing it. Most NPF research has relied heavily on statistical methods to test the hypotheses about the role of narratives in the policy process. Given that the majority of NPF applications are conducted at the meso level and utilize content analysis, the analytical techniques have predominantly involved statistical testing (Jones et al. 2022a, b). Many NPF studies have employed basic descriptive statistical techniques, such as frequency distributions, probability density functions, measures of central tendency, and dispersion metrics (*see* Shanahan et al. 2014). These methods are often used to identify group mean differences through techniques like two-sample t-tests, analysis of variance (ANOVA), and related approaches (Shanahan et al. 2013). Relational analyses, such as cross-tabulations with chi-square tests and correlation analysis, are also frequently applied to explore relationships within the data (*see* McBeth et al. 2012; Crow and Berggren 2014). Beyond descriptive and relational techniques, some research has incorporated more advanced predictive methods, including regression analysis (Kirkpatrick and Stoutenbourogh 2018; Shanahan et al. 2014; Jones 2014a, b; Lybecker et al. 2016; Peterson 2020), causal mediation analysis (Guenther and Shanahan 2020; Zanocco et al. 2018), and Bayesian posterior simulation (Jorgensen et al. 2018). Emerging studies are now exploring the application of network analysis to NPF research (Weible et al. 2016), broadening the methodological toolkit available for understanding the effect of narratives on public policy.

THE FUTURE OF THE NPF

Our overview of the evolution of the NPF points to two primary questions that have seemingly steered the trajectory of the NPF's overall development:

> *If narratives are tools for constructing one version of reality, is it possible to identify any generalizable narrative structures that can transcend contexts? Can narratives be integrated with positivist and empirical applications to provide a more robust and objective policy analysis, bridging the divide between opposing schools of thought?*

The NPF has successfully addressed the first question. Nearly two decades of research have demonstrated that not only are there generalizable elements within narratives, but that different narrative structures can lead to different policy outcomes. This conclusion affirms that narratives are a crucial component of policy studies, and that their role in policymaking is variable.

Regarding the second question, the NPF has partially addressed the challenge. The framework was initially, and continues to be, grounded in empirical and positivist methodologies, largely in response to Sabatier's initial concerns about narrative relativism. As a result, much of the NPF's early work focused on demonstrating that there is a scientific basis for analyzing storytelling (*see* the edited collection by Jones et al. 2014a, b) and that the framework is clear enough to be empirically tested and proven wrong. However, in the pursuit of falsifiability, the framework has encountered a degree of "objective paralysis". While there are notable exceptions (*see* Gray and Jones 2016), much of the NPF research agenda has concentrated on operationalizing and developing key narrative elements and understanding their impact and role within specific policy domains or processes. This focus has often led to the omission of a more holistic view of narratives, leaving a large gap in building the bridge between structuralist and post-structuralist approaches.

Emery Roe and Maarten Hajer's works were both based on the notion that narratives are not isolated units but interconnected elements that flow together to form a broader narrative arc—through which we can understand policy reality. As the NPF continues to evolve, the framework should draw on the early post-structuralist insights and the concept of the additive nature of narratives. The NPF no longer needs to justify its empirical legitimacy; instead, it can confidently rely on its strong empirical foundation while remaining flexible enough to accommodate some degree of relativism.

References

Alamsyah, Alamsyah. 2022. Collaborative practice during forest fires disaster: a narrative policy framework. *Journal of Disaster and Emergency Research.* https://doi.org/10.18502/jder.9744.

Bacchi, Carol Lee. 2009. *Analysing policy: what's the problem represented to be?* Frenchs Forest, NSW: Pearson Australia.

Barker, David C., and James D. Tinnick. 2006. Competing visions of parental roles and ideological constraint. *American Political Science Review* 100 (2): 249–263. https://doi.org/10.1017/S0003055406062149.

Bertrand, Ariell Rose, Melissa Arnold Lyon, and Rebecca Jacobsen. 2024. Narrative spillover: a narrative policy framework analysis of critical race theory discourse at multiple levels. *Policy Studies Journal* 52 (2): 391–423. https://doi.org/10.1111/psj.12523.

Blair, Benjamin D., and Larkin McCormack. 2016. Applying the narrative policy framework to the issues surrounding hydraulic fracturing within the news media: a research note. *Research & Politics* 3 (1): 2053168016628334. https://doi.org/10.1177/2053168016628334.

Boscarino, Jessica E. 2019. From three mile island to fukushima: the impact of analogy on attitudes toward nuclear power. *Policy Sciences* 52 (1): 21–42. https://doi.org/10.1007/s11077-018-9333-5.

Brewer, Adam M. 2019. A bridge in flux: narratives and the policy process in the pacific northwest. *Review of Policy Research* 36 (4): 497–522. https://doi.org/10.1111/ropr.12343.

Bruner, Jerome. 1991. The narrative construction of reality. *Critical Inquiry* 18 (1): 1–21. https://doi.org/10.1086/448619.

Chomsky, Noem. 1957. *Syntactic structures*. Oxford, England: Mouton.

Clemons, Randy, and Mark K. McBeth. 2020. *Public policy praxis: a case approach for understanding policy and analysis*, 4th ed. New York: Routledge. https://doi.org/10.4324/9780367444495.

Crespy, Amandine, and Camille Nessel. 2022. Discursive analysis, framing, and the narrative policy framework. In *Elgar encyclopedia of European union public policy*, ed. Paolo Roberto Graziano and Jale Tosun, 495–505. Edward Elgar Publishing. https://doi.org/10.4337/9781800881112.ch51.

Crow, Deserai A., John Berggren, Lydia A. Lawhon, Elizabeth A. Koebele, Adrianne Kroepsch, and Juhi Huda. 2017a. Local media coverage of wildfire disasters: an analysis of problems and solutions in policy narratives. *Environment and Planning C: Politics and Space* 35 (5): 849–871. https://doi.org/10.1177/0263774X16667302.

Crow, Deserai A., Lydia A. Lawhon, John Berggren, Juhi Huda, Elizabeth Koebele, and Adrianne Kroepsch. 2017b. A narrative policy framework analysis of wildfire policy discussions in two colorado communities. *Politics & Policy* 45 (4): 626–656. https://doi.org/10.1111/polp.12207.

Crow, Deserai A., and Andrea Lawlor. 2016. Media in the policy process: using framing and narratives to understand policy influences. *Review of Policy Research* 33 (5): 472–491. https://doi.org/10.1111/ropr.12187.

Crow, Deserai Anderson, and John Berggren. 2014. Using the narrative policy framework to understand stakeholder strategy and effectiveness: a multi-case analysis. In *The science of stories*, ed. Michael D. Jones, Elizabeth A. Shanahan, and Mark K. McBeth, 131–56. New York: Palgrave Macmillan US. https://doi.org/10.1057/9781137485861_7.

Crow, Deserai, and Michael Jones. 2018. Narratives as tools for influencing policy change. *Policy & Politics* 46 (2): 217–234. https://doi.org/10.1332/030 557318X15230061022899.

deLeon, Peter. 1992. The democratization of the policy sciences. *Public Administration Review* 52 (2): 125–129. https://doi.org/10.2307/976465.

Derrida, Jacques, Alan Bass, and Henri Ronse. 1981. *Positions*. Chicago: University of Chicago Press.

Edelman, Murray J. 1964. *The symbolic uses of politics*. Illini books ed. Urbana: University of Illinois Press.

Edelman, Murray J. 1990. *Constructing the political spectacle*. Chicago: University of Chicago Press.

Finucane, Melissa L., and Theresa A. Satterfield. 2005. Risk as narrative value: a theoretical framework for facilitating the biotechnology debate. *International Journal of Biotechnology* 7 (1–3): 128–146. https://doi.org/10.1504/IJBT.2005.006450.

Fischer, Frank. 2003. *Reframing public policy: discursive politics and deliberative practices*. Oxford, New York: Oxford University Press.

Fischer, Frank, and John Forester. 1993. The argumentative turn in policy analysis and planning. *Duke University Press*. https://doi.org/10.2307/j.ctv122 0k4f.

Flores, Andrew, Daniel Boden, Donald Haider-Markel, Daniel Lewis, Patrick Miller, and Jami Taylor. 2023. Taking perspective of the stories we tell about transgender rights: the narrative policy framework. *Policy Studies Journal* 51 (1): 123–143. https://doi.org/10.1111/psj.12475.

Franzosi, Roberto. 1998. Narrative analysis—or why (and how) sociologists should be interested in narrative. *Annual Review of Sociology* 24 (1): 517–554. https://doi.org/10.1146/annurev.soc.24.1.517.

Galloway, Ben, Chad Zanocco, Geoboo Song, and Michael Jones. 2024. The effect of policy narratives on policy elite versus public preferences for hydraulic fracturing regulation. *Review of Policy Research* 41 (4): 613–634. https://doi.org/10.1111/ropr.12563.

Genette, Gérard. 1983. *Narrative discourse: an essay in method*. 1. publ., 4. print. Ithaca: Cornell University Press.

Golding, Dominic, Sheldon Krimsky, and Alonzo Plough. 1992. Evaluating risk communication: narrative vs. technical presentations of information about radon. *Risk Analysis* 12 (1): 27–35. https://doi.org/10.1111/j.1539-6924.1992.tb01304.x.

Gottlieb, Madeline, Ernst Bertone Oehninger, and Gwen Arnold. 2018. 'No fracking way' vs. 'Drill Baby Drill': a restructuring of who is pitted against whom in the narrative policy framework. *Policy Studies Journal* 46 (4): 798–827. https://doi.org/10.1111/psj.12291.

Gray, Garry, and Michael D. Jones. 2016. A qualitative narrative policy framework? *Examining the policy narratives of US Campaign Finance Regulatory Reform. Public Policy and Administration* 31 (3): 193–220. https://doi.org/10.1177/0952076715623356.

Guenther, Sara K., and Elizabeth A. Shanahan. 2020. Communicating risk in human-wildlife interactions: how stories and images move minds. *PLoS ONE* 15 (12): e0244440. https://doi.org/10.1371/journal.pone.0244440.

Gupta, Kuhika, Joseph Ripberger, and Wesley Wehde. 2018. Advocacy group messaging on social media: using the narrative policy framework to study twitter messages about nuclear energy policy in the United States. *Policy Studies Journal* 46 (1): 119–136. https://doi.org/10.1111/psj.12176.

Hajer, Maarten. 1997. *The politics of environmental discourse: ecological modernization and the policy process.* https://doi.org/10.1093/019829333X.001.0001.

Hajer, Maarten A. 1993. Discourse coalitions and the institutionalization of practice: the case of acid rain in Britain. In *The argumentative turn in policy analysis and planning*, ed. Frank Fischer and John Forester, 43–76. Duke University Press. https://doi.org/10.2307/j.ctv1220k4f.

Hajer, Maarten A. 2005. *The politics of environmental discourse: ecological modernization and the policy process.* Repr. Oxford: Clarendon Press.

Hampton, Greg. 2004. Enhancing public participation through narrative analysis. *Policy Sciences* 37 (3–4): 261–276. https://doi.org/10.1007/s11077-005-1763-1.

Herman, David. 2009. *Basic elements of narrative*, 1st ed. Wiley. https://doi.org/10.1002/9781444305920.

Hindess, Barry. 1977. *Philosophy and methodology in the social sciences.* Hassocks: Harvester Press.

Huda, Juhi. 2019. Policy narratives across two languages: a comparative study using the narrative policy framework. *Review of Policy Research* 36 (4): 523–546. https://doi.org/10.1111/ropr.12344.

Huisman. Narrative structures in language and literature. In *The Routledge companion to semiotics and linguistics*, ed. Paul Cobley.

Huisman, Rosemary. 2005. From structuralism to post-structuralism. In *Narrative and media*, ed. Anne Dunn, Helen Fulton, and Julian Murphet, 28–44. Cambridge: Cambridge University Press. https://doi.org/10.1017/CBO9780511811760.003.

Hukkinen, Janne Ilmari, Emery Roe, and Gene I. Rochlin. 1990. A salt on the land: a narrative analysis of the controversy over irrigation-related salinity and toxicity in California's San Joaquin valley. *Policy Sciences* 23 (4): 307–329.

Jones, Michael D. 2014a. Communicating climate change: are stories better than 'Just the Facts'? *Policy Studies Journal* 42 (4): 644–673. https://doi.org/10. 1111/psj.12072.

Jones, Michael D. 2014b. Cultural characters and climate change: how heroes shape our perception of climate science. *Social Science Quarterly* 95 (1): 1–39. https://doi.org/10.1111/ssqu.12043.

Jones, Michael D. 2018. Advancing the narrative policy framework? The musings of a potentially unreliable narrator. *Policy Studies Journal* 46 (4): 724–746. https://doi.org/10.1111/psj.12296.

Jones, Michael D. Heroes and villains: cultural narratives, mass opinions, and climate change. Ph.D. The University of Oklahoma. https://www.proquest. com/docview/305218173/abstract/A7245ED4EC9A4C52PQ/1. Accessed on 29 August 2024.

Jones, Michael D., and Claudio M. Radaelli. 2015. The narrative policy framework: child or monster? *Critical Policy Studies* 9 (3): 339–55. https://doi. org/10.1080/19460171.2015.1053959.

Jones, Michael D., and Mark K. McBeth. 2010. A narrative policy framework: clear enough to be wrong? *Policy Studies Journal* 38 (2): 329–353. https:// doi.org/10.1111/j.1541-0072.2010.00364.x.

Jones, Michael D., Mark K. McBeth, and Elizabeth A. Shanahan. 2014. Introducing the narrative policy framework. In *The science of stories: applications of the narrative policy framework in public policy analysis*, ed. Michael D. Jones, Elizabeth A. Shanahan, and Mark K. McBeth, 1–25. New York: Palgrave Macmillan US. https://doi.org/10.1057/9781137485861_1.

Jones, Michael D., Mark K. McBeth, Elizabeth A. Shanahan, Aaron Smith-Walter, and Geoboo Song. 2022. Conducting narrative policy framework research: from theory to methods. In *Methods of the policy process*, ed. Christopher M. Weible and Samuel Workman. Routledge.

Jones, Michael D., Aaron Smith-Walter, Mark K. McBeth, and Elizabeth A. Shanahan. 2022. The narrative policy framework. In *Theories of the policy process*. New York, NY: Routledge.

Jones, Michael D., and Geoboo Song. 2014. Making sense of climate change: how story frames shape cognition. *Political Psychology* 35 (4): 447–476. https://doi.org/10.1111/pops.12057.

Jones, Michael, Elizabeth Shanahan, and Mark McBeth. 2014. *The science of stories: applications of the narrative policy framework in public policy analysis*. Springer. https://books.google.com/books?hl=en&lr=&id=ceoaBgAAQ BAJ&oi=fnd&pg=PP1&dq=info:Y2FgyvammO0J:scholar.google.com&ots= EdZJ-KWUp4&sig=98SOZDkYT6G1dWzBKnJb_0KInaY. Accessed on 29 August 2024.

Jorgensen, Paul D., Geeboo Song, and Michael D. Jones. 2018. Public support for campaign finance reform: the role of policy narratives, cultural predispositions, and political knowledge in collective policy preference formation. *Social Science Quarterly* 99 (1): 216–230. https://doi.org/10.1111/ssqu.12357.

Kear, Andrew R., and Dominic D. Wells. 2014. Coalitions are people: policy narratives and the defeat of Ohio senate bill 5. In *The science of stories: applications of the narrative policy framework in public policy analysis*, ed. Michael D. Jones, Elizabeth A. Shanahan, and Mark K. McBeth, 157–84. New York: Palgrave Macmillan US. https://doi.org/10.1057/9781137485861_8.

Kirkpatrick, Kellee J., and James W. Stoutenborough. 2018. Strategy, narratives, and reading the public: developing a micro-level theory of political strategies within the narrative policy framework. *Policy Studies Journal* 46 (4): 949–977. https://doi.org/10.1111/psj.12271.

Kuenzler, Johanna, and Bettina Stauffer. 2023. Policy dimension: a new concept to distinguish substance from process in the narrative policy framework. *Policy Studies Journal* 51 (1): 11–32. https://doi.org/10.1111/psj.12482.

Kuhlmann, Johanna, and Sonja Blum. 2021. Narrative plots for regulatory, distributive, and redistributive policies. *European Policy Analysis* 7 (S2): 276–302. https://doi.org/10.1002/epa2.1127.

Lakoff, George. 2016. *Moral politics: how liberals and conservatives think.* University of Chicago Press.

László, János. 2008. *The science of stories.* Routledge. https://doi.org/10.4324/9780203894934.

Lawlor, Andrea, and Deserai Crow. 2018. Risk-based policy narratives. *Policy Studies Journal* 46 (4): 843–867. https://doi.org/10.1111/psj.12270.

Levi-Strauss, Claude. 1958. *Structural anthropology.* Revised ed. edition. Basic Books.

Liu, Li-Yin, and Wei-Ting Yen. 2024. Why do individuals in democratic societies support stringent policies? a narrative policy framework analysis. *Policy & Politics* 52 (3): 453–76. https://doi.org/10.1332/030557324X17049690476008.

Lybecker, Donna L., Mark K. McBeth, and James W. Stoutenborough. 2016. Do we understand what the public hears? Stakeholders' preferred communication choices for discussing river issues with the public. *Review of Policy Research* 33 (4): 376–392. https://doi.org/10.1111/ropr.12182.

Majone, Giandomenico. 1989. *Evidence, argument, and persuasion in the policy process.* Nachdr. New Haven: Yale Univ. Press.

McBeth, Mark K., and Donna L. Lybecker. 2018. The narrative policy framework, agendas, and sanctuary cities: the construction of a public problem. *Policy Studies Journal* 46 (4): 868–893. https://doi.org/10.1111/psj.12274.

McBeth, Mark K., Donna L. Lybecker, and James W. Stoutenborough. 2016. Do stakeholders analyze their audience? the communication switch and stakeholder personal versus public communication choices. *Policy Sciences* 49 (4): 421–44. https://doi.org/10.1007/s11077-016-9252-2.

Mcbeth, Mark K., Donna L. Lybecker, and Kacee A. Garner. 2010. The story of good citizenship: framing public policy in the context of duty-based versus engaged citizenship. *Politics & Policy* 38 (1): 1–23. https://doi.org/10.1111/j.1747-1346.2009.00226.x.

McBeth, Mark K., Donna L. Lybecker, and Jessica M. Sargent. 2022. Narrative empathy: *a narrative policy framework study of working-class climate change narratives and narrators*. *World Affairs* 185 (3): 471–499. https://doi.org/10.1177/00438200221107018.

McBeth, Mark K., Donna L. Lybecker, James W. Stoutenborough, Sarah N. Davis, and Katrina Running. 2017. Content matters: stakeholder assessment of river stories or river science. *Public Policy and Administration* 32 (3): 175–196. https://doi.org/10.1177/0952076716671034.

Mcbeth, Mark K., and Elizabeth A. Shanahan. 2004. Public opinion for sale: the role of policy marketers in greater yellowstone policy conflict. *Policy Sciences* 37 (3–4): 319–338. https://doi.org/10.1007/s11077-005-8876-4.

McBeth, Mark K., Elizabeth A. Shanahan, Ruth J. Arnell, and Paul L. Hathaway. 2007. The intersection of narrative policy analysis and policy change theory. *Policy Studies Journal* 35 (1): 87–108. https://doi.org/10.1111/j.1541-0072.2007.00208.x.

McBeth, Mark K., Elizabeth A. Shanahan, Molly C. Arrandale Anderson, and Barbara Rose. 2012. Policy story or gory story? Narrative policy framework analysis of buffalo field campaign's YouTube videos. *Policy & Internet* 4 (3–4): 159–83. https://doi.org/10.1002/poi3.15.

McBeth, Mark K., Elizabeth A. Shanahan, Paul L. Hathaway, Linda E. Tigert, and Lynette J. Sampson. 2010. Buffalo tales: interest group policy stories in greater yellowstone. *Policy Sciences* 43 (4): 391–409. https://doi.org/10.1007/s11077-010-9114-2.

McBeth, Mark K., Elizabeth A. Shanahan, and Michael D. Jones. 2005. The science of storytelling: measuring policy beliefs in greater yellowstone. *Society & Natural Resources* 18 (5): 413–429. https://doi.org/10.1080/08941920590924765.

McComas, Katherine, and James Shanahan. 1999. Telling stories about global climate change: measuring the impact of narratives on issue cycles. *Communication Research* 26 (1): 30–57. https://doi.org/10.1177/009365099026001003.

McGovern, Rachel, and Michael D. Jones. The narrative policy framework and institutions. *Review of Policy Research* n/a(n/a). https://doi.org/10.1111/ropr.12616.

McMorris, Claire, Chad Zanocco, and Michael Jones. 2018. Policy narratives and policy outcomes: an NPF examination of oregon's ballot measure 97. *Policy Studies Journal* 46 (4): 771–797. https://doi.org/10.1111/psj.12263.

Merry, Melissa K. 2016. Constructing policy narratives in 140 characters or less: the case of gun policy organizations. *Policy Studies Journal* 44 (4): 373–395. https://doi.org/10.1111/psj.12142.

Merry, Melissa K. 2018. Narrative strategies in the gun policy debate: exploring proximity and social construction. *Policy Studies Journal* 46 (4): 747–770. https://doi.org/10.1111/psj.12255.

Merry, Melissa K. 2019. Angels versus devils: the portrayal of characters in the gun policy debate. *Policy Studies Journal* 47 (4): 882–904. https://doi.org/10.1111/psj.12207.

Merry, Melissa Kate. 2020. *Warped narratives: distortion in the framing of gun policy*. University of Michigan Press.

Mishler, Elliot G. 1995. Models of narrative analysis: a typology. *Journal of Narrative and Life History* 5 (2): 87–123. https://doi.org/10.1075/jnlh.5.2.01mod.

Morrill, Calvin, Madelaine Adelman, Cindy Bejarano, Christine Yalda, and Michael Musheno. 2000. Telling tales in school: youth culture and conflict narratives. *Law & Society Review* 34 (3): 521–565. https://doi.org/10.2307/3115137.

O'Donovan, Kristin Taylor. 2018. Does the narrative policy framework apply to local policy issues? *Politics & Policy* 46 (4): 532–570. https://doi.org/10.1111/polp.12265.

O'Leary, Renée, Ron Borland, Tim Stockwell, and Marjorie MacDonald. 2017. Claims in vapour device (e-Cigarette) regulation: a narrative policy framework analysis. *International Journal of Drug Policy* 44: 31–40. https://doi.org/10.1016/j.drugpo.2017.03.004.

Olofsson, Kristin L., Christopher M. Weible, Tanya Heikkila, and J. C. Martel. 2018. Using nonprofit narratives and news media framing to depict air pollution in Delhi, India. *Environmental Communication* 12 (7): 956–72. https://doi.org/10.1080/17524032.2017.1309442.

Peterson, Holly L. 2018. Political information has bright colors: narrative attention theory. *Policy Studies Journal* 46 (4): 828–842. https://doi.org/10.1111/psj.12272.

Peterson, Holly L. 2023. Narrative policy images: intersecting narrative & attention in presidential stories about the environment. *Policy Studies Journal* 51 (1): 53–77. https://doi.org/10.1111/psj.12447.

Peterson, Holly L., and Michael D. Jones. 2016. Making sense of complexity: the narrative policy framework and agenda setting. In *Handbook of public policy agenda setting*, ed. Nikolaos Zahariadis. Edward Elgar Publishing. https://doi.org/10.4337/9781784715922.00015.

Propp, V. 1968. *Morphology of the folktale*, 2d ed. Austin: University of Texas Press.

Raile, Eric D., Elizabeth A. Shanahan, Richard C. Ready, Jamie McEvoy, Clemente Izurieta, Ann Marie Reinhold, Geoffrey C. Poole, Nicolas T. Bergmann, and Henry King. 2022. Narrative risk communication as a lingua franca for environmental hazard preparation. *Environmental Communication* 16 (1): 108–24. https://doi.org/10.1080/17524032.2021.1966818.

Richardson, Laurel. 1990. Narrative and sociology. *Journal of Contemporary Ethnography* 19 (1): 116–135. https://doi.org/10.1177/089124190019001006.

Ricketts, Mitch. 2007. The use of narratives in safety and health communication.

Roe, Emery. 1994. *Narrative policy analysis: theory and practice*. Durham London: Duke Univ. Press.

Roe, Emery M. 1992. Applied narrative analysis: the tangency of literary criticism, social science and policy analysis. *New Literary History* 23 (3): 555. https://doi.org/10.2307/469220.

Ruff, Jonathan W. A., Gregory Stelmach, and Michael D. Jones. 2022. Space for stories: legislative narratives and the establishment of the US space force. *Policy Sciences* 55 (3): 509–553. https://doi.org/10.1007/s11077-022-09455-5.

Sabatier, Paul A. 1991. Toward better theories of the policy process. *PS: Political Science & Politics* 24 (2): 147–56. https://doi.org/10.2307/419923.

Sabatier, Paul A. 1999. Fostering the development of policy theory. In *Theories of the policy process*, ed. Paul A. Sabatier, 261–76. Boulder, Colo.: Westview Press. 0813399866.

Sabatier, Paul A., and Christopher M. Weible. 2007. The advocacy coalition framework: innovations and clarifications. In *Theories of the policy process, Second Edition*, Routledge.

Sager, Fritz, Karin Ingold, and Andreas Balthasar. 2017. *Policy-analyse in der Schweiz: Besonderheiten, Theorien, Beispiele*. NZZ Libro.

de Saussure, Ferdinand. 1916. *Course in general linguistics*. New York: McGraw-Hill.

de Saussure, Ferdinand. 2005. *Course in general linguistics*. Nachdr. ed. Charles Bally. New York: McGraw-Hill.

Schattschneider, E. E. 1975. *The semisovereign people: a realist's view of democracy in America*. Hinsdale, Ill: Dryden Press.

Schlaufer, Caroline, Johanna Kuenzler, Michael D. Jones, and Elizabeth A. Shanahan. 2022a. The narrative policy framework: a traveler's guide to policy stories. *Politische Vierteljahresschrift* 63 (2): 249–273. https://doi.org/10.1007/s11615-022-00379-6.

Schlaufer, Caroline, Marina Pilkina, Tatiana Chalaya, Tatiana Khaynatskaya, Tatiana Voronova, and Aleksandra Pozhivotko. 2022b. How do civil society organizations communicate in an authoritarian setting? A narrative analysis of the Russian waste management debate. *Review of Policy Research* 39 (6): 730–751. https://doi.org/10.1111/ropr.12492.

Schwartz, Noah S. 2023. Taking stock: the contribution of policy studies to our understanding of gun policy. *Politics & Policy* 51 (3): 415–425. https://doi.org/10.1111/polp.12530.

Shanahan, Elizabeth A., Ann Marie Reinhold, Eric D. Raile, Geoffrey C. Poole, Richard C. Ready, Clemente Izurieta, Jamie McEvoy, Nicolas T. Bergmann, and Henry King. 2019. Characters matter: how narratives shape affective responses to risk communication. ed. Fritz Breithaupt. *PLOS ONE* 14 (12): e0225968. https://doi.org/10.1371/journal.pone.0225968.

Shanahan, Elizabeth A., Stephanie M. Adams, Michael D. Jones, and Mark K. McBeth. 2014. The blame game: narrative persuasiveness of the intentional causal mechanism. In *The science of stories: applications of the narrative policy framework in public policy analysis*, ed. Michael D. Jones, Elizabeth A. Shanahan, and Mark K. McBeth, 69–88. New York: Palgrave Macmillan US. https://doi.org/10.1057/9781137485861_4.

Shanahan, Elizabeth A., Michael D. Jones, and Mark K. McBeth. 2011a. Policy narratives and policy processes. *Policy Studies Journal* 39 (3): 535–561. https://doi.org/10.1111/j.1541-0072.2011.00420.x.

Shanahan, Elizabeth A., Michael D. Jones, and Mark K. McBeth. 2018a. How to conduct a narrative policy framework study. *The Social Science Journal* 55 (3): 332–345. https://doi.org/10.1016/j.soscij.2017.12.002.

Shanahan, Elizabeth A., Michael D. Jones, Mark K. McBeth, and Ross R. Lane. 2013. An angel on the wind: how heroic policy narratives shape policy realities. *Policy Studies Journal* 41 (3): 453–483. https://doi.org/10.1111/psj.12025.

Shanahan, Elizabeth A., Michael D. Jones, Mark K. McBeth, and Claudio M. Radaelli. 2018. the narrative policy framework. In *Theories of the policy process*, Routledge, 173–213. https://www.taylorfrancis.com/chapters/edit/10.4324/9780429494284-6/narrative-policy-framework-elizabeth-shanahan-michael-jones-mark-mcbeth-claudio-radaelli. Accessed on 29 August 2024.

Shanahan, Elizabeth A., Mark K. Mcbeth, and Paul L. Hathaway. 2011b. Narrative policy framework: the influence of media policy narratives on public opinion. *Politics & Policy* 39 (3): 373–400. https://doi.org/10.1111/j.1747-1346.2011.00295.x.

Shanahan, Elizabeth A., Mark K. McBeth, Paul L. Hathaway, and Ruth J. Arnell. 2008. Conduit or contributor? The role of media in policy change theory. *Policy Sciences* 41 (2): 115–138. https://doi.org/10.1007/s11077-008-9058-y.

Shanahan, Elizabeth A., Eric D. Raile, Kate A. French, and Jamie McEvoy. 2018c. Bounded stories. *Policy Studies Journal* 46 (4): 922–948. https://doi.org/10.1111/psj.12269.

Smith, Kevin B., and Christopher W. Larimer. 2009. *The public policy theory primer*. Boulder, CO: Westview Press.

Smith, Kevin B., Kevin B. Smith, and Christopher W. Larimer. 2017. *The public policy theory primer*, 3rd ed. Boulder, Colorado: Westview Press.

Smith-Walter, Aaron, Emily Fritz, Shannon O'Doherty, Michael D Jones, Mark K. McBeth, and Elizabeth A. Shanahan. 2022. Chapter 7: Sanctuary cities, focusing events, and the solidarity shift: a standard measurement of the prevalence of victims for the narrative policy framework. In *Narratives and the policy process: applications of the narrative policy framework*, Montana State University Library. https://oer.pressbooks.pub/scienceofstoriesv2/chapter/sanctuary-cities-focusing-events/. Accessed on 29 August 2024.

Smith-Walter, Aaron, Michael D. Jones, Elizabeth A. Shanahan, and Holly Peterson. 2020. The stories groups tell: campaign finance reform and the narrative networks of cultural cognition. *Quality & Quantity* 54 (2): 645–684. https://doi.org/10.1007/s11135-019-00884-8.

Smith-Walter, Aaron, Holly L. Peterson, Michael D. Jones, and Ashley Nicole Reynolds. Marshall. 2016. Gun stories: how evidence shapes firearm policy in the United States. *Politics & Policy* 44 (6): 1053–1088. https://doi.org/10.1111/polp.12187.

Stauffer, Bettina. 2023. What's the grand story? A macro-narrative analytical model and the case of Swiss child and adult protection policy. *Policy Studies Journal* 51 (1): 33–52. https://doi.org/10.1111/psj.12465.

Stauffer, Bettina, Johanna Kuenzler, and Michael D. Jones. 2024. Narrative policy framework and policy implementation. In *Handbook of public policy implementation*, eds. Fritz Sager, Céline Mavrot, and Lael R. Keiser. Edward Elgar Publishing, 193–203. https://doi.org/10.4337/9781800885905.00024.

Stephan, Hannes R. 2020. Shaping the scope of conflict in Scotland's fracking debate: conflict management and the narrative policy framework. *Review of Policy Research* 37 (1): 64–91. https://doi.org/10.1111/ropr.12365.

Stone, Deborah. 2012. *Policy paradox: the art of political decision making*, 3rd ed. New York: W.W. Norton & Co.

Stone, Deborah A. 1997. *Policy paradox: the art of political decision making*. New York: W.W. Norton.

Thompson, M., Richard Ellis, and Aaron B. Wildavsky. 1990. *Cultural theory*. Boulder, Colo: Westview Press.

Troiani, Vanessa, Sherry Ash, Jamie Reilly, and Murray Grossman. 2006. The neural correlates of narrative discourse: an investigation using arterial spin-labeling. *Brain and Language* 99 (1–2): 204–205. https://doi.org/10.1016/j.bandl.2006.06.110.

Wagenaar, Hendrik. 2014. *Meaning in action: interpretation and dialogue in policy analysis: interpretation and dialogue in policy analysis.* Routledge. https://doi.org/10.4324/9781315702476.

Weible, Christopher M. 2018. *Introduction: the scope and focus of policy process research and theory.* In Theories of the Policy Process: Routledge.

Weible, Christopher M., Kristin L. Olofsson, Daniel P. Costie, Juniper M. Katz, and Tanya Heikkila. 2016. Enhancing precision and clarity in the study of policy narratives: an analysis of climate and air issues in Delhi, India. *Review of Policy Research* 33 (4): 420–441. https://doi.org/10.1111/ropr.12181.

Weible, Christopher, Saba Siddiki, Jonathan Pierce, and Paul Sabatier. 2009. Contesting rationality: a target population and devil shift approach to evaluate collaborative policymaking.

Weiss, Jens. 2020. The evolution of reform narratives: a narrative policy framework analysis of German NPM reforms. *Critical Policy Studies* 14 (1): 106–23. https://doi.org/10.1080/19460171.2018.1530605.

Williams, Teshanee T., and Jennifer Kuzma. 2022. Narrative policy framework at the macro level—cultural theory-based beliefs, science-based narrative strategies, and their uptake in the canadian policy process for genetically modified salmon. *Public Policy and Administration* 37 (4): 480–515. https://doi.org/10.1177/09520767211065609.

Wolters, Erika Allen, Michael D. Jones, and Duvall. 2021. A narrative policy framework solution to understanding climate change framing research. In *Narratives and the policy process: applications of the narrative policy framework,* eds. Michael D. Jones,Mark McBeth, and Elizabeth Shanahan. Montana State University, 222–242. https://doi.org/10.15788/npf9.

Wolton, Laura P., Deserai A. Crow, and Tanya Heikkila. 2022. Chapter 3: Stepping forward: towards a more systematic NPF with automation. https://doi.org/10.15788/npf3.

Young, Kay, and Jeffrey L. Saver. 2001. The neurology of narrative. *SubStance* 30 (1/2): 72. https://doi.org/10.2307/3685505.

Zanocco, Chad, Geoboo Song, and Michael Jones. 2018. Fracking bad guys: the role of narrative character affect in shaping hydraulic fracturing policy preferences. *Policy Studies Journal* 46 (4): 978–999. https://doi.org/10.1111/psj.12278.

The Policy Transaction Perspective: A New Pragmatist Approach to Policy Processes

Philippe Zittoun, Christopher Ansell, Patrick Hassenteufel, and Jennifer Dodge

In the last fifteen years, a new pragmatist approach has emerged to better grasp the complex, fragmented, underdetermined, and uncertain nature of contemporary policy processes. Early policy studies in the 1930s and 1940s were heavily influenced by the philosophy of pragmatism (Dunn 2019; Deleon 1988), but this influence declined with the ascendence of positivist approaches to decision-making and the policy process. A new

P. Zittoun (✉)
LAET-ENTPE, University of Lyon, Lyon, France
e-mail: pzittoun@gmail.com

C. Ansell
University of California-Berkeley, Berkeley, CA, USA
e-mail: cansell@berkeley.edu

P. Hassenteufel
University of Paris Saclay-Printemps, Gif-Sur-Yvette, France
e-mail: Patrick.hassenteufel@uvsq.fr

J. Dodge
University at Albany, Albany, NY, USA

© The Editor(s) (if applicable) and The Author(s), under exclusive   253
license to Springer Nature Switzerland AG 2026
B. G. Peters and P. Zittoun (eds.), *Contemporary Approaches to Public
Policy*, International Series on Public Policy,
https://doi.org/10.1007/978-3-032-06026-6_11

pragmatism emerged beginning in the 1980s, influenced by the development of argumentative, interpretative, and constructivist approaches to policy studies (Jobert and Muller 1987; Stone 1989; Rochefort and Cobb 1994; Fischer 2003; Haas 2004; Wagenaar 2011; Fischer and Gottweis 2012; Lejano 2012) and the rediscovery of the pragmatist tradition in the social sciences in the U.S. and in Europe beginning in the 1980s (Bernstein 1992; Boltanski and Thévenot 1991; Stengers and Debaise 2007; Rorty 2013). Pragmatism points to the limits of classical policy concepts like "policy sub-system", "problem definition", or "policy coalition" for understanding the complexity of policy processes today.

The new pragmatism perspective seeks to renew our understanding of the policy process by focusing on how state and non-state actors define, discuss, argue about, and criticize policy proposals. However, rather than looking for fixed beliefs, values, and interests to explain the behavior of policymakers, this approach emphasizes the fluidity of individual and collective values and interests as policy actors explicate, test, negotiate, agree upon, and dispute. From this perspective, policy statements (or stories, narratives, arguments, etc.) are not emblems of pre-established interests or values, but rather moves in the co-construction of identities and alliances. Consequently, instead of starting from the perspective of clearly demarcated policy subsystems, new pragmatism follows the career of policy statements through a succession of empirical situations as they intersect with the formation of identities and alliances.

Inspired by the concept of "transaction" developed originally by Dewey and Bentley (1946), we call this new pragmatism approach the "Policy Transaction Approach" (Ansell et al., 2024). According to Dewey and Bentley, transactions occur in concrete situations at the micro-level of analysis where individuals test and modify definitions, values, knowledge, and even their own identity in order to persuade, enroll, or dispute their relationship to others and to themselves. Applied to policy processes, policy transactions are situated engagements of policy actors that relationally shape—or "co-construct"—their interests and values. The policy process is thereby conceptualized as a sequence of transactions that take place not only in the public sphere but also in multiple discrete venues, such as in the bureaucracy, cabinet meetings, interest group offices, etc.

---

e-mail: jdodge@albany.edu

In these venues, select groups of policy actors discuss the definition of public problems and their solutions and dispute their ownership, and in so doing construe the relationship between state and society.[1]

The policy transaction approach does not focus, however, on the concept of "problem" or "public" or "policy" in isolation, but rather stresses the relational processes through which these perspectives become entangled or co-defining. Thus, while the "problem definition" or "social construction of problems" approaches to policymaking are perhaps our nearest progenitors, the policy transaction approach emphasizes that defining a problem is always simultaneously and provisionally a determination of what "public" and "policy" mean and vice versa. Like three-dimensional chess, a transactional perspective stresses that any move along one policy dimension is likely to entail or have implications for other dimensions. Thus, while the policy transaction approach emphasizes the situational logic of the policy process, it understands policy actions in any given situation as being likely to entail or have implications for other situations.

This chapter introduces how the new pragmatist approach understands and conceptualizes the policy process. It begins with a discussion of the pragmatist origins of policy studies, thereby situating new pragmatism in a long tradition of policy inquiry. It then elaborates on new pragmatism, first by explaining policy transactions—particularly problematization and policy formulation practices—and then by elaborating on policy situations and the ways in which policy meanings evolve across various situations in a broader policy field.

THE PRAGMATIST ORIGINS OF POLICY STUDIES

As Peter Deleon (1988) and William Dunn (2019) suggest, early policy studies were heavily influenced by the philosophy of pragmatism. Authors such as Harold Lasswell, Abraham Kaplan, and Daniel Lerner, as well as the broader Chicago School of Political Science, were well-versed in

---

[1] For example, this processual and experimental view was expressed by Lasswell in his "power as a process" perspective, while Bentley redefined "pressure" as "a process of influence." In the same way, Kaplan and Lasswell emphasize actors-in-environment versus actors in an environment (Lasswell and Kaplan 1950), while unpacking the ways actors define environments and environments define actors in a specific context. Pragmatism thus emphasizes the importance of observing policy practices in situ, as practitioners build knowledge and apply tools to define policy processes.

and frequently cited the works of John Dewey and William James (Simon 1987; Almond 2004; Monroe 2004; Heaney and Hansen 2006). Charles Merriam, who became an assistant professor in 1900, met the "friendly John Dewey" (Karl 1974) and mentioned Dewey's book "The Public and its Problems". Since then, Dewey's work has been cited by many important authors, including Simon, Lindblom, and Truman, among others (Farr 1999). The pragmatist tradition was significant in the early twentieth century in the U.S. but was overshadowed by the success of positivism after World War II. It was rediscovered in the U.S. and in Europe beginning in the 1980s (Bernstein 1992; Stengers and Debaise 2007; Rorty 2013).

To gain a better understanding of the multiple influences of pragmatism on policy studies, it is important to revisit some fundamental issues. The founding pragmatists sought to break from classical philosophical traditions that sought to clarify the definition of concepts based solely on logic and reason and they eschewed the clear demarcation between subject and object advocated by Compte's positivism. Instead, the pragmatist perspective understands perception as intertwined with the social world. Peirce defined pragmatism as a method to clarify concepts through the observation of their expected effect, while William James defined them in terms of the observation of unexpected consequences (Misak 2018; Frega and Silva 2011). John Dewey proposed to develop an inquiry that includes experimentation, which he considered the only method to build knowledge (Mateo 2021; Dewey 1922).

This approach has influenced a pragmatist approach to policy studies along three important dimensions. First, pragmatism focuses attention on "processes", "situations", and "events" rather than on timeless "entities". As evoked by their book *Power and Society*, Lasswell and Kaplan (1950, xiv) suggest that the "subject matter of political science [can be expressed] in terms of a certain class of events rather than timeless institutions." They proposed to study "power as a process" instead of power as an entity. Indeed, this idea had been expressed fifty years earlier by another famous political scientist, Arthur Bentley, who followed courses by both John Dewey at the University of Chicago and Georg Simmel at the University of Berlin. Ten years later, Bentley proposed to study "pressure" as a process of influence as "legislating-administrating-adjudicating" rather than "law" or "administration", rejecting any fixed "class" or "group" in favor of "group activity" and "a way of action in which many people participate". These pragmatist roots of policy studies led it to focus on dynamic processes of policymaking rather than on fixed or structural characteristics of the State and the Administration.

A second dimension of pragmatist influence concerns the importance given to the empirical observation of practices in their specific situation. Kaplan and Lasswell argued that political science needs to be an "empirical science" based on "the principle of indetermination". Concepts and taxonomy are not a substitute for, but "an instrument of political inquiry". Dewey proposes that "knowing" results from inquiry. These authors propose that the researcher has to focus on empirical practices of knowledge-making practices and reflexive practices such as taxonomizing, valuation, symbolizing, analyzing, and defining in the policy process.

A third dimension of pragmatism is the rejection of epistemological dualism, which encourages a sharp distinction between object and subject, individual and society, thinking and acting, action and environment, or speech and the identity of the speaker. By contrast, pragmatism focuses on the objectivation by the subject rather than the object, the "individual-in-society" rather than the individual distinct from society, the "actors-in-an-environment" rather than action in an environment, the actor-issue rather than actors and issues as isolated phenomena, etc. In their book, Lasswell and Kaplan (1950, 4) propose considering seriously the "situation" as "a pattern of actors-in-an-environment".

While the pragmatist philosophy of Pierce, James, and Dewey played a significant role in the development of policy studies, the dominant positivism in social sciences eventually obscured the pragmatist perspective. The first generation of Policy Process theories in the 1970s, as well as the second generation in the 1980s and 1990s, were dominated by a causal perspective based on fixed variables such as tools, beliefs, ideas, interests, and institutions and on stable institutional arrangements such as a "system" or "subsystem". These perspectives enable us to grasp aspects of policy processes that are considered relatively stable but can obscure uncertainty and fragmentation in policy processes; the ways actors are variously and complexly defined by policy content and visa versa across situations; contingency, contradiction, and heterogeneity in policy processes; as well as the ways policy processes nonetheless construe the relationship between state and society as habits and customs are formed and reinforced, not as fixed entities but as repertoirs to creatively draw on in policy situations. The renewal of pragmatism in philosophy over the past thirty years, and in sociology and political science over the past twenty years, suggests new ways to think about the policy process to gain a deeper understanding of these dyanmics of the policy process.

THINKING LIKE A NEW PRAGMATIST

The new pragmatism emphasizes two main concepts: transactional practices and creative syncretism. As described above, transactional practices involve the relational co-construction of meanings in specific contexts. We further break down these transactional practices into two that, on the surface, are familiar to policy scholars but are viewed from a fresh perspective within new pragmatism: problematization practices (more commonly recognized as problem definitions) and policy formulation practices (more commonly understood as defining policy solutions). These transactional practices illuminate the meaning-making that occurs in micro-level policy processes.

The concept of creative syncretism draws on the work of Berk and Galvan (2009), which constructs a phenomenological perspective on institutional change that challenges more structural accounts. Building directly on Dewey's analysis of habit, they argue that people reorganize and redirect meanings and resources to meet certain situational demands. This process is "syncretic" because, like bricoleurs, actors creatively combine and recombine meaning. Creative syncretism is useful for thinking about transformations both within and across policy situations. Within policy situations, it suggests that policy actors creatively transform policy statements (problematizations, policy formulations, claims about the relationship between state and society, etc.) by situationally reorganizing and redirecting their meanings. Working across policy situations, these actors draw meaning and experience learned in one situation forward to new situations. The profound implication of this perspective is that we can trace a genealogy of transactions across situations.

In the following sections, we elaborate on these ideas, integrating concepts of power throughout and providing illustrations to clarify the focus of analysis in new pragmatism.

UNDERSTANDING & OBSERVING
POLICY TRANSACTIONAL PRACTICES

The pragmatist approach invites us to take into account the practices developed by actors through relationships with others. Bentley and Dewey proposed using the concept of "transaction" to better understand this relationship. They interpret a transaction "to refer to situations where systems of description and naming are used to deal with aspects and phases of action, without making a final attribution to 'elements' or other presumptively detachable or independent 'entities,' 'essences,' or 'realities,' and without isolating presumptively detachable elements" (Dewey and Bentley 1946, 509). They distinguish a "transaction" from an "interaction" or a "self-action". While discussing modern physics, they argue that the traditional mechanistic view of interactions in physics as two entities colliding is limiting and instead, they stress the quantum physics interpretation by which the definition of each entity changes through their relationship.

When studying transactions, individuals and society cannot be understood independently of each other, even in relationships, and must be considered as conjoint definitional processes. In other words, individuals and society co-construct each other, and understanding them in this way transcends the dualism between the individual and society. From this perspective, the researcher's task is not to determine the relationship between an individual and the environment but to understand that society is made up of individuals who are intertwined with the society (environment) to which they belong. The concept of "individual-society" is used to reject the dualism between individual and society. In the policy process, it encourages us to consider definitional processes—such as valuation, problematization, and problem-solving—as related to identify formation and the articulation of state-society relationships. From a pragmatist perspective, when policy actors argue about a policy instrument, they are also conjuring value, staking out identities, and claiming state prerogatives.

The concept of transaction also allows us to understand how individuals involved in a relationship do not merely exchange points of view, information, or material resources, but also transform themselves through the process of interacting. A statement or argument does not simply transmit information but also comes to define the identity of the speaker. Therefore, rather than thinking of given values that individuals uphold or exchange, a transactional approach regards "valuation" as a process where value is provisionally defined through the transaction. Similarly, the term "problem" is replaced with "problematization" to underline how policy actors transform an undetermined situation into a problem, and the terms "role" and "interest" are replaced by "enrolment" and "interessement" to highlight how policy actors shape a role, an interest and an identity, and so on.

Power within a transactional perspective is exercised through shaping the direction of defining self-in-relationship, creating value that binds individuals and coalitions, or problematizing bad situations in such a way that compels action (and may also further build coalitions). This is what it means to view power as a process enacted through transactional practices.

Building on this initial idea, the concept of "transactional policy practices" allows us to focus on the relational practices of actors from a new perspective. It can help us to understand how individuals define the world around them and its complex relationship with the State. Key transactional policy practices relevant to the policy sciences include problematization and policy formulation practices.

Observing Problematization

One of the most important transactional practices is to problematize a situation by defining a problem and claiming ownership of it. Problematization calls attention to how individuals transform an undefined situation into an unacceptable problem that generates victims and announces a tragic future that the State needs to address. It encompasses analytical practices by which actors identify themselves, for example as policymakers who formulate public policies that enable the State to solve problems, transform victims into beneficiaries, condemn culprits, and design a better future. Drawing on the constructivist perspective, a problem does not exist as an entity. Instead, it should be considered as a construction based on a definitional process developed by some actors to attract media attention, to get an issue on the government's agenda, or simply to understand what is happening.

New pragmatism builds upon insights from a rich tradition in the policy sciences of giving attention to problem definition and problem framing. From Easton and Wildavsky to Kingdon, and through the work of Rochefort and Cobb and Stone, the political science literature has long acknowledged definitional processes by which "claimants" transform a situation into a public problem and propagate their definition to attract attention as central to agenda-setting. Easton, for example, argued that an "input" is a combination of desires transformed into "demands" that receives enough support to influence policy. Wildavsky (1987, 42) argued that "a difficulty is a problem only if something can be done on it" and Kingdon (2010, 109) discusses "problem definition" as a way "conditions become defined as problems when we come to believe that we should do something about it". Rochefort and Cobb (1994, 14) call attention to "the struggles for problem ownership" and Stone (1989) stresses the "causal stories" that attribute responsibility for problems.

The concept of problematization has also been usefully articulated in the public policy literature by Carole Bacchi (2009). Building on the work of Foucault, Bacchi (2009, 2012, 2015) presents a framework for thinking about problematization in policy studies guided by six questions: First, "what's the problem...represented to be in a specific policy?" (WPR); second, "what presuppositions or assumptions underpin this representation of the 'problem'?"; third, "how has the representation of this 'problem' come about?"; fourth, "what is left unproblematic in this representation of this problem representation?"; fifth, "what effects are produced by this representation of the 'problem'?"; and finally, "how/where has this representation of the 'problem' been produced, disseminated, and defended?".

What does new pragmatist contribute to this already rich literature on problem definition and problematization? As useful as it is, the prior literature treats problem definition and problematization as acts that occur unilaterally when a policy actor seeks to construe an issue to their advantage. While this often appears to be the case, the policy transaction approach stresses that such constructions are relational processes where the meaning that I construct is intertwined with the meaning you construct—or what Karl Weick (1969) calls the "double interact" (see also Dewulf and Bouwen 2012). The policy transaction approach also suggests that problem definition or problematization is not only a "mobilization of bias" or a form of marketing spin, but also entails enactments of social or political order. We do not mean that problem definitions or problematization are ideologies, at least in the typical understanding of that term. Rather, we mean that any framing move (Abolafia 2004) must dynamically align itself with or engage other meaning constructions, such as the identity of opponents, situational rules of engagement, or commitments about what is good, right, or just. Put another way, problematizations are invariably networks of meaning rather than univocal statements of principle or position.

New pragmatism's focus on creative syncretism illuminates this dynamic construction of social and political order by stressing how meanings are combined and recombined to meet the demands and context of particular situations. This is achieved by coupling different elements from problematic circumstances. The concept of "coupling" should not be considered as either rationalistic or random (Kingdon 2010; Zittoun et al. 2021) but rather as a chaining or arrangement of meaning. This implies that actors not only attach different elements to build a problem statement but also take into account the capacity to give meaning to this language game (Wittgenstein 2014). They do so by joining five main activities related to problematization:

- Naming a phenomena "problematic" is a political act that assigns meaning and value to an uncomfortable situation. Problematizations are given various types of labels, some with negative connotations such as "homelessness", "pollution", "inequalities", and others where actors add the word "problem" such as "the housing problem". Naming is never neutral and can be the result of political controversies, as seen in the debate between "climate change" and "global warming" (Shi et al. 2020; Whitmarsh 2009), or the labeling of Covid-19 variants using the Greek alphabet instead of geographical origin as with "Chinese virus" or "UK variant".
- Identifying a public of victims or of culprits qualifies them as elements of social disorder. As Dewey mentioned, the public of victims emerges through knowledge tools, which are mobilized to shape and make visible the part of society victimized by unexpected consequences of human activities. This identification generally requires a normative perspective to recognize and differentiate victims from non-victims, and to order society accordingly.
- Dramatizing a problem occurs by integrating it into a narrative form that includes a past where the problem did not exist with an unfolding tragic process with a future whereby the tragic process continues to amplify. Dramatization emphasizes that a problem is rarely, if ever, defined by a singular event but rather is a part of a larger phenomenon that may repeat and amplify in the future.
- Politicizing a problem designates a public authority as responsible for solving it and preventing a tragic future. The politicization of the

issue articulates not only the need for the State to solve the problem but also a critique of its failure to do so earlier.

- Identifying problem owners makes specific policy actors responsible for either the creation or the clean up of problems. Identification can be useful in policy processes in many ways. For example, by publicizing identifications, policy actors can impose or put the problem on the media agenda, or pin down certain authorities to take action to address it. Or they can identify themselves or others as gatekeeper of the problem (Rochefort and Cobb 1994; Gusfield 1981) thus creating "problem ownership".

Coupling the meaning of these elements allows a policy actor to build a tragic problem statement as a means to bring about certain policy effects. Power as process is exercised in the successful (convincing) way policy actors weave these meanings of policy problems together to build broader coalitions of support and compel action.

To illustrate, a successful policy statement is necessary but not sufficient for problem owners to put the problem on the media agenda. For example, when air pollution was first put on the media agenda in Paris in July 1995, it resulted from linking problematization with other meanings. Environmental experts coupled air pollution, and the need to measure it, with a large number of Parisian victims with health issues, identifying cars as main culprits and the municipality as responsible for responding to pollution alerts. The equipment to measure the pollution was installed a few months before the first alert, making the pollution visible. The media questioned the mayor about his plans to solve this problem as the responsible party (Zittoun 2008).

OBSERVING POLICY FORMULATION PRACTICES TO TAME WICKED PROBLEMS AND DESIGNATE POLICY-MAKERS

A second important transactional practice is defining a solution statement and identifying policymakers who support it. While most scholars accept the constructivist perspective of problem agenda-setting, they differ on how to conceptualize the formulation of policy solutions. Some focus on the list of available instruments (Margetts and Hood 2016) or on "the short list of ideas" (Kingdon 2010, 139) rather than on the process of defining solutions. Even Rochefort and Cobb who approached problem definition from a constructivist perspective emphasized that finding solutions depended on their "availability" (Rochefort and Cobb 1994, 25). The definition of a policy solution continues to be an enigma or at least a black box (Zittoun 2014). The transactional perspective opens this black box by observing the main definitional activities associated with policy problems, again focusing on how meanings are creatively combined and recombined within and across situations:

- Naming the solution means actors label their proposal to bestow meaning and fight against alternative interpretations. For example, in France, when proposing a law authorizing same sex marriage, the government developed the term "marriage for all" while the opposition referred to it as "gay marriage". A policy can often take the name of the policymaker as with "Obamacare", demonstrating the co-construction of a policy instrument and its owner.
- Instrumentation requires attaching the solution to technical, social, and political tools to shape and modify the relationship between public authorities and the human or non-human behaviors they want to influence. These tools are known as "effecting" tools by Hood. Instrumentation should be viewed as a normative process that defines both the beneficiaries and condemns culprits. Lowi referred to distributive tools such as drivers' licenses, which distinguish those who have the right to drive from those who do not. He also referred to redistributive tools that transfer resources such as money through taxation from one group to another.
- Taming wicked problems through cause-shifting occurs when a seemingly intractable problem is redefined as a tractable one, and can take the form of replacing a problem with its cause. This rests on the notion that a problem requires a solution to be defined as a problem, and similarly a solution (such as a specific policy instrument) also requires a problem to become defined as a "solution". In contrast with Kingdon's multiple streams framework, in which a moment occurs when problems and solutions "out there" become aligned, coupling from a new pragmatist perspective occurs when problems and solutions are co-defined. The meaning dimension of coupling is crucial to understanding the dynamic of defining a solution and transforming the problem. For example, when the French president proposed to reform the labor code, he justified it by stating that it would solve one of the main causes of unemployment: the

rigidity of the labor code. The rigidity of the labor code is not only the "cause" of the problem, it is also a new treatable problem that can replace unemployment as a problem.

- Securing support for a policy solution involves designating a public authority as capable of solving a problem or wicked problem. In this way, defining a policy solution involves not just clarifying a response to a problem, but also legitimizing the State by convincingly articulating its ability to prevent a future tragedy and reenchant the tragic future, perhaps by "making something great again".

- Shaping policymakers occurs when policy owners not only advance a policy statement but also identify themselves as policymakers implicated in the policy statement—that is, as persons capable of influencing the policymaking process by imposing a new solution. Based on this epistemological inseparability between the definition and its definers, the definition of a policy solution is also a powerful process that designates not only who the decision-makers are but also who can influence them.

Syncretizing these meanings through the transactional process of policy formulation makes it possible to build a dramatic policy statement in which the State becomes the one that can change the future and prevent the anticipated tragedy. It must also be seen as a necessary condition to allow its owners to put a formulated policy on the governmental agenda. Again, power is exercised in situ through the convincing articulation of policy solutions in ways that link meanings related to naming, instrumentation, cause-shifting, politicizing, and (re)defining policymakers. For example, before the subprime crisis, there was an important debate within the Ministry of Economy between those who argued that the French government must adopt a Keynesian stimulus policy based on temporary and targeted budgetary tools to combat the economic recession while others preferred to wait and use fiscal stabilizers to counter the economic slowdown. Each solution statement linked a specific name, certain economic tools, a different definition of the problem, and specific set actors who support them.

Policy transactions practices—problematization as well as policy formulating—do not occur in isolated, singular policy venues but flow across various "situations" within which they are transformed, a topic we turn to next.

THE SITUATIONAL AND TRANS-SITUATIONAL LOGIC OF NEW PRAGMATISM

While most policy theories prefer to observe the policy process and policy transformation at the meso-level emphasizing structure—in a particular, policy subsystem, policy stream, or policy venue—new pragmatism proposes to start by identifying empirical situations when and where policy transactional practices concretely take place. A "situation" can be understood as an occurrence at the micro-level—such as a specific meeting, discussion, or public discourse—whereby different actors who, at a specific time and space, enact a relationship between themselves, the situation with its formal and informal rules and resources, and an audience or public. This focus on the "situation" allows researchers to investigate micro-processes by which problematization and policy formulation occur, tracing policy transformations as they progress along the policy process. Situations may involve a policy statement's resistance to critique, its propagation through the enrolment of new "policymakers", and the redefinition work they do.

Taking "Situation" Seriously as an Empirical Central Time–Space Perspective

The concept of "situation" as that of "event", "eventful", or "eventuation" (Dewey and Bentley 1964, 143) stresses the importance of not separating time and space when trying to grasp transactional practices. Bentley talked of "behavioral space–time" to highlight the importance of finding an observable place-time in social relationships and the meaning built into those relationships (Dewey and Bentley 1964, 35). In the same way, Dewey insists on the logic of inquiry within a "situation" as each event produces its own consequences through time and space. Influenced by Einstein's revolution in physics to rethink the relationship between space and time, Dewey and Bentley conceived the concept of "situation" as having the capacity to grasp both space and time together.

The main idea of this micro-level perspective is to observe the empirical situation where and when policymakers deploy their transactional policy practices. Policy transactions take place at a certain time and place—a press conference, a committee meeting, or a public hearing, etc. These specific situations or events tend to elicit certain kinds of transactions, such as conviction, persuasion, negotiation, or struggles between different policymakers. A central implication of this stress on situation or event is that the policy transaction approach adopts a more fine-grained micro-analysis of policy change than do contemporary policy process theories, which adopt a more meso-level, systemic perspective.

This centrality of the "situation" as a temporal site corresponds to the importance given to the transactional practices and their impacts on the definition of statement and identity. Contrary to determinist theories, which consider that phenomena can be explained by grasping the phenomena that precede them as a "cause", the transactional approach gives a centrality to what is happening during the phenomena itself (relational co-construction). It focuses on how each situation can be observed through its capacity to transform the definition of the problem or policy statement and/or its capacity to transform the coalition that supports it. Each situation can be understood as a specific experience in which actors test, but also modify, their statements and arguments.

As Majone reminded us, actors argue all the time and at every step during the policy process (Majone 1989). If we observe policymakers, their main activity is an argumentative one whereby they defend their policy proposals. Argumentative can be an exercise of power by contributing to the death of a proposal. Majone insisted, in particular, on the "feasibility argument", a main weapon mobilized by experts to kill a proposal. The feasibility argument can be legal, budgetary, or about the unexpected impact of the proposal. A proposal that is considered "unfeasible" by the experts can disappear from the government agenda. For example, in an interview with former French Minister for the Economy Christine Lagarde, she explained how every time she proposed a policy solution in front of departmental directors, someone always said: "Madame Minister, it is an excellent idea, but unfortunately it is not feasible".

Given the multiplicity and diversity of situations, the main idea of the pragmatist approach is to focus on the situations where transformations of policy statements and/or supporting configurations of actors take place. If each situation can be understood as an experience in which policymakers test their policy statements, some situations can be seen as occasions in which the policy statements attached to specific policymakers change. In other words, either changes in problem or solution definitions and/or changes in the configuration of actors, or both, can be observed.

To understand this transactional process, we can take the empirical example of the Paris tramway as a solution to the problem of air pollution. The debate about the problem and the solution took place across situations where actors discussed, negotiated, and fought. In one situation, the mayor organized various meetings with his main collaborators to discuss which policy solution could be coupled with the problem of air pollution. During these meetings, different proposals were supported by different experts and bureaucrats were in competition. The tramway was proposed by the Transport Department, recycling an old project that they had developed 20 years ago for a different problem and that had failed to get on the agenda then. Through redefinition work, they coupled the tramway to the problem of pollution, with themselves as the new policymakers and the Mayor as the new decision-maker.

Situations Cue the Transaction

Even though each situation is a unique time–space venue, the situations we are interested in share some common characteristics that allow us to construct a kind of ideal type. A situation in the policy process is characterized not only by its physical location and its specific time, but also by a configuration of actors, a discursive regime of discussion, an audience, and a regulatory process. To illustrate, we can distinguish between a situation with a small audience and a limited number of participants, who deliberate and negotiate among themselves to find a common understanding or position, and a situation with a large audience and a large number of participants where discourse is generally addressed to an audience beyond the participants, with the hope of convincing or influencing them. As observed by Perelman and Olbrechts-Tyteca (2008), speaking in front of a large audience has an immediate impact on the modality and structure of the situation's purpose (Perelman and Olbrechts-Tyteca 2008). If a small audience allows the exchange and the mutual understanding through discussion, the purpose of the public discourse is to convince a public that cannot really react.

By combining these characteristics, we arrive at three ideal-type situations with different mixes of power, authority, and public engagement: public forums, policy atriums, and policy arenas.

Public situations as **"public forums"** organize public debate or opinion. As the privileged space for the publicization of problems and proposals, the media forum is the most important public forum. In this forum, the publicization of problems and proposals statement depends both on the complex rules that restrict access to the media, guarded by a world of journalists, and on the strategies of their owners who structure their subject and choose their temporality in an attempt to master the process. It should be noted, for example, that problem-owners tend to publicize their problem definitions as soon as possible in order to give them importance, while the mediatization of policy proposals usually takes place at the end of conflictual agenda-setting processes. While public forums are primarily visible, debate is more discrete and less visible in other situations.

Both hermetic atriums and discrete arenas are situations in which debate occurs, such as an official meeting, where the list of participants and invitees is limited and fixed, or an informal meeting limited to two or three people. **Policy atriums** are restricted and closed debates where access is more limited than in public forums. These atriums are based on asymmetric configurations of actors dominated by certain actors, often experts, and by a particular system of debate of which they are the guarantors. The policy atrium is a situation where problem or solution claimants lead discussions in order to impose their regime of debate, with themselves as the dominant actors. For example, regarding shale gas policy in France, the Ministry of Energy, as the lead agency on this issue, was composed of legal and technical specialists who held a monopoly on the issue within the State bureaucracy. When questions came from members of parliament and the Minister's cabinet about the environmental problem of fracking and the possibility of freezing some licenses, they discussed and wrote an answer in their policy atrium. In this atrium, the claimants believed that drilling for shale gas was not a problem and that freezing was legally impossible. There was no disagreement, discussion was ended, and this answer was given to the Minister of Environment, which she repeated later in a public forum to a member of parliament (Zittoun and Chailleux 2022).

In contrast, **policy arenas** lack dominant actors, a specific system of debate and a legitimate and institutionalized form of regulation. These arenas are places of conflict where outcomes are not determined in advance, and around which power relations emerge, are constantly tested, and may become established. In arenas of debate, policy proposals and owners are therefore subjected to a variety of tests related to the "feasibility" of proposals and the "legitimacy" of their owners. In the policy process in France, for example, most policy proposals defended by a ministry and/or minister have to be discussed in inter-ministerial meetings. In these meetings, organized by the Prime Minister's Cabinet, there are often conflicts between different ministries. If it is a costly proposal, for instance, it might pit the Ministry of Transportation against the Ministry of the Budget. In the case of the shale gas policy, it was between the Ministry of Industry and the Ministry of the Environment. In this case, there were no dominant actors, no clear rules of regulation, and no unique regime of debate. On the contrary, it is a struggle between two coalitions developing their own strategies.

Drama and Creative Syncretism as Trans-Situational Logics

A situational approach might appear to focus on the trees (situations) rather than the forest (the policy process), but situations are not necessarily understood in isolation. Indeed, the policy transaction approach raises an intriguing set of questions not fully addressed by other policy process theories. Why or how do certain situations or events materialize in the first place? Contemporary public policy theories rightfully point to major focusing events or windows of opportunity as key turning points in policy change, but they lack a finer-grained account of important policy-making episodes. How or why does a meeting between a public agency and group of lobbyists come about in the first place? Why is it followed by a public meeting and why is there a rush to hold that meeting before the election? A policy transaction approach suggests that we view policy-making as an interactive sequence of situations in which each situation is contingent not only upon the creativity, power, skill, and capacity of the convening policy actors, but also on the outcome of prior events.

In general, a proposal is discussed many times before it becomes a government decision. Each discussion can be seen as a test for the proposal and its owners, who have to argue, defend, and involve other actors they consider important. Sometimes a proposal can die because it cannot withstand criticism. Sometimes a proposal has to be transformed to allow agreement between participants. The proposal statement and its owner follow what Gusfield called a "career" when the proposal and its owner need to be propagated, to enroll new actors and to resist critiques (Gusfield 1981). From a new pragmatism perspective, the success of this career depends on the ability of meanings and strategies to mutate across situations in order to facilitate its propagation. Here, power is exercised when meanings of policy problems, solutions, and the like are linked across, and transformed through, situations. As should be clear, a transactional approach highlights the relationship between power and transformation: ideas do not flow unchanged from one venue to another but are reworked and changed. Power is not the ability for an idea to endure in its original form, but to morph over time in ways that gain more adherents.

While a policy statement may have a career, the policy transaction approach does not fundamentally conceive of this career as a "path" or even a "stream" (in the manner these terms are typically used in Policy Studies). Rather, the sequence of situations is characterized by pivots, leaps, and dead ends. Imagine a policy atrium where policy actors come together to address a particular issue. Their transaction in this atrium produces a particular outcome—perhaps a statement of principle that mobilizes a certain provisional alliance. Critical actors may then react to this outcome by mobilizing a public forum to air this statement of principle in the hope of generating dissent. The second situation is contingent upon the first. This forum, however, is a dead end: it fails to produce a clear counterstatement and is unsuccessful in mobilizing significant opposition. So, the critical actors pivot and engage their opponents directly in a different policy arena. Acting as creative syncretists, they try to leap over their opponents, embracing certain limited aspects of the original statement, criticizing others, but proposing certain overriding principles that surpass the original statement.

As this analysis suggests, new pragmatism spotlights how the relationship between problems and solutions is reworked in the movement across situations. As we have seen, the definition of the problem includes the designation of an authority as responsible. When some actors want to couple a solution to a problem, they do not have to merely associate two concepts, but rather must glue them together by arguing how the solution responds to the problem, which generally implies a redefinition of the problem, a transformation of victims into beneficiaries, a transformation of the designated responsible party into a presumed decision-maker capable of solving the problem, and a redefinition of the expected future.

While such a sequence of policy transactions may appear disordered, even chaotic, the policy transaction approach anticipates that a trans-situational logic of sorts may emerge in the form of a dramatic perspective. Dramas establish a narrative relationship between certain symbols, meanings, and roles. Such dramatic policy narratives are already a central feature of the Narrative Policy Framework, however the Policy Transaction Approach specifically points to how these narratives *emerge* and *change* through situations and their interaction. For example, one transaction may yield claims about victims and oppressors. Another may turn the tables and proclaim the oppressors "heroes". Recognizable dramatic narratives begin to form in which a given situation may "play its role". An intriguing implication of this perspective is that while policy problems and their solutions may become increasingly complex as new situations produce new layers of meaning, policy disputes might at the same time be increasingly represented by stylized dramatic forms.

As should be clear by now, instead of thinking of a stable "advocacy coalition that defends a proposal as a fact, the pragmatist approach opens the double black box of coalition building and proposal making. In different situations, one actor tries to convince another of the relevance of his proposal, to fight against the critics and feasibility arguments, and to enroll new allies through discussion and negotiation. One may, in this situation, transform the proposal to allow enrolment of new supporters. By analogy, coalitions are similar to a viral epidemic, where what matters is less the macro number of people affected than the micro-dynamics of propagation, where one actor affects another through direct contact, starting with the famous patient 0, and how and where in the process the virus mutates to facilitate propagation. In other words, the success of enrolment depends on the capacity of a proposal to transform itself in order to integrate new members.

Let's conclude this section with an example. In Zittoun and Chailleux's (2022) study of legislation banning shale gas in France, they observed revisions to many articles of the law. Interestingly, each modification appears as a condition to include new actors in the agreement or to prevent criticism. For example, in a debate about the first article, discussion centered on what must be prohibited in the ban. In order to get the agreement of the legal experts, the lawmakers withdraw the term "shale gas", explaining that there is no legal definition. The lawyers made a second version with "non-conventional gas", but they were challenged by some companies that practice non-conventional extraction of coal gas and who wanted to maintain their activities. They proposed to ban "fracking" to avoid this opposition, but geothermal companies protested because they also use fracking. They finally decided to ban "fracking for oil and gas" in order to reach an agreement. Legislators were criticized by some political opponents for not banning the importation of shale gas, but the opposition was not sufficient to create a new modification. The trajectory of the article through different versions contributed to its survival and its growing coalition.

CONCLUSION

As developed in this chapter, a new pragmatist perspective makes a series of interrelated propositions about how to understand and analyze policy processes. First, it proposes that to better grasp the policy process, we should try not to think of policy actors as "billiard balls" with fixed interests, values, and perspectives that merely collide with one another. Instead, we should become more sensitive to how policy actors and their policy positions co-construct each other in the course of what we call "policy transactions". Second, we must examine how these policy trans-actions are creatively forged in situ. To do this, we must observe and methodologically reconstruct the empirical micro-situations where poli-cymakers discuss, argue, negotiate, and critique, not only in public spaces but also in more discrete spaces within or between bureaucracies, interest groups, politicians, and so on. Third, we must appreciate how problema-tization and policy formulation are processes of creatively combining and recombining the ideational resources at hand and that they are linked to wider claims about social and political order. In other words, policy prob-lems and solutions are best conceived as networks of meaning. Fourth, we propose that policy problems and solutions have a career. We can trace their genealogy as they are reworked and rearticulated across situations, which requires (and produces) a more fine-grained temporal analysis than other contemporary policy process. The policy transaction approach thus addresses complexity, fragmentation, and uncertainty in policy processes, while also allowing the possibility that social orders nonetheless emerge from these dynamic processes to generate insights about the relation between state and society.

REFERENCES

Abolafia, Mitchel Y. 2004. Framing moves: Interpretive politics at the Federal Reserve. *Journal of Public Administration Research and Theory* 14 (3): 349–370. https://doi.org/10.1093/jopart/muh023

Almond, Gabriel A. 2004. Who lost the Chicago school of political science? *Perspectives on Politics* 2 (1): 91–93.

Ansell, C., Hassenteufel, P., and Zittoun, P. 2024. The policy transaction perspective: A pragmatist-constructivist approach to the policy process. *European Policy Analysis*.

Bacchi, C. 2009. Analysing policy: What's the problem represented to be? Pearson Australia.

Bacchi, C. 2012. Why study problematizations? Making politics visible. *Open Journal of Political Science* 2 (1): 1–8.

Bacchi, C. 2015. The turn to problematization: Political implications of contrasting interpretive and poststructural adaptations. *Open Journal of Political Science* 5 (1): 1–12.

Berk, G., and D. Galvan. 2009. How people experience and change institutions: A field guide to creative syncretism. *Theory and Society* 38: 543–580.

Bernstein, Richard J. 1992. The resurgence of pragmatism. *Social Research* 813–40.

Boltanski, Luc, and Laurent Thévenot. 1991. *De la justification: Les économies de la grandeur*. Paris: Gallimard.

Deleon, Peter. 1988. *Advice and consent: The development of the policy sciences*. Russell Sage Foundation.

Dewey, John. 1922. Valuation and experimental knowledge. *The Philosophical Review* 31 (4): 325–351.

Dewey, John, and Arthur F. Bentley. 1946. Interaction and transaction. *The Journal of Philosophy* 43 (19): 505–517.

Dewey, John, and Bentley, Arthur F. 1964. *John Dewey and Arthur F. Bentley: A philosophical correspondence, 1932–1951*. Rutger University Press.

Dewulf, A., and R. Bouwen. 2012. Issue framing in conversations for change: Discursive interaction strategies for "doing differences." *The Journal of Applied Behavioral Science* 48 (2): 168–193.

Dunn, William N. 2019. *Pragmatism and the origins of the policy sciences: Rediscovering Lasswell and the Chicago School*. Cambridge University Press.

Farr, James. 1999. John Dewey and American political science. *American Journal of Political Science* 43 (2): 520–541. https://doi.org/10.2307/2991805.

Fischer, Frank. 2003. *Reframing public policy: Discursive politics and deliberative practices*. First Edition. OUP Oxford.

Fischer, Frank, and Herbert Gottweis. 2012. *The argumentative turn revisited: Public policy as communicative practice*. Duke University Press.

Frega, Roberto, and Filipe Carreira da Silva. 2011. Pragmatism and the social sciences. *European Journal of Pragmatism and American Philosophy* III (2). https://doi.org/10.4000/ejpap.812.

Gusfield, Joseph R. 1981. *The culture of public problems: Drinking-driving and the symbolic order*. Chicago: University of Chicago Press.

Haas, Peter. 2004. When does power listen to truth? A constructivist approach to the policy process. *Journal of European Public Policy* 11 (4): 569–592. https://doi.org/10.1080/1350176042000248034.

Heaney, Michael T., and John Mark Hansen. 2006. 'Building the Chicago School'. *American Political Science Review* 589–96.

Jobert, Bruno, and Pierre Muller. 1987. *L'Etat en action: Politiques publiques et corporatismes*. Presses universitaires de France.

Karl, Barry Dean. 1974. *Charles E. Merriam and the study of politics*. Chicago: University of Chicago Press.

Kingdon, John W. 2010. *Agendas, alternatives, and public policies, update edition, with an epilogue on health care*. 2nd ed. Longman.

Lasswell, Harold D., and Abraham Kaplan. 1950. *Power and society: A framework for political inquiry*. New Haven: Yale University Press.

Lejano, Raul Perez. 2012. *Postpositivism and the policy process*. Routledge: Routledge Handbook of Public Policy.

Majone, Giandomenico. 1989. *Evidence, argument and persuasion in the policy process*. New Haven: Yale University Press.

Margetts, Helen, and Christopher Hood. 2016. Tools approaches. In *Contemporary approaches to public policy*, 133–54. Springer. http://link.springer.com/chapter/https://doi.org/10.1057/978-1-137-50494-4_8.

Mateo, Joaquín Fernández. 2021. John Dewey's theory of inquiry. Quantum Physics, ecology and the myth of the scientific method. *Agora: Papeles de Filosofía* 40 (1): 133–154.

Misak, Cheryl. 2018. *Cambridge pragmatism: From Peirce and James to Ramsey and Wittgenstein*. Oxford and New York: Oxford University Press.

Monroe, Kristen Renwick. 2004. The Chicago School: Forgotten but not gone. *Perspectives on Politics* 2 (1): 95–98.

Perelman, Chaïm, and Lucie Olbrechts-Tyteca. 2008. *Traité de l'argumentation : La Nouvelle Rhétorique*. 6e édition. Université de Bruxelles.

Rochefort, David A., and Roger W. Cobb. 1994. *The politics of problem definition: Shaping the policy agenda*. Lawrence, KS: University Press of Kansas.

Rorty, Richard. 2013. Wittgenstein and the Linguistic Turn. *From Ontos Verlag: Publications of the Austrian Ludwig Wittgenstein Society-New Series (Volumes 1–18)* 3.

Shi, Wen, Haohuan Fu, Peinan Wang, Changfeng Chen, and Jie Xiong. 2020. # Climatechange vs.# Globalwarming: Characterizing two competing climate discourses on twitter with semantic network and temporal analyses. *International Journal of Environmental Research and Public Health* 17 (3): 1062.

Simon, Herbert Alexander. 1987. *Charles E. Merriam and the" Chicago School" of Political Science*. Urbana, Ill.: Department of Political Science, University of Illinois at ....

Stengers, Isabelle, and Didier Debaise. 2007. 'William James: Une Éthique de La Pensée?' *Vie et Expérimentation: Peirce, James, Dewey*, 147–74.

Stone, Deborah A. 1989. Causal stories and the formation of policy agendas. *Political Science Quarterly* 104 (2): 281–300.

Wagenaar, Hendrik. 2011. *Meaning in action: Interpretation and dialogue in policy analysis*. Routledge.

Weick, Karl. 1969. *The social psychology of organizing*. New York: McGraw Hill.

Whitmarsh, Lorraine. 2009. What's in a Name? Commonalities and differences in public understanding of "climate change" and "global warming." *Public Understanding of Science* 18 (4): 401–420. https://doi.org/10.1177/096 3662506073088.

Wildavsky, Aaron. 1987. *Speaking truth to power: The art and craft of policy analysis*. Reprint. Transaction Publishers.

Wittgenstein, Ludwig. 2014. *Recherches philosophiques*. Paris: Gallimard.

Zittoun, Philippe. 2008. One policy for two problems: The controversy surrounding the Parisian tramway. *Planning Theory & Practice* 9 (4): 459–474.

Zittoun, Philippe. 2014. *The political process of policymaking: A pragmatic approach to public policy*. Palgrave Macmillan.

Zittoun, Philippe, and Sébastien Chailleux. 2022. *The politics of meaning struggles: Shale gas policy under pressure in France*. Cheltenham, UK ; Northampton, MA, USA: Edward Elgar Publishing Ltd.

Zittoun, Philippe, Frank Fischer, and Nikolaos Zahariadis. 2021. *The political formulation of policy solutions : Arguments, arenas and coalitions*. Bristol University Press. https://www.brownsbfs.co.uk/Product/Zittoun-Philippe-University-of-Lyon/The-Political-Formulation-of-Policy-Solutions--Argume nts-/9781529210347.

Conclusion: Public Policy Theory and Democracy: The Elephant in the Corner

Helen Ingram, Peter deLeon, and Anne Schneider

INTRODUCTION

We are, in many ways, living in an environment of academic riches in terms of public policy theory. A series of notable texts and highly regarded national and international conferences reflect its importance. A serious caveat to this sanguine assessment is warranted, however. It is, of course, the elephant in the corner—the wounded and sagging figure of democracy. Democracy is both central to the governance of many countries and in trouble, but public policy scholars (especially the American school)

This chapter is a substantial revision of the keynote address Helen Ingram presented to the 1915 International Conference on Public Policy in Milan, Italy, July 2. Many thanks to Martin Nekola, whose review and suggestions helped us make this chapter less US-centric.

H. Ingram · P. deLeon · A. Schneider (✉)
University of Pittsburgh, Lyon, France
e-mail: Anne.Schneider@asu.edu

H. Ingram
e-mail: hingram@uci.edu

B. G. Peters and P. Zittoun (eds.), *Contemporary Approaches to Public Policy*, International Series on Public Policy,
https://doi.org/10.1007/978-3-032-06026-6_12

appear not to see it, or conveniently restrict it to the analytic margins. The voices of privileged, well-regarded citizens are loud and influential in policy-making, while ordinary citizens speak with a whisper that is mainly ignored. The public policies that emerge from and fuel uneven participation and representation perpetuate the problem. Yet, few public policy studies even mention democracy (or its absence) and certainly do not use it as a criterion for evaluating policy. We thus pose the straightforward question: How has it happened that the study of public policy theory has flourished, and yet the critical issue of policy implications for democracy is unnoticed? With collective hindsight that extends backward many decades, we reflect on the roots and reasons for the neglect of democracy by policy scholars.

In this chapter, we provide a basic understanding of democracy and trace its roots as a topic in public policy studies to the birth of the field. We then probe why and how policy scholars turned away from the topic and examine its insignificant stature as a subject in contemporary policy frameworks, including those described in this book. A policy scholar of great standing, Ted Lowi, provides reasons that democracy came to be slighted in public policy analysis, and we examine the extent to which his criticisms remain relevant. We then identify what we see as the greatest threat to democracy today in the USA and many other democracies. We provide our own democratic policy framework that focuses on the two-way relationships between policy and citizens, and highlights the dangers of policies conveying messages damaging to participation. Finally, we provide suggestions for what policy scholars might do to drag the elephant that is democracy out of the corner, and analyze how policy scholars can contribute to curing its ills. Democracy is a kind of cant to which we pay homage but take the word's meaning for granted. For the purpose here, we must break the idea down to some fundamentals: democracy is a system of government in which the members of a community by and large participate, directly or indirectly, in making decisions that affect them all (deLeon 1997, p. 14). Policies should not consistently discriminate against and marginalize certain kinds of citizens. Critical to democracy is the notion that all vantage points for reflecting on policy get represented (Dryzek and Niemeyer 2008). Public policy should involve, enable, and inspire citizen participation (Mettler and Soss 2004). These fundamentals of democracy are not being achieved even in Western industrialized nations where democracy is supposed to be most deeply embedded. There are many reasons that the US' performance, in particular, is especially egregious: an exceptionally high incarceration rate that deprives current and many former inmates of basic rights like voting and freedom of assembly, widespread racial discrimination and biased laws that repress voting, and the dominance of money in elections. Even the federal court system—historically the guardian of America's democratic heritage—has all but endorsed the perception that personal funds can anonymously sway the American body politic (see *F.E.C. v. Citizens United*, as well as *Buckley v. Vellajo*).

European states also fall short, and findings of the Council of Europe (2014) state that ethnic discrimination against minorities, especially the Roma, is widespread; there is a lack of equal opportunity for political contestants in elections; the right to peaceable assembly is not observed by a number of countries; and there are threats to freedom of expression and media freedom, including violence against journalists. This is true not only of consolidated liberal democracies but also of post-communist countries that are fragile and imperfect. There are also democracies being threatened in Latin America and other parts of the world. Mexico, for instance, suffers from a lack of rule of law and excessive corruption (*The Economist* 2014). These signals of democracies in trouble mainly go unheeded by policy researchers. While democracy is a major topic for some respected scholars,[1] the topic is not a central concern in the vast majority of policy studies.

This neglect was certainly not intended when policy studies emerged as a separate enterprise in the 1940s. When the field of public policy first emerged, democracy and public policy were closely linked. In 1948, Harold Lasswell founded the field as the *Policy Sciences of Democracy*, with the aim of providing information that would clarify the processes of policy-making and supply needed data on policy questions. He offered three criteria for policy studies: that they be interdisciplinary, problem oriented, and explicitly normative (deLeon 1998). In Lasswell's words, the policy sciences of democracy were directed toward gathering knowledge to improve the practice of democracy (deLeon 1997, p. 7). His interest was in serving a democratic elite, but he envisioned the elite as embracing the whole community (deLeon 2009, p. xi). Sadly, Lasswell fell out of fashion in political science despite an active research agenda

---

[1] Among them, notably, John Dryzek, Frank Fischer, James Fishkin, Deborah Stone, John Forester, Suzanne Mettler, Joe Soss, Steven R. Smith, Genevieve Johnson, and James Morone.

that produced 50 books and over 1000 articles. Public policy as a subject became almost nonexistent. Instead, scholars focused on political behavior as it was exhibited in voting and legislative action, highlighting narrowly gauged, testable propositions without risking value judgments.

In the 1960s, about the only courses offered to students in the USA with the word *policy* in them were foreign policy courses. Some pluralist political scientists were concerned with democracy, but primarily in relation to the political system, not in relation to policy content.[2] As the 1960s ended, things began to change and several trends came together to more firmly legitimize the study of public policy within the discipline of political science. Edited books by Austin Ranney (1968) and Ira Sharkansky (1970) helped make a place for policy process studies within political science in the USA; and shortly thereafter the policy studies organization was created with the help of scholars like Chuck Jones and Tom Dye, with multiple "implementation" studies. In 1973 by Jeffrey Pressman and Aaron Wildavsky (1973), many policy-oriented researchers found a home among "implementation" scholars. The comparative state studies of Dye, Sharkansky, and Hofferbert treated the American states as miniature experiments in democracy and tested comparative propositions relating policy process to policy outcomes, including democratic ones, such as how states managed to adopt (or not adopt) policies representing the interests of the have-nots. Hofferbert in exasperation wrote—

> "For sometime it has been my habit to ask colleagues from that corner of the craft which they call 'political theory' the following: How can policy-makers use their tools to maximize a country's chances of getting and/or keeping a democracy?" My political theory colleagues respond with: "You are asking the wrong question."
> "No, I am not, blast it!". (Hofferbert 1986, p. 234)

That said, the early link to democracy Lasswell founded was generally not carried forward in the rebirth of policy studies, and most of

---

[2] We learned from Dahl and Lindblom that US democracy is a pluralist system in which no group always wins or loses, but the system persistently moves back toward a stable equilibrium characterized by incremental change. We learned from Phillip Converse that the stability of the US system is at least partly because of cross-cutting cleavages and the two-party system, which produces legislation generally acceptable to the public. V.O. Key taught us that a competitive two-party system was essential if a state was to have public policy outcomes that benefited the have-nots of society.

the more narrow-gauge theories or frameworks that emerged distanced themselves from any concern with democracy entirely. Others examined only one aspect of democracy. Furthermore, until the development of policy design, the actual content, including tools, rules, and implementation structures, policy was considered the purview of other fields of study, certainly not within the purview of political science (Bobrow and Dryzek 1987; Schneider and Ingram 1990; Ingram and Schneider 1990). Without some attention to the actual content of policy, it was almost impossible to link policy itself to democratic outcomes. Treating policy process as an input and impacts on democracy as an outcome simply left the policy itself as a black box and led to the implicit assumption (common to pluralist theory) that a competitive two-party system with universal suffrage and separation of powers would (of course) produce public policy that serves democracy.

ROLE OF DEMOCRACY IN CONTEMPORARY FRAMEWORKS AND APPROACHES TO PUBLIC POLICY

Some of the major frameworks in contemporary policy studies have basically no linkages to democracy; some have weak or implicit linkages; and only the framework presented later in this chapter was intentionally created to highlight the relationship of policy to democracy.

Arguably the most prominent framework in the policy studies field—indeed its creator won the Nobel prize in economics for it—is the Institutional Analysis and Development (IAD) framework of Elinor Ostrom, following on the influential work of her husband, Vincent Ostrom. This framework was grounded in fundamental issues of democratic governance, but its more current applications have deemphasized the linkages with democracy or entirely abandoned them in favor of narrowly focused arguments.

Although firmly grounded in public choice theory and "bounded rationality," E. Ostrom became convinced from her early work that the economists were wrong in their belief that self-interested individuals combined with democratic governing would destroy the commons. After years of painstaking collection and coding of case studies from all over the world, she demonstrated in *Governing the Commons* that self-interested individuals in a democracy do not result in Hardin's "tragedy of the commons" because individuals (or agencies of government) are usually able to come together, compromise, reach agreements that are responsive to the public, and govern the commons without destroying it.

The core questions, then, would seem to be the conditions under which democratic governance is (or is not) able to reach such agreements. Nevertheless, it seems the value orientation of the IAD framework too often has been lost with its attention to definitions, categories, and discussion of the difference between frameworks, models, and theories. A second well-known framework, the Advocacy Coalition Framework (ACF), has intentionally excluded consideration of democracy or other value-based judgments. As explained by Weible and Jenkins-Smith (Chapter 2), the ACF focuses on policy process (not policy content), explaining how coalitions are formed, how policy learning occurs, and how policy changes. Most of those who use this framework remain "value-free" and make no effort to determine whether the policy processes being studied improve or detract from democracy or even who benefits and who loses from the changes that are being observed. Chapter 2 in this volume emphasizes that the framework is especially useful in studying contentious policy issues, and the authors point out that the causal linkages almost certainly will differ depending on the type of government—authoritarian regimes will not necessarily demonstrate the same patterns as democratic ones or highly centralized systems. This is, of course, a connection to democracy, but it is not one that attempts to explain how democratic governance is maintained or lost. The big questions connecting policy and democracy are not the concern of the ACF.

Punctuated Equilibrium Theory (PET) originated with an explicit connection to democracy, but the linkage tends to be somewhat vague and distant, as applications have focused on narrow aspects of policy change generally disconnected from democracy. As explained nicely by Eissler, Russell, and Jones (Chapter 6), PET began because the existing theories of incremental change did not fit with empirical observations. Instead, observations of the system indicated that sometimes the US system of government experienced sudden punctuations as it lurched from one dominant perspective to another. PET scholars sometimes saw this as a fundamental flaw in democracy, as it was unable to change smoothly in response to external events, and some of the scholars were especially interested in why disfavored groups had such a difficult time breaking into the policy agenda itself. Thus, there was an initial implicit assumption in PET that a democracy should be able to adjust to changes in its environment (including changes in public preferences) in a way that is relatively stable, incremental, and easy to reverse if needed. Staying largely in the positivist tradition, however, most applications of PET have been more interested in noting the difficulty in making accurate predictions that are apparently needed for a mature science rather than exploring the danger posed to democracy by an inability to adapt to changing circumstances. With but a few exceptions, PET does not consider who benefits and who loses from policy punctuations.

Discursive policy analytic frameworks are among the approaches that emerged from critical theory that introduced several innovative ideas into the philosophy and practice of public policy scholarship (Fischer 2003a, b; Yanow 1998; Dryzek and Niemeyer 2008; Durnova et al., this volume, Chapter 3). Rejecting most of the positivist and neo-positivist agenda, critical theory focuses not on explaining and predicting policy processes, designs, or change but on revealing systems of oppression. The goal of a critical perspective on policy—at least in principle—is to produce social change that will empower, enlighten, and emancipate all people (Schneider and Ingram 1997, p. 51). Even so, one can legitimately question whether most critical policy analysis actually puts at its core the implications of public policy for democracy.

One of the variants of discursive policy analysis, the "argumentative turn" (see Durnova et al., Chapter 3, this volume) focuses the attention of policy scholars on the actual arguments that participants were making and through these observations calls to attention the fact that problems were often "wicked" in the sense of highly complex, multiply perspectival, ambiguous, and uncertain about the consequences of various actions. In these situations, the more scientifically oriented efforts to find a few causal variables and predict which policies would be chosen or which would have better consequences were doomed to failure and actually became antidemocratic. As Durnova et al. (this volume, Chapter 3) say, arguments have to be held up against higher normative standards so that the policy analyst does not simply collect the data but rather situates, interprets, and gives them meaning. Policies are not simply judged by whether they work, but also whether they are relevant to the situation and how they impact the basic values and normative ideals of the society.

As the field has developed, however, the linkage to democracy often has become increasingly hard to discern. Even though discourse, for example, is to be judged in terms of a "higher-level" normative critique (Durnova et al., this volume, Chapter 3), it is not self-evident that this critique involves democracy, nor is it self-evident that "improving arguments" will also improve democracy. Many (perhaps most) critical theorists envision a form of participatory, consensus-based decision-making seldom actually found even in small groups, much less in whole nations. Durnova and colleagues (this volume, Chapter 3) write, "The best decision is frequently not the most efficient one. Instead, it is the one that has been deferred until all disagreements have either been discursively resolved or placated, at least enough to be accepted in specific circumstances." Public policy and institutions generally are viewed with suspicion if not outright disdain as these are part of the problem, not the solution. Sometimes critical analysis seems to imply that problems are immutable and public policy is not only too weak to help solve them, but continually sustains the oppression and anti-democratic character of the society. Some critical approaches have generally abandoned the idea of democracy and instead focus much of their attention on discrediting the continued use of positivist and neo-positivist methodologies.

There is no question critical approaches such as discourse analysis, narrative analysis, deliberative policy analysis, and the social construction movement broadly understood have brought many new ideas into the field of policy analysis but it is important for these approaches not to lose their grounding to endless critique of contemporary institutions and processes, but focus in addition on how public policy can contribute to a more democratically governed society.

The kind of governance that a society creates and sustains over time depends on how people think, the values they hold, how they make decisions, resolve differences, and the institutional cultures within which they work. Several of the most distinctive frameworks in policy analysis have focused their attention on issues such as these. Zahariadis (this volume, Chapter 9) describes the evolution of ideas about "bounded" rationality and how the "multiple streams" approach offers a compelling explanation of policy processes, but it does not deal effectively with issues of political power or democratic ideals. Instead, Zahariadis says that in the multiple streams approach (this volume, Chapter 9), "democracy is exercised by celebrating intent and the efficacy of collective action." Guy Peters provides an excellent summary of the various institutional approaches to policy analysis that reminds us of the overwhelming influence institutions have on the way people arrive at their values and make decisions. Institutions affect public policy, and public policy affects institutions, Peters writes; but explicit linkages among institutions, policy, and democracy are largely missing. More narrowly focused is the "instruments and tools" approach, nicely summarized in this volume by Helen Margetts and Christopher Hood (Chapter 8), which examines the application, strengths, and limitations of several different kinds of "tools" frameworks; but most of the discussion is on how to categorize the various tools, rather than on how they contribute to or thwart democracy.

In contrast to the largely value-neutral tools and instruments frameworks, Peter John (Chapter 7, this volume) lays out in clear detail the promise and problems of the new behavioralism and how it impacts the tools and instruments used by decision-makers and those that citizens can use to "nudge" policy-makers. The promise offered by the many insights from social psychology on how people make decisions, John says, is that knowledge of how various tools and instruments of policy design will impact people's behavior will enable decision-makers to create better public policy—more efficient and more accepted—without limiting citizens' freedom or rights. The great danger, however, is that experts who gain more knowledge about the specific ways in which the people in a certain location and situation will respond to various cues will then use that knowledge to manipulate people. Nevertheless, he concludes on a positive note about the prospects of the growing knowledge about why people behave the way they do: "There is a lot to trust, but it is possible that the better understanding of the sources of behavior will help policy-makers produce better policies and in turn assist citizens in a self-reinforcing cycle."

PROBING THE ROOTS OF THE NEGLECT OF DEMOCRACY

Even as public policy studies have flourished, the relationship of this research to democracy has languished. As we have discussed, questions of democracy in some approaches and frameworks were so sidelined as to be trivial. Many of the frameworks that have evolved to study public policy could make the linkages to democracy, but too often researchers have become distracted or lost sight of the larger question of the implications of public policy for a democratic society.

Over the years, there has been little acknowledgment by major figures in public policy[3] of the import of this neglect, with a notable exception, the presidential address of Theodore Lowi to the American Political

---

[3] The additional exception of Hofferbert was noted above.

Science Association in 1992. Lowi's address, subtitled *"How We Become What We Study,"* suggested that, like the elephant in the corner, big changes that were threatening democracy (Lowi called them transformations) were being overlooked by political scientists and its major subfields including public policy (1992). We revisit some of those arguments in this chapter, explaining them and assessing whether they persist.

In 1992, Lowi declared that economic thinking and analysis were swallowing up the field. Economics was the new language of the state, and policy analysis was serving the state very well with its emphasis on efficiency and effectiveness. Now it can be said that economics is still influential in policy studies, but so are many other disciplines, including sociology, geography, planning, psychology, history, communications, and others. Moreover, many of the best policy scholars today have multiple disciplinary identities. Our orientation is that of political scientists who are reaching out to other disciplines, but for better or worse our critique emanates from political science.

Another complaint remains partly pertinent. Lowi deplored the brand of positivist science that dominated political science. He said it disparaged value-oriented research and robbed the discipline of its passion. Lowi said that science dictated that analysis must be neutral, rational, and microscopic. As a consequence, attention was drawn to the smallest unit, the variable, about which it was difficult to be passionate. We turn to a talk given by Deborah Stone to reinforce this point. The title Deborah Stone (2013) chose for her keynote to the Interpretive Policy Conference, "Taking Emotions Seriously" suggests that we policy scholars are still neglecting emotions. She stated, "We now know from cognitive science that there is no such beast as pure rational thinking, absent emotion. Everyone in the interpretive policy community and many who aren't roundly reject positivist science, the rational/emotional dichotomy and the possibility of objectivity." She goes on to write that even postpositivist interpretive scholars are at pains to prove they are serious and scientific. Terms like rigorous, *systematic, methodological, careful, analytical,* and *dispassionate* are often buzzwords or what Stone calls "belonging words" that we utter like secret passwords so we can be admitted to the social science club and permitted to stay.

We agree with Deborah Stone that playing down the emotional underpinnings of human behavior costs us mightily in terms of insight (see also Durnova et al., this volume, Chapter 3). Some of the notable work related to emotions comes from other study areas like geopolitics and social psychology. Dominique Moisi (2010) argues that the emotions of fear, humiliation, and hope are reshaping the world. Psychologists have revealed to us all that moral judgments are emotion- and affect-driven, with reason relegated to a secondary role (Lewis 2013; See John, this volume, Chapter 7). Haidt (2012) argues that moral impulses guide human behavior, including in-group loyalty that dictates being true to the group and being suspicious of outsiders and the betrayal of in-group members.

Yet the field of public policy studies is overcoming many of the troublesome constraints Lowi thought science imposed. As Deborah Stone indicated, she and many others of us are quite comfortable operating outside the positivist tradition. Ethnographic methodologies are widely embraced by those who base their work on interviews and observation. Discourse analysis has a firm place in public policy studies. Narrative policy analysis draws from work in the humanities. Many people embrace a variety of methodologies, some that might be termed interpretive and others not. Q-methodology is widely used for studies of subjective experience. We observe that the best of public policy work today adopts multiple methodologies.

Lowi's most damning criticism was that public policy and the other hegemonic subfields were too slow to recognize the fundamental changes that were altering the nature of American Democracy in 1992. Lowi argued that the failure to address big issues rather than microscopic questions resulted in a tendency to interpret each small change as consistent with our existing model of the political system taken by definition as democratic. Researchers were blinded to the accumulation of actions that fundamentally changed the regime.

Lowi further contended that the language of analysis itself has to be microscopic, that is, translated into the language of variables. For Lowi, the tyranny of the microscopic crowds out topics with which we should be seriously engaged. He concludes that we need a level of discourse worthy of the problems. Lasswell would have deplored work that was ferociously focused on a specific phenomenon. Policy science was not science in his view unless it was in service of democratic society (deLeon 2009, p. xi). Yet research in public policy often does focus on small issues, and only rarely traces implications to large issues like democracy.

Policy studies have evolved in important ways since Lowi's criticisms of 1992. It has escaped the domination of economic thinking, and institutional economics and behavioral economics have acted as buffers against economic imperialism. We have embraced multiple disciplines, approaches, and methods. However, some of Lowi's concerns continue to be relevant. Much of the field has yet to embrace emotions as a part of analysis. Deference to narrow ideas of the scientific method still drives many to a microscopic focus in their studies. Failure to take seriously the value commitment underlying the aims that originally motivated the policy sciences of democracy—that is, providing information to policy actors to improve decisions and processes—has caused many in the field to be uncritical. Perilous trends threatening democracy have been overlooked. The dangerous change Lowi thought had been missed in his presidential essay was the growth and power of bureaucracy in an administrative state in which specialists and experts made many of the decisions affecting citizens without their participation and input. In our opinion, the threats to democracy existing today are very different, but the topic of democracy does not yet get nearly the attention it deserves.

A Democracy-Centered Approach to Policy Analysis

Theorists who study democracy have differing notions of what the relationship between citizens, who are also targets of policy, and various stages of the policy cycle should be. There are some who believe that people in a democracy need protection from government. Others believe that government should liberate citizens to express their preferences effectively. The first conception, which Peter deLeon (1995) calls Madisonian democracy, is intended to defend citizens from tyranny. Madison feared the pernicious effects of political factions and domination by the majority. The other, more recent, conception to which we subscribe holds that people in a democracy should be able to engage in policy-making and enact policy preferences (for a discussion of deliberative democracy, see Johnson 2015). Some such scholars are focusing on reforming policy governing election eligibility and voting rights. They fashion and experiment with promising alternatives for representation outside voting, such as discursive representation, citizen forums, and other mechanisms to increase meaningful participation in policy. This work is important, but such changes in laws will by themselves not redress the existing ways in which policy is damaging democracy.

Democracy is built and torn down by the creation of categories that carve out target groups in public policy. In many contemporary policy designs, bias based on labels, stereotypes, and stigma creates and justi-fies categories and plays a prominent role in determining who wins and who loses. Portrayals of target populations in the policy cycle are often socially constructed and may become so embedded that people think they are "real." When social constructions are deceptive and discriminatory, they clearly breach bedrock principles of fairness and equal treatment and alienate some citizens from participation. Policies determined by emotionally based branding of particular groups as deserving or unde-serving inform some that their interests are automatically consonant with the public interest, while alienating and discouraging others. At each stage in the policy cycle, the discourse in policy formulation, the provisions in legislation and rules, the ways laws are implemented, and the impact of policy all carry powerful messages about who matters, and whom govern-ment serves and punishes. These messages teach citizens whether their problems are public problems related to public welfare or are their own to solve, as well as telling them whether they are to be treated with respect, ignored, or punished. They teach whether participation matters or whether government is something to be avoided. Of course, the allo-cation of material benefits and burdens by policy also affects the time and resources targets have to participate in policy-making. Thus, some people are strongly and successfully motivated by policy to participate in politics. Others are sidelined and repelled by policy. The system is degenerative because the next round of policy-making reproduces the same pathologies that become even more entrenched in the policy processes and institu-tions of the society. Instead of a self-correcting system of governance, as the pluralists posited, the problems build on themselves.

Figure 1 places citizens at the center of analysis since it is their atti-tudes and behavior that are critical to democracy. The figure identifies some key points for policy engagement. That engagement may be partici-pation in policy processes *and* the messages sent by policy affecting citizen attitudes and orientation. It is important to observe that the arrow works both ways, and it is the policy feedback/feed-forward relationship that has been so neglected. The basic point we are making is that the discourse in policy debates, the provisions in legislation and rules, the ways laws are implemented, and impact of policy all carry powerful messages about who matters, and whom government serves and punishes. By using the policy cycle in Fig. 1, we are not assuming that the policy process is either linear or stage-based (see Weible and Jenkins-Smith, this volume, Chapter 2). Rather, we are suggesting that the politics, including actors and messages to targets, may vary from one setting to another. For instance, ideas and norms of institutions affect how agencies interpret policy and treat clients (see Peters, this volume, Chapter 4; Araral and Amri, this volume, Chapter 5).

Elsewhere we have argued that social construction of target populations is a process through which values and meanings become attached to persons and groups that enable interpretation of their worthiness and provides rationales for treating them well or badly (Schneider and Ingram 1993; Schneider et al. 2013). Political power refers to something very different, including electoral support, authority, skill, and economic and

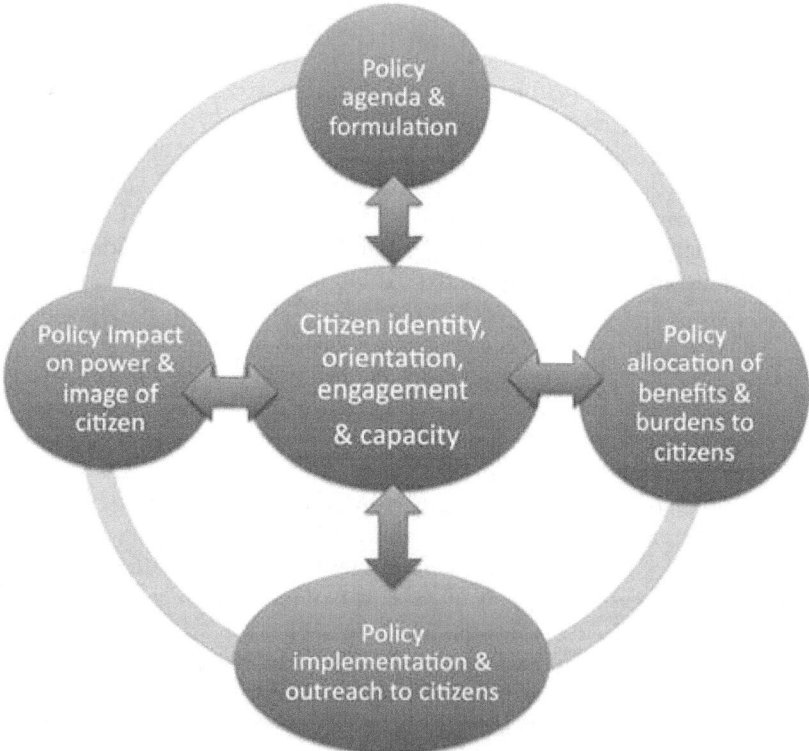

Fig. 1   Two-way relationships of policy and citizens

other resources. There is no reason to reprise the power/social construc-tions matrix that we began to develop over 20 years ago to categorize different populations and that has been widely applied in the policy liter-ature. It is sufficient for our purposes to observe that when some people with certain characteristics in terms of power and positive images always get benefits while others almost never do, the kind of equal and fair repre-sentation and treatment we expect of democracy is not taking place. How bad consequences flow from policies that are too generous or too stingy, or that hide benefits, is what we will discuss next. We will then go on to discuss the equally bad things that happen when policies impose excessive costs and intrusive rules that demean the beneficiaries of policies.

Biased Allocation of Benefits

At a time when budgets are tight, it would seem that overgenerous bene-fits even to well-regarded, powerful groups might be at risk of being attacked. Yet, benefits to advantaged populations such as property owners or senior citizens in the USA do not attract such criticism. Property ownership and good citizenship have long been co-associated in America. The Homestead Act that built much of the American West was fueled by the notion that property ownership drained the teeming tenements in big cities and resettled people on the land, where they could form demo-cratic communities and become true Americans. In the Depression, home ownership was threatened by large numbers of foreclosures, and govern-ment responded with guaranteed low-interest loans and other measures. More importantly, homeownership offers a number of tax benefits. The cost of the tax benefits for owner-occupied housing adds up to about $175 billion annually, with the mortgage-interest deduction alone costing the Treasury roughly $100 billion. The five-year costs of these tax bene-fits total well over $1 trillion. To put this amount in perspective, one year of tax benefits for owner-occupied housing costs more than the discretionary budgets of the departments of Education, Homeland Secu-rity, Energy, and Agriculture combined. These subsidies, however, do not even increase the rate of homeownership and are highly skewed toward wealthier people in suburbs (Hanson et al. 2014).

Clearly tax subsidies do not make much instrumental sense today because many people treat their houses as an investment, move often, and do not form ties to the community. Yet the people who are benefit from this policy would be very reluctant to admit that their benefits are not justified. Public subsidies that favor some homeowners clearly exist in other countries besides the USA. Homeowners in Spain and The Netherlands, where homeownership is high, are clearly favored with tax breaks and investments. In contrast, investors in rental housing in Germany are privileged because private investors were included in the subsidization scheme from the beginning, which laid the foundation for a large private rental housing market (Voigtländer 2009).

In a similar way, senior citizens protected by social security in the USA are a powerful and well-regarded group. In fact, attacks on the benefits to seniors are viewed as the "third rail" of politics—sure death! Yet in England, while it appears that seniors are well regarded, they lack the kind of political power they enjoy in the USA (Vincent et al. 2001). This highlights the important fact that the social construction of a group is a matter for empirical verification, not something to be "taken for granted" that holds across all countries or throughout time. Social constructions can change. Benefits for the disadvantaged that are too miserly send the message that recipients' needs are relatively unimportant to government. At the same time, other populations arguably just as deserving as homeowners and seniors, but without political power, receive benefits that are too small to really be helpful. More than 50 years after Lyndon Johnson declared war on poverty, aid to the poor is insufficient to get to the root of their problems. When the poor do get help, it is often way too little for them to make much headway. Poverty emerged as an issue after John Kennedy visited Appalachia during the 1960 presidential primaries and was shocked into awareness of the problem. Last year, after half a century of struggles against poverty in Appalachia, the poverty rate of families with children is now 43%, and the median family income is only $22,000 (Gabriel 2014). Poverty and stingy benefits are a considerable challenge in other developed democracies, especially those attempting to deal not only with the collapse of Communism but also with association with the European Union (EU) and the draconian austerity programs that followed the worldwide financial collapse of 2008. Romano, for example (2014), explores how poverty in Central and Eastern Europe is socially and politically constructed, as are the approaches to it, and how various groups have come to be considered part of either the "deserving" or "undeserving" poor (Romano 2014). In the UK, where welfare benefits have been sharply reduced and are under attack from conservatives, at least a sixth of households are considered poor, a fifth of the people find it difficult to cope with the recent economic crisis, and a third of all families contain at least one person experiencing mental health problems (Dorling 2015). Being a poor immigrant greatly increases the likelihood of receiving too few policy benefits. In Denmark, for example, immigrants who had come as temporary guest workers in the 1960s and then settled in Denmark gradually came to be seen as deviants rather than dependents. Stereotypes were strengthened by the fact that many immigrant workers, who were redundant in the labor market, made a better living from the social benefits they received in Denmark than by returning and working in their home country. Even though such benefits were established rights, immigrants were perceived as being less deserving than other needy people (Jørgensen and Thomsen 2013).

Hidden benefits and regulatory relief granted to powerful clientele with negative reputations teach citizens that influence peddling and lobbying in obscure arenas pays off better than more democratic, above-the-board processes. Suzanne Mettler in her book *The Submerged State* (2011) argues that influential lobbies are able to protect complicated tax breaks and regulatory lapses benefiting the wealthy. Without knowledge of who is winning and losing, ordinary citizens are unable to mobilize against unfair policies. Much of the complicated and generally invisible tax code tilts the scales in favor of the well-off.

Recent research on affluence and influence in the USA shows that economic elites and organized groups representing business interests have substantial independent impacts on US government policy, while mass-based interest groups and average citizens have little or no independent influence (Gilens 2009). Attempts to curb shady practices of the powerful that abuse their position often fail. Banks were widely thought to be culpable for the 2008–2009 financial meltdown. Excessive bonuses and other perverse financial incentives encouraged banks to take risks by lending to unqualified borrowers. Yet, today, corrective action is weak. No limit on executive pay has occurred, and implementation of regulatory reform is being undercut in practice. The Dodd–Frank banking reform law required regulators to write hundreds of rules and conduct dozens of studies within agencies before the laws reforms could be put in place. The result of all the nearly invisible activity has been delays, weak rules, and regulatory setbacks (Grosse 2012).

Costs—Including Fines, Incarceration, and Negative Regulations—Are Even More Biased in Their Distribution than Benefits

As public officials have become constrained by tight budgets and are less able to build support by allocating good things to "good" people, they have turned to doing bad things for those who are considered negatively. Deviant stereotypes and negative policies are often inflicted on hated minorities. Czech authorities were found to be violating the human rights of Romani children in schools across the country. Romani children are segregated in mainstream education in Roma-only separate classes, buildings, and schools and are even placed in schools for pupils with "mild mental disabilities" (Amnesty International 2015).

Young black offenders are remarkable for the punitive policies directed against them in the USA. Approximately 25% of young black men aged between 16 and 24 who did not finish high school are incarcerated in juvenile detention, jail, or prison as compared with only 6% of Whites. Police–citizen encounters feature derogatory remarks and the use of physical force. Weaver and Lerman (2010) found that punitive encounters with the state foster mistrust of political institutions and weak attachments to the political process. Criminal justice policies send consistent messages that prisoners are unworthy of equal citizenship and create an enduring demarcation between law-abiding citizens and those branded as deviants. From the 1970s to the mid-1990s in the USA, the "war on crime" prescribed mandatory sentences and long incarceration for many offenses. As the cost of incarceration has climbed, legislatures have responded by backing away somewhat from more long-term sentencing, but have not relented when it comes to arrests and fines, barring access to benefits, and breach and suspension of civil rights.

Terrorists are the quintessential example of over-allocation of costs. Elected leaders seem willing to make very large allocations of resources to punish them. As of June 2015, a total of 122 prisoners remained at Guantanamo despite the international uproar and costs approaching 3 million dollars to jail each prisoner for a year (compared with $34,000 for other federal prisoners).[4] Fifty-four of these were approved for release,

---

[4] This number has been reduced gradually during the last years of the Obama administration.

but transfers are being blocked for a variety of reasons, including Congressional opposition (Human Rights First 2015). Long-term incarceration without trial or conviction, or after convictions have been overturned in courts, certainly does not meet standards of fairness. Excessively harsh laws directed against suspected terrorists already exist and are increasingly being promulgated in Europe. Murphy (2012) argues convincingly that EU counterterrorism is weakening the rule of law and bypassing democratic safeguards in favor of a system emphasizing coercive control over individual autonomy.

Intrusive Rules Demean Recipients

Policies allowing invasions of privacy and limitations on liberty are supposed to promote democracy and good, responsible citizenship. There are many examples. In the wake of the Charlie Hebdo killings, students and parents must sign a charter of *Laicite,* or a ban of public exercise of religion such as the wearing of headscarves. Among the larger French population, these laws and regulations are considered essential to the maintenance of democracy. Muslims, on the other hand, feel have been specifically targeted by the act since the Christian calendar of holidays is still observed and exceptions are granted to other groups. The *New York Times* quoted sociologist Jean Bauberot as stating, "This new *Laicite,* which I would call repressive rather than strict, is no longer that of 1905. It risks being draconian and counterproductive, leading to feelings of victimhood. We don't need such things in the current situation." Dominique Moisi, whom we quoted earlier about emotions and politics, said, "*Laicite* has become the first religion of the Republic, and it requires obedience and belief. But, I care more for democracy than for the republic" (Erlanger and De Fretas-Tamura 2015).

Welfare reform begun during the Clinton administration was supposed to get people off the welfare roles and into productive work. Efforts at welfare reform, such as requiring work and limiting the time period of payments, have decreased the number of people on the welfare rolls, but have not improved the reputations of welfare clients. Further, Congress allocated to states the ability to condition the receipt of benefits from numbers of social programs, including not just welfare but the Supplemental Nutritional Assistance Program, Medicaid, unemployment insurance, and disability; and state legislatures have required mandatory drug testing. In some states, up to 20% reduction in welfare rolls are due to drug testing. Yet research has found that other problems like mental illness, poor academic skills, and poor physical health are more influential causes of poverty than addiction (Metsch and Pollack 2005). Drug testing all of the poor without cause or suspicion of drug use is demeaning and alienating. Further, such a policy further portrays recipients of social programs aimed at the poor and disadvantaged as largely responsible for their own problems and not worthy of sympathy. The whole group tends to be labeled as deviant. For example, there is a widespread public perception that most mothers on welfare are alcoholics and drug addicts. Happily, such social constructions and discriminatory rules are not universal. A study (Brucker 2009) using a framework of social construction performed a qualitative comparative analysis of how the national disability systems of eight countries—Australia, Canada, Germany, Japan, The Netherlands, South Africa, Sweden, the UK, and the USA—address issues of substance abuse. The USA is the only country among the focal countries that does not currently allow disability benefits to be awarded to those with primary conditions of substance-abuse disorders.

Policy Portrayal Affects Participation

Experience with policy is among the most significant influences on the identity of citizens and therefore upon participation in politics, including voting. On its face, the connection between policy effects and participation would seem to be obvious since government spending accounts for one-third to one-half of the gross domestic product of Western industrialized nations. In addition to this spending, government regulations directly affect the lives of workers, consumers, and community members (Mettler and Soss 2004). Yet Susanne Mettler and Joe Soss (2005) observe that with few exceptions, political science and public policy have had little to say about the impact of public policy on democratic citizenship. Studies that do exist show a strong relationship between experience with policies and participation. Negative experience alienates and marginalizes potential participants. For example, Joe Soss (2005) found that a majority of welfare clients in the USA report feeling humiliated and vulnerable in their encounters with the welfare agency, which they have come to see as a pervasive threat in their lives. In a national elections study, Soss (2005) reportedly found that welfare recipients have considerably lower levels of political efficacy. Moreover, welfare recipients are deeply estranged from one another. Welfare recipients buy into the negative stereotypes directed toward their group and want to separate themselves as much as possible from interaction with others who they think deserve the label while they do not. Such alienation from their fellows makes them extremely difficult to mobilize. Tellingly, recipients of disability payments who have quite different relationships with a donor agency that is not paternalistic and invasive have a much higher opinion of government in general and are much more likely to participate (Soss 2005).

Experience with Policy Impacts and Messages Can Restrict Participation as well as Foster It

Contact with the criminal justice system in the USA has quite a negative impact on political participation, voting, involvement in civic groups, and trusting the government. This is true not just for young black men, who are incarcerated in large numbers, but also for the general young adult population (Weaver and Lerman 2010). People are likely to be more positive about government and likely to participate if the benefits directed toward them are portrayed as deserved (not handouts or charity).

Social security benefits in the USA, where beneficiaries make contributions, have clearly increased the voting and participation of the elderly. Veterans' benefits in the USA after World War II were depicted as fair and justified, and signaled that veterans were valued citizens. Suzanne Mettler (2005) found that benefits helped returning veterans earn college degrees; train for vocations; support young families; and purchase homes, farms, and businesses. Recipients also became more engaged citizens. Compared to veterans who did not use education and training benefits, recipients reported involvements in 50% more civic associations and became significantly more politically active.

Implementation That Engages Recipients and Encourages Them to Voice Their Concerns Sends Democratic Messages

Joe Soss (2005) found that mothers with children in Head Start, an early-education program, participate in the program's educational mission and decision-making and have a more positive orientation toward government. We need much more research on how certain policy designs can counteract stigma and stereotypes, and how such policies can send democratic and participatory resources and messages. For instance, we would profit from knowing whether the Affordable Care Act increases the likelihood that people previously without insurance will vote and participate to protect their gains.

Impact of Multiple Policies on Participation

Current research on citizen participation and voting indicates that a constellation of factors affects participants' choices. Deciding whether or not to vote is not just a decision but also an expression of identity. It is not a purely self-interested act, but an inherently social act that fulfills basic needs of affiliation and belonging to a larger group (Rogers et al. 2013). Since multiple policies send the same kinds of messages to those with similar power and social image, a whole array of policies must change to effect changes in participation. Discovering how those policies interact and reinforce one another requires an examination of clients in the context of these policies.

Several recent studies are exemplary of what kinds of work might be done and what has so far been neglected. Alice Goffman's fine book *On the Run: Fugitive Life in an American City* (2013) looks at how problems with the law affect every aspect of the lives of the 6th Street boys, a group of poor, uneducated, young, urban black men, with whom she became embedded for her story. She documents how every aspect of their lives, including education, health, housing, employment, friendships, partnerships, family, and race relations, is ruled by the omnipresence of a repressive regime of interlinked policies (Goffman 2014). In the book, Goffman concentrates on policing policies, but her study demonstrates that many other policies are implicated. Similar research that deeply embeds researchers with policy recipients and traces the effects of policy is badly needed.

Robert Putnam's book *Our Kids: The American Dream in Crisis* (2015) treats more broadly the growing gap in life experiences of the rich and poor. With the hollowing-out of the middle class in America, Putnam documents how a gulf has developed between those who prosper in America and participate in politics and those who fail and have no voice. Politics is the last thing on the minds of many of the people he identifies as belonging to the lower social class. Like Goffman, Putnam sees the alienation from politics of non-voters as the product of many factors developing over decades, including family structure, schools, child development and parenting, and neighborhood where people live. He offers a number of suggestions for improvements; interestingly many of these require policy changes. Maddeningly, however, he does not implicate specific policies that have had a large role in breaking up families, communities, educational institutions, and unions as well as destroying economic opportunities for those far down on the economic ladder. We need to understand better the legacy of multiple policies and how they interact to send messages destructive of democracy and participation. What does citizenship mean for people who are consistently subjected to labeling and stereotyping?

CONCLUSION: TREATING DEMOCRACY AS INTEGRAL TO POLICY STUDIES

Serving democracy by finding better answers is a fundamental obligation of policy researchers. From the beginning Lasswell made serving democracy by informing and enlightening citizens, and inspiring their participation, a core responsibility. Of course, we all write for our colleagues, hoping our ideas and findings will attract scholarly attention. But we must also serve more fundamental and less personal values. It is time for us to collectively move the elephant to the center of the room, examine it closely, and see what can be done to improve the health of democracy through better-informed public policy. In this chapter, we have suggested a number of things public policy scholars need to do.

Our review of the contemporary policy approaches included in this book has shown that for a variety of reasons, democracy is treated as marginal, irrelevant, or an afterthought. Some frameworks that in the beginning afforded democracy some attention, over time, drifted away from value-oriented questions. Others ignore the content of public policy and therefore cannot trace its implications. Yet others focus so much on criticism that policy actions to improve the prospects for democracy are not considered, and democracy is not held up as any kind of ideal.

It is important that contemporary scholars using these frameworks rediscover the democratic impulse that inspired Lasswell. We suggest that frameworks be modified to address democracy in a meaningful and nontrivial way. The democracy-centered approach to public policy outlined above, which focuses on the feed-forward/feedback effects of policy on citizens' orientations, beliefs, and participation, is quite flexible and can be adapted so as to be compatible with and integrated into other approaches. We have listed a number of longstanding impediments to taking democracy seriously among policy scholars, including the mistaken commitment to be value-neutral; the neglect of emotions, passion, and sensory experience as factors in policy; the excessively microscopic focus on many studies and the lingering effects of positivism that shackle many studies to quantitative, to the exclusion of qualitative, methods. Policies that create and perpetuate stigma and stereotypes that discourage participation should be acknowledged. Policy scholars need to be much more aware of the cumulative impacts of many policies that send similar undemocratic messages to people who have the most to gain by policy participation yet participate the least. Much more ought to be done to identify policy designs that foster more positive images of government and encourage democratic participation.

The core of our argument is that public policies have a powerful role in teaching citizens who is served by a policy and who is not, who can benefit and who is left out, and whether demeaning encounters and disappointments with government are the norm or the exception. When the messages and lessons of public policy are at odds with democracy, policy scholars should be at the vanguard of those raising the alarms.

REFERENCES

Amnesty International. 2015. *Czech Republic systematically discriminates against Romani children in schools.* https://www.amnesty.org/en/latest/news/2015/04/czech-republic-systematic-discrimination-against-romani-children-in-schools/.

Bobrow, D. B., and J. Dryzek. 1987. *Policy analysis by design.* Pittsburg: University of Pittsburg Press.

Brucker, D. 2009. Social construction of disability and substance abuse within public disability benefit systems. *International Journal of Drug Policy* 20 (5): 418–423.

Council of Europe. 2014. *State of democracy, human rights and the rule of law in Europe: Report by the Secretary General of the Council of Europe.* www.coe.int.

deLeon, P. 1995. Democratic values and the policy sciences. *American Journal of Political Science* 39 (4): 886.

deLeon, P. 1997. *Democracy and the policy sciences.* Albany: State University of New York Press.

deLeon, P. 1998. *Advice and consent: The development of the policy sciences.* New York: The Russell Sage Foundation.

deLeon, P. 2009. Introduction to the transaction edition in H. D. Lasswell. In *Power and personality*. New Brunswick: Transaction Publishers.

Dorling, Danny. 2015. *Why social inequality still persists*. Bristol: Policy Press.

Dryzek, J., and S. Niemeyer. 2008. Discursive representation. *American Political Science Review* 102 (4): 481–493.

Erlanger, S., and K. DeFretas-Tamura. 2015. Old tradition of secularism clashes with France's new reality. *New York Times*, February 5, p. 1.

Fischer, F. 2003a. Beyond empiricism: Policy analysis and deliberative practice. In *Deliberative policy analysis: Understanding governance in a networked society*, ed. M. Hajer and H. Wagener, 209–227. Cambridge: Cambridge University Press.

Fischer, F. 2003b. *Redefining policy analysis*. Oxford: Oxford University Press.

Gabriel, T. 2014. 50 Years into the war on poverty, hardship hits back. *New York Times*, April 20. http://nyti.ms/QyiHKt. Downloaded 24 April 2015.

Gilens, M. 2009. Preference gaps and inequality in representation. *PS: Political Science and Politics* 42 (2): 335–341.

Goffman, A. 2014. *On the run: Fugitive life in an American City*. Chicago: The University of Chicago Press.

Grosse, R. 2012. Bank regulation, governance and the crisis: A behavioral finance view. *Journal of Financial Regulation and Compliance* 20 (1): 4–25.

Haidt, J. 2012. *The righteous mind: Why good people are divided by politics and religion*. New York: Pantheon.

Hanson, A., I. Brannon, and Z. Hawley. 2014. Rethinking tax benefits for home owners. *National Affairs* no 19, Spring.

Hofferbert, R. 1986. Policy analysis and political morality: A rejoinder to Anne E Schneider's critique of my prescription for scholarly division of labor. *Policy Studies Review* 6 (2): 234.

Human Rights First. 2015. *Guantanamo by the numbers*. https://www.humanrightsfirst.org/sites/default/files/gtmo-by-the-numbers.pdf.

Ingram, H., and A. Schneider. 1990. Improving implementation through framing smarter statutes. *Journal of Public Policy* 10 (1): 67–88.

Johnson, Genevieve Fugi. 2015. *Democratic Illusion: Deliberative democracy in Canadian public policy*. Toronto: University of Toronto Press.

Jørgensen, M.B., and T. L. Thomsen. 2013. Crises now and then—Comparing integration policy frameworks and immigrant target groups in Denmark in the 1970s and 2000s. *Journal of International Migration and Integration* 14 (2): 245–262.

Lewis, P.G. 2013. *Policy thinking, fast and slow*. Annual Political Science Association Meeting, August.

Lowi, T. J. 1992. The state in political science: How we become what we study. *The American Political Science Review* 86 (1): 1–7.

Metsch, L., and H. Pollack. 2005. Welfare reform and substance abuse. *The Milbank Quarterly* 83 (1): 65–99.

Mettler, S., and J. Soss. 2004. The consequences of public policy for democratic citizenship: Bridging policy studies and mass politics. *Perspectives on Politics* 2 (1): 55–73.

Mettler, S. 2005. *Soldiers to citizens: The G.I. Bill and the making of the greatest generation.* New York: Oxford University Press.

Mettler, S. 2011. *The submerged state: How invisible government policies undermine American democracy.* Chicago: University of Chicago Press.

Moisi, D. 2010. *Geopolitics of emotion: How cultures of fear humiliation, and hope are reshaping the world.* New York: Anchor Books (Moisi has a .. over the I but I do not know how to insert it).

Murphy, C.C. 2012. EU counter terrorism law: Preemption and the rule of law. In *Modern studies in European Law.* Oxford: Hart.

Pressman, J., and A. Wildavsky. 1973. *Implementation: Or, how great expectations are dashed in Oakland….* Berkeley: University of California Press.

Putnam, R. D. 2015. *Our kids: The American dream in crisis.* New York: Simon & Schuster.

Ranney, A. 1968. *Political science and public policy.* Ontario: Markham.

Rogers, T., C.R. Fox, and A.S. Gerber. 2013. Rethinking why people vote: Voting as dynamic social expression. In *The behavioral foundations of policy,* ed. E. Shafir. Princeton: Princeton University Press.

Romano, Serena. 2014. *The political and social construction of poverty: Central and East European countries in transition.* Bristol: University of Bristol Press; Chicago: University of Chicago Press.

Schneider, A. L., and H. Ingram. 1990. Behavioral assumptions of policy tools. *Journal of Politics* 52 (2): 510–529.

Schneider, A. L., and H. Ingram. 1993. The social construction of target populations: Implication for politics and policy. *The American Political Science Review* 87 (2): 334–347.

Schneider, A. L., H. Ingram, and P. deLeon. 2013. Democratic policy design: Social construction of target populations. In *Theories of the policy process,* ed. P. Sabatier and C. M. Weible, 105–149. Boulder: Westview Press.

Schneider, Anne, and Helen Ingram. 1997. *Policy design for democracy.* Lawrence, KS: University of Kansas Press.

Sharkansky, I. 1970. *Policy analysis in political science.* Ontario: Markham.

Soss, J. 2005. Making clients and citizens: Welfare policy as a source of status, belief, and action. In *Deserving and entitled: Social construction of public policy,* ed. A. L. Schneider and H. Ingram, 291–328. Albany: State University of New York Press.

Stone, D. 2013. *Keynote address to interpretive policy analysis conference,* Vienna.

The Economist. 2014. Reforms and democracy but no rule of law (November 15). http://www.economist.com.

Vincent, John A., MGuy Patterson, and Karen Wale. 2001. *Politics and old age: Older citizens and political processes in Britain.* Aldershot: Ashgate.

Voigtländer, Michael. 2009. Why is the German homeownership rate so low? *Housing Studies* 24 (3): 355–372. https://doi.org/10.1080/026730309028 75011.

Weaver, V., and A. E. Lerman. 2010. Political consequences of the carceral state. *American Political Science Review.* https://doi.org/10.1017/S00030554100 00456.

Yanow, D. 1998. The communication of policy meanings: Implementation as interpretation and text. *Policy Sciences* 16 (1): 41–61.

INDEX

B. G. Peters and P. Zittoun (eds.), *Contemporary Approaches to Public Policy*, International Series on Public Policy, https://doi.org/10.1007/978-3-032-06026-6

305